D1112631

Social Entrepreneurship

Social Entrepreneurship

Edited by Johanna Mair, Jeffrey Robinson and Kai Hockerts

First published 2006 by
PALGRAVE MACMILLAN
Houndmills, Basingstoke, Hampshire RG21 6XS and
175 Fifth Avenue, New York, N. Y. 10010
Companies and representatives throughout the world

PALGRAVE MACMILLAN is the global academic imprint of the Palgrave
Macmillan division of St. Martin's Press, LLC and of Palgrave Macmillan Ltd.
Macmillan® is a registered trademark in the United States, United Kingdom
and other countries. Palgrave is a registered trademark in the European Union
and other countries.

ISBN-13: 978–1–4039–9664–0   hardback
ISBN-10: 1–4039–9664–4   hardback

This book is printed on paper suitable for recycling and made from fully
managed and sustained forest sources.

A catalogue record for this book is available from the British Library.

Library of Congress Cataloging-in-Publication Data
    Social entrepreneurship / edited by Johanna Mair, Jeffrey Robinson &
Kai Hockerts.
        p. cm.
    "This book results from an international conference held at IESE
Business School, Barcelona, in March 2005"–Introd.
    Includes bibliographical references and index.
    ISBN 1–4039–9664–4 (cloth)
    1. Social entrepreneurship–Congresses. I. Mair, Johanna, 1967–
II. Robinson, Jeffrey, 1971– III. Hockerts, Kai, 1970– IV. Universidad de
Navarra. Instituto de Estudios Superiores de la Empresa.

HD60.S59 2006
306.3'42–dc22

                                                        2005056487

10   9   8   7   6   5   4   3   2   1
15   14 13 12 11 10 09 08 07 06

Transferred to digital printing 2006

Contents

v

List of Tables

List of Figures

List of Appendices

Notes on Contributors

James Austin
Dr Austin holds the Snider Professorship of Business Administration at the Harvard Business School. He has been a member of the Harvard University faculty since 1972. His Doctor of Business Administration and MBA degrees are from Harvard University. Professor Austin was the cofounder of the School's Social Enterprise Initiative. He has authored 16 books, dozens of articles, and over a hundred case studies on business organizations. His most recent award-winning book is *The Collaboration Challenge: How Nonprofits and Business Succeed through Strategic Alliances.* Dr Austin has given seminars and served as an advisor to managers and government officials around the world, including being a special advisor to the White House. He has served on many nonprofit and corporate boards.

Albert Cho
Albert Cho is an independent researcher. He received an A.B. in Social Studies, *summa cum laude* and Phi Beta Kappa, from Harvard College, and received an MS in development economics and an MBA with distinction from the University of Oxford, where he was a Rhodes Scholar. He has worked at the World Resources Institute and the United Nations Millennium Project, where he conducted research on education, health and the environment Millennium Development Goals. He has published research on international trade and environmental policy, social entrepreneurship, and identity politics. Albert is now an Associate in the Washington, DC office of McKinsey & Co. and splits his time between DC and Brooklyn, NY.

Anne Clifford
Anne Clifford runs a marketing and development department for a UK-based charity. After a career in the entertainment industry, she recently completed an MBA at Kingston Business School. She also spent several very enjoyable months volunteering for Green-Works, the organization on which the research in this book was based.

Geoffrey Desa

Geoffrey Desa is a doctoral student of technology entrepreneurship and strategic management at the University of Washington Business School in Seattle. He holds a BS in Electrical Engineering from Georgia Institute of Technology and a MS in Electrical Engineering from Stanford University. His research interests lie at the intersection of technology and social entrepreneurship, to understand how social entrepreneurs use new technologies in resource limited environments. He teaches strategic management and entrepreneurship in the undergraduate business program. Geoffrey has worked in R&D at Hewlett-Packard, Agilent Research Laboratories and Novera Optics, in Silicon Valley, California.

Sarah E. A. Dixon

Sarah E. A. Dixon is a principal lecturer in strategic management at Kingston Business School, London, UK. She is subject leader for strategy and organizes the Strategy into Practice guest lecture series. She holds an MBA from Kingston Business School and is studying for her DBA at Henley Management College. She is a Fellow of the Chartered Management Institute. She worked for 23 years for Shell in various management positions including expatriate postings as business manager in Austria and Russia and roles in strategic planning and mergers and acquisitions in London. Her research interests are focused on two main areas – organizational transformation in transition economies, in particular the Russian oil industry, and social and ecological entrepreneurship.

Kate Ganly

Kate Ganly is a research assistant at IESE Business School, Barcelona. She holds a BA in English and Anthropology from the University of Sydney, Australia. Kate has worked as a marketing manager in book retailing and is currently pursuing a career in the publishing industry in London.

Helen Haugh

Helen Haugh is a lecturer at the Judge Business School, University of Cambridge. She holds a BS Management Sciences (UMIST), MA European Marketing Management (Brunel) and PhD in Management (Aberdeen). Dr Haugh is Course Director for the Masters in Community Enterprise at the Judge Business School – the first postgraduate management qualification for community enterprise practitioners to be delivered in the UK. Her research interests and teaching responsibilities embrace entrepreneurship, management and strategy and she has a specific interest in the potential of organizations (private, public and nonprofit) to contribute to economic, social and environmental regeneration. During her academic career, Dr Haugh has also worked as a management consultant and executive educator.

Kai Hockerts

Kai Hockerts is Adjunct Professor and Senior Research Programme Manager at INSEAD's Centre for the Management of Environmental and Social Responsibility (CMER) in Fontainebleau, France, where he is heading a team of six research associates. His primary research focus is on corporate sustainability strategy and environmental entrepreneurship research. He teaches a course on 'Blended Value Strategies – Transforming the Non-Profit Sector' as well as on 'Environmental Sustainability and Competitive Advantage'. He has given numerous talks to academic audiences and practitioners on a broad variety of topics linked to corporate sustainability, environmental management, and social responsibility. Dr Hockerts holds a PhD in Management from the University St Gallen, Switzerland and a Diploma in Business Administration from the University of Bayreuth, Germany. Kai's business experience includes work as a management consultant for Life Cycle Assessments and Eco-Design at Ecobilan S.A., Paris.

Suresh Kotha

Suresh Kotha is Professor of Management and Organization, and Faculty Director of the Center for Technology Entrepreneurship, at the University of Washington Business School. Dr Kotha holds the Battelle/Oleson Excellence Endowed Chair in Entrepreneurship and specializes in technology, strategic management and corporate entrepreneurship. He has published over 40 articles, many in peer-reviewed journals. Suresh has been quoted in the Wall Street Journal, National Public Radio, the Stanford Business school magazine, The Seattle Times and The Post Intelligencer. Suresh has taught at the Stern School of Business at New York University, the International University of Japan, the University of Pretoria, and the Indian School of Business, India.

Johanna Mair

Johanna Mair is Assistant Professor of General Management at IESE, the Business School of the University of Navarra in Barcelona, Spain. She earned her PhD in Management with a specialization in Strategy from INSEAD (Fontainebleau, France) and publishes in strategy and entrepreneurship journals. Professor Mair teaches strategy and social entrepreneurship in the MBA program, executive programs and the PhD program at IESE. Her current research focuses on the intersection of traditional strategy and social entrepreneurship. As such she is interested in entrepreneurial activity that aims at economic *and* social value creation, both in the context of established and newly created organizations. Professor Mair collaborates closely with the Schwab Foundation and Ashoka on research and teaching and is involved in a global Teaching Innovation Program by the Aspen Institute. She is also the coordinator of an EU-sponsored program that fosters exchange and mobility between Asia and Europe in the area of social entrepreneurship.

Ignasí Martí

Ignasí Martí is a doctoral candidate of management with a specialization in organization theory at the IESE Business School in Barcelona, Spain. He holds a BS both in Economics and in Philosophy from the University of Barcelona, an MS in Management from the IESE Business School and an MS in Philosophy from the University of Barcelona. His research lies at the intersection of organization theory, sociology and entrepreneurship research: how by creating new institutions and by transforming, deinstitutionalizing and replicating existing ones, social entrepreneurs can enable the poor and the excluded to participate more actively in society.

Ernesto Noboa

Ernesto Noboa recently joined IDE Business School in Ecuador as Professor in the Business Policy Department. He teaches several courses in the Executive MBA and other management programs including corporate strategy, strategy implementation and social entrepreneurship. Professor Noboa's research and teaching interests include corporate strategy and social entrepreneurship. He is a PhD candidate in General Management at IESE Business School (Barcelona, Spain) and has an MBA from MIT Sloan School of Management (Massachusetts, USA) and a Mechanical Engineering degree from the University of Dayton (Ohio, USA). Before becoming a professor, Noboa worked for several years as an executive in a consumer goods company in Ecuador.

Francesco Perrini

Francesco Perrini is Associate Professor of Management, CSR and Sustainability Innovation at the 'Giorgio Pivato' Management Department of Bocconi University. He is also Senior Professor of Corporate Finance at the SDA Bocconi School of Management. Since 1990 his research has focused on strategic and innovation management and social issues in management such as corporate governance, sustainability, social responsibility and social entrepreneurship. Prof. Perrini is director of CSR group at SDA Bocconi; and a member of several boards including the Advisory Board of SPACES, Bocconi's, research center for 'Security, Protection And Corporate Social Responsibility and Entrepreneurial Sustainability' and the Board of the Italian Centre for Social Responsibility (I-CSR), Milan. In 2004–2005 Prof. Perinni spent the academic year at the Business Ethics Department, Wharton School, University of Pennsylvania, as Visiting Associate Professor and has collaborated on several international research initiatives including the CSR Initiative, KSG at Harvard University and the Multinational Enterprises Program at the International Labour Organization in Geneva. He holds postgraduate degrees in Protection Management and Financial Management, and a laurea degree in Business Administration from Bocconi University.

Jeffrey Robinson

Jeffrey A. Robinson is Assistant Professor of Management at the Stern School of Business, New York University. He holds a BS in Civil Engineering and a BA in Urban Studies from Rutgers, The State University of New Jersey; a MS in Civil Engineering Management from Georgia Institute of Technology and a PhD from Columbia University's Graduate School of Business. Professor Robinson spends much of his time writing and researching about the role of entrepreneurs and entrepreneurship in society and in developing the competitive advantage of regions and nations. He is committed to research and informed policy making in the areas of community economic development, social ventures, and social and institutional barriers to markets. In 2001 he cofounded BCT Partners, a firm that provides management, technology and policy consulting to nonprofits, foundations, corporations and various government entities as they plan and implement change strategies and improve organizational effectiveness.

Christian Seelos

Christian Seelos recently joined the Malik Management Centre, St Gallen and is a Senior Researcher and Lecturer at IESE Business School and other European schools in Business Strategy and Social Entrepreneurship. He received his PhD from the University of Vienna and his MBA from the University of Chicago, GSB. He previously held positions as Head of Corporate Social Responsibility at BT Global

Services and as Senior Consultant at Siemens Business Services. He led the Biological Weapons disarmament work in Iraq for the United Nations Special Commission for several years and helped in the build-up of an IT company as Vice President of Business Development. Beginning his research career as Assistant Professor at the Medical Faculty in Vienna, Christian has published a number of original papers in leading science journals.

Clodia Vurro

Clodia Vurro is a PhD student of Business Administration and Management at Bocconi University, Milan, Italy. She also works as Research Assistant at Findustria – Centre for Finance and Industry Study and SPACES Bocconi, Research Centre on 'Security, Protection And Corporate Social Responsibility & Entrepreneurial Sustainability'. She is Teaching Assistant of Business Management and CSR & Sustainability Innovation. Her primary research interests are socially responsible corporate behavior and social entrepreneurship. She is committed to research in the areas of tools and methods for the evaluation and measurement of social and environmental performance and on the analysis of organizations dealing with complex social problems through an innovation mindset and an entrepreneurial lens. She holds a laurea degree in Economics and Management for Arts, Culture and Communication from Bocconi University.

Acknowledgments

This book would not have been possible without the help of many contributors. We are indebted to the authors for their work and their willingness to contribute to this project; their hard work has made this book possible. Special thanks to all of the participants at the first International Social Entrepreneurship Research Conference (ISERC), held at IESE Business School, University of Navarra in Barcelona, Spain, 22–24 April 2005, who supported this work and made a vital contribution to this book.

This conference provided the opportunity for the exchange of views on social entrepreneurship among the more than sixty participants gathered there. It was supported by the Anselmo Rubiralta Center of Globalization and Strategy at IESE, and we would like to thank the many people at IESE who actively supported the conference: Guillermo Nesi, Claudia Thurner, and Gemma Golobardes. Additional support for the conference was received from the Berkley Center for Entrepreneurial Studies of NYU Stern School of Business and the CSR Platform, a collaborative effort of the European Academy of Business in Society and 12 academic partner institutions, funded by the European Commission Sixth Framework Research Program.

Finally, we are especially grateful to Kate Ganly. Her support in organizing the conference and most of all her assistance in writing the book made this project possible.

1
Introduction

Johanna Mair, Jeffrey Robinson and Kai Hockerts

What is social entrepreneurship?

The concept of social entrepreneurship (SE) is, in practice, recognized as encompassing a wide range of activities: enterprising individuals devoted to making a difference; social purpose business ventures dedicated to adding for-profit motivations to the nonprofit sector; new types of philanthropists supporting venture capital-like 'investment' portfolios; and nonprofit organizations that are reinventing themselves by drawing on lessons learned from the business world. In the past decade 'social entrepreneurship' has made a popular name for itself on the global scene as a 'new phenomenon' that is reshaping the way we think about social value creation. Some of these practices are uniquely new however many have been around for a long time having finally reached critical mass under a widely endorsed label.

SE as a field of research on the other hand is a relatively recent phenomenon. Although the development of this field from a research perspective will be discussed later in this introduction; we simply wish to highlight here that although a large number of events have been organized bringing together disparate audiences interested in the topic, to date there have been few opportunities for scholars to gather and discuss papers, themes and concepts relating specifically to the study of SE.

Why produce this book?

This book results from an international conference held at IESE Business School, Barcelona in March 2005, the first in a series devoted specifically to SE research.

The number of books, newsletters, and magazine articles written on SE could easily fill several bookcases: why another handbook and yet another event series? Given all that has been said and written about SE it is surprising that very little rigorous research has been conducted on the issue. Most of the work published so far has been based on anecdotal evidence or was targeted to promote specific initiatives. The conference series that has led to this volume's publication was initiated by us to help create space for academic researchers and thus to jumpstart serious debate about this important field. By bringing established academic theories and research methods to the domain of SE, scholars can provide much needed framing and scrutiny of an area of research that is still in its infancy. At the same time we are convinced that the academic study of SE will have profound impact on many of the established management theories.

The idea for this conference series first emerged at the June 2004 Babson Kauffman Entrepreneurship Research Conference in Glasgow. The first planning meeting followed just weeks later at the Academy of Management's annual conference in New Orleans in August. Being able to produce this volume just a little more than a year after this initial meeting of the minds fills us with a sense of achievement. Such an endeavor would have been impossible without the excellent work done by the Barcelona team that organized and hosted our first International Social Entrepreneurship Research Conference (ISERC), as well as the generous sponsorship of the Anselmo Rubiralta Center for Globalization and Strategy at the IESE Business School.

Obviously a handbook such as this would have come to nothing without the contribution of the many scholars who participated in the meeting and subsequently contributed to this handbook. They are testimony to the fact that there is already a growing body of academic scholars conducting academically rigorous research work.

Antecedents and development of the field

In many ways, SE as a field of study is in startup mode. The creation of a new field of study is exciting work and to that end, there have been prelaunch activities. For example, some of the elements of what we call the field of SE research were acquired from studies of nonprofit leadership and management and the research being conducted at the intersection of social issues (including environmental issues) and management. Some of the studies on the nonprofit sector examined how business-like practices were being used to achieve their noteworthy objectives. Other studies focused on the revenue generating strategies of nonprofit organizations. Studies categorized as social issues management focused on the efforts of large multinational corporations and their corporate social responsibility programs and performance. None of these antecedents however discussed the creation of new organizations.

The extensive literature on entrepreneurship has only recently embraced the idea that entrepreneurial actors may be driven by more than a profit motive. Some scholars have discussed the role of entrepreneurship in economic development. In our mind, all of these efforts are the primordial soup out of which scholarship about SE has risen.

Throughout this primordial stage, there were several papers written that declared the arrival of a new set of ideas. Our scan of the previous work in this area uncovered a handful of academic articles that used the term 'social entrepreneurship' and were published in peer-reviewed journals between 1990 and 2004. During this period, several interesting books on the subject also appeared. Many reports have appeared on-line that describe small scale surveys of social ventures in various regions. These reports and the books have provided important and influential contributions to the discussion but might not meet the rigorous standards necessary to push forward knowledge in an academic context.

The contents of this volume

The objective of the conference and this book is to stimulate scholarly discourse. In 1999 Paul Hirsch and Daniel Levin wrote a wonderful paper on the life cycle of scholarly constructs in which they describe the tension between researchers who advocate broad 'umbrella constructs' and researchers who prefer narrowly defined issues and assume the role of 'validity police' (Hirsch and Levin, 1999). They further describe how academic constructs undergo different phases from an initial phase of excitement, through a phase of validity checks and then one where typologies are dominant, before they either collapse or become permanent. Applying their insights to the evolution of SE as an academic field we are clearly now in the 'emerging excitement' phase. Over the last five years SE has received increasing attention from many different sources – elites and politicians such as Tony Blair, businesspeople such as e-Bay founder Jeff Skoll, and institutions such as the World Economic Forum.

Table 1.1 Definitions of social entrepreneurship concepts within this volume

Author/s	Ch.	Title	Definition
Austin	3	Three avenues for social entrepreneurship research	'Social entrepreneurship is innovative, social value creating activity that can occur within or across the nonprofit, business, and public sectors.'
Cho	4	Politics, values and social entrepreneurship: a critical appraisal	'...a quite general working definition of social entrepreneurship: a set of institutional practices combining the pursuit of financial objectives with the pursuit and promotion of substantive and terminal values.'
Perrini/ Vurro	5	Social entrepreneurship: Innovation and social change across theory and practice	'...social entrepreneurs are change promoters in society; they pioneer innovation within the social sector through the entrepreneurial quality of a breaking idea, their capacity building aptitude, and their ability to concretely demonstrate the quality of the idea and to measure social impacts.' 'We define SE as a dynamic process created and managed by an individual or team (the innovative social entrepreneur), which strives to exploit social innovation with an entrepreneurial mindset and a strong need for achievement, in order to create new social value in the market and community at large.'
Robinson	7	Navigating social and institutional barriers to markets: How social entrepreneurs identify and evaluate opportunities	'...I define social entrepreneurship as a *process* that includes: the identification of a specific social problem and a specific solution... to address it; the evaluation of the social impact, the business model and the sustainability of the venture; and the creation of a social mission-oriented *for-profit* or a business-oriented *nonprofit* entity that pursues the double (or triple) bottom line.'

Table 1.1 Definitions of social entrepreneurship concepts within this volume – *continued*

Author/s	Ch.	Title	Definition
Mair/Noboa	8	Social entrepreneurship: How intentions to create a social venture are formed	'...we define social entrepreneurship as the innovative use of resource combinations to pursue opportunities aiming at the creation of organizations and/or practices that yield and sustain social benefits.'
Hockerts	10	Entrepreneurial opportunity in social purpose business ventures	'Social purpose business ventures are hybrid enterprises straddling the boundary between the for-profit business world and social mission-driven public and nonprofit organizations. Thus they do not fit completely in either sphere.'
Desa/Kotha	11	Ownership, mission and environment: An exploratory analysis into the evolution of a technology social venture	'TSVs [technology social ventures]... develop and deploy technology-driven solutions to address social needs in a financially sustainable manner... TSVs address the twin cornerstones of social entrepreneurship – ownership (financial return) and mission (social impact) using advanced technology.'
Haugh	12	Social enterprise: beyond economic outcomes and individual returns	'Social enterprise is a collective term for a range of organizations that trade for a social purpose. They adopt one of a variety of different legal formats but have in common the principles of pursuing business-led solutions to achieve social aims, and the reinvestment of surplus for community benefit. Their objectives focus on socially desired, nonfinancial goals and their outcomes are the nonfinancial measures of the implied demand for and supply of services.'
Clifford/Dixon	14	Green-Works: A model for combining social and ecological entrepreneurship	'... the term "ecopreneur"...[defines] an ecopreneurial organization as one that is a "system-transforming, socially

5

Table 1.1 Definitions of social entrepreneurship concepts within this volume – *continued*

Author/s	Ch.	Title	Definition
			committed...break-through venture", a definition that seems to encompass both ecological and social enterprise. However [this term] draws the focus too narrowly upon the environmental aspects, and we therefore apply the term **"social ecopreneur"** ... to encompass the triple drivers of these organizations: environmental, social and economic, the latter being inherent in the concept of entrepreneurship.'
Seelos/Ganly/ Mair	15	Social entrepreneurs directly contribute to global development goals.	The Schwab Foundation [source of the study population] defines a **social entrepreneur** as someone who [among other things]: "identifies and applies practical solutions to social problems...; innovates by finding a new product, service or approach...; focuses... on social value creation...; resists being trapped by the constraints of ideology or discipline; [and] has a vision, but also a well-thought out roadmap as to how to attain the goal.'

The emerging excitement surrounding the topic of SE is evident in the large number of definitions that are currently used to describe the phenomenon. This is also reflected by the variety of definitions present in this volume (Table 1.1).

The proliferation of definitions, and also different naming conventions, mirrors the multiple facets of the phenomenon. Narrowing SE down to a uniformly agreed upon definition would probably make it applicable only to a limited set of problems and issues. As Albert Cho points out in Chapter 4 of this book, restrictive definitions at this early stage seem to cause more problems than they solve, 'not least because the research community continues to explore new forms and avenues for SE'.

A look at the different papers presented here also reveals pluralism not only in terms of definition but also in terms of particular themes covered.

The chapters in Part I are generally concerned with setting an agenda for future research; they attempt an overall analysis of what has already been written in the field of SE and offer suggestions for new theoretical directions.

- *James Austin* (Chapter 3) proposes three areas for future research: comparative analysis along five possible dimensions of time, place, form, actor and practice; studies of SE in the corporate sector; and studies of collaborations in SE such as social purpose alliances and networks. To conclude, Austin suggests interdisciplinary research as a fruitful path towards achieving these aims.
- *Albert Cho* (Chapter 4) stresses the importance of taking politics and values into consideration when researching SE. He maintains a deliberately broad definition of the phenomenon but also points out that a deconstruction of the term 'social' is integral to understanding what we mean by the term 'social entrepreneurship'. Cho offers an important critique of SE and warns against conceptualizing it as a panacea for what ails society. He argues that relying on SE to plug the gaps left open by markets or social welfare systems avoids a more discursively mediated process in the broader sphere which could lead to more inclusive and integrated systemic solutions.
- *Francesco Perrini and Clodia Vurro* (Chapter 5) begin by asking: what is SE? They examine the literature to date, extracting what they believe to be the essential elements of the social entrepreneurial process and identifying the differences from what could be called 'business' or traditional entrepreneurship. A large number of socially

entrepreneurial ventures are then analyzed and the commonalities mapped to each of these essential elements to produce a descriptive framework of the SE process. The authors conclude that, while most studies to date have focused on separate elements of the process such as opportunity recognition and organizational form, a fruitful area of research might be to explore the links and relationships between these elements.

Part II concentrates on an area of research derived from existing entrepreneurship theory: that of opportunity. The chapters represented here offer an empirical approach which examines the sociological aspects behind the exploitation of social entrepreneurial opportunities and a conceptual paper theorizing the behavioral impetus which initiates such exploitation in the first place.

- *Jeffrey Robinson* (Chapter 7) examines the interplay between the economic, social and institutional barriers to market entry for social entrepreneurs and how these impact on the evaluation of entrepreneurial opportunities. He brings an important sociological dimension to bear on the relationships among three main factors: the decision to enter a particular market, the social networks in which the entrepreneur and the initiative are embedded and the types of institutions (both formal such as laws, and informal such as language and culture) that exist (or do not exist) which can help or hinder the development of the initiative. These observations and analyses are born out by the in-depth study of six social ventures.
- *Johanna Mair and Ernesto Noboa* (Chapter 8) draw on established literature in the fields of behavioral psychology and entrepreneurship as well as anecdotal evidence on social entrepreneurs to postulate a model for the formation of intentions to create a social venture. They suggest that such intentions develop from a perception of desirability which, in turn, is affected by emotional and cognitive attitudes such as empathy and moral judgment, combined with perceptions of feasibility, which are backed by enabling factors such as self-efficacy and social support.

In Part III we turn to the structures, strategies and outcomes of social entrepreneurial ventures, in other words: how do social entrepreneurs turn opportunities into successful initiatives, what are the benefits they generate and whom do they serve?

- Focusing on 'social purpose business ventures', typically mission-driven and socially innovative for-profit businesses, *Kai Hockerts* (Chapter 10) identifies three main sources of social entrepreneurial opportunity: activism, self help and philanthropy. Each of these provides an economic and a social value proposition which supports the entrepreneurial intention to turn an idea into a reality. His framework suggests that different sources of opportunity might lead to different operational models and strategies and could provide fertile ground for further research.

- *Geoffrey Desa and Suresh Kotha* (Chapter 11) study the evolution of projects within a startup technology social venture, Benetech in California, to uncover ways in which such a venture manages technology in a resource limited environment. Their findings suggest that, as the organization evolves, sources of opportunity shift from the experience, networks and resources available to the founder toward an interaction with the socio-political dynamic – the activist, philanthropic and volunteer communities – and the necessity of developing long term relationships with stakeholders, often entailing a parallel evolution in the organization's mission.

- In a longitudinal study of six social enterprises in rural north-east Scotland, *Helen Haugh* (Chapter 12) observes and records the economic, social and environmental outcomes generated by these initiatives over time. Her findings indicate that, not only do such initiatives generate direct benefits but also indirect economic, social and environmental benefits such as raising the skill level of individuals in the local community and an increased sense of empowerment and overall community vibrancy. Haugh's work correlates the positive impacts with the outcomes created by social enterprises and suggests that this approach to exploiting market opportunities in a resource poor environment offers a valuable tool for promoting social and economic regeneration.

Part IV broadens the scope of this volume to integrate sustainability and the environment into the discussion and should be taken as indicative of the many different approaches and lenses with which to view this complex phenomenon.

- *Anne Clifford and Sarah Dixon* (Chapter 14) analyze the business model of an environmental-social enterprise, GreenWorks in London, to uncover the strategies and processes that help it to balance a triple bottom line. Based on their observations and analysis the authors conclude that successful 'ecopreneurship' is related to the mission-driven values and ideals of the founder and to creating networks of mutually benefiting stakeholders.

- *Christian Seelos, Kate Ganly and Johanna Mair* (Chapter 15) propose that social entrepreneurs are making valuable contributions to achieving the Millennium Development Goals proposed by the United Nations in 2000. Their study analyzes 73 initiatives world-wide and reveals that 68 per cent of these initiatives are impacting one or more of the goals and that 60 per cent of this group are operating in the countries with the lowest levels of human development where such an impact is most needed and can have the greatest effect. The authors conclude by suggesting that, with their talent for combining scarce resources and creating value networks under the harshest of conditions, such social entrepreneurs could provide a novel set of partners for multilateral development agencies who are struggling to achieve the Millennium Development Goals by the target year of 2015.

The chapters in this volume represent a broad range of subject areas and theoretical perspectives within SE research. However, to move forward as a field of academic discovery SE will have to face a validity challenge. We do not mean to imply that convergence to unified paradigm is needed here but rather more rigorous research that also captures the complexity of the phenomenon. Going deeper into the motivations, structures and outcomes of SE will provide a special challenge.

Directions for the future of SE research

This book consists mainly of conceptual papers and studies based on a qualitative research design. We hope that the next volume resulting from the second International Social Entrepreneurship Research Conference will take on the validity challenge by incorporating different methods and more robust theoretical foundations. We believe that SE is in a great position to face validity challenges as it attracts the interest of outstanding scholars and receives the support of practitioners who consistently provide us with reality checks.

Is SE an important area of scholarship? In this volume, we make the case for the importance of this research and invite others to join us. We believe that this research is significant and important for several reasons. First, we believe it is essential to furthering scholarship across the disciplines of sociology, economics, political science or psychology. This is achieved by the development of conceptual, theoretical and empirical papers that challenge the prevailing constructs and ideas in a changing society.

Second, we see the potential for scholarship in SE to influence business schools. Business schools which are concerned about corporate social responsibility will also benefit from encouraging their students and stakeholders to become involved in social entrepreneurial activity. By understanding the phenomenon we can bring a new perspective to the existing theories of organizations, strategy, marketing, finance and entrepreneurship.

Third, we believe that this research has great social relevance. Conducting research in the area of SE will have practical implications that may influence the outcomes of social entrepreneurs and those that support or fund them. We hope that this has an impact on the significant issues these actors are attempting to address.

Recently, scholars have lamented that there is a lack of research in top-tier journals that demonstrates the social impact of organizations (Hinnings and Greenwood, 2002; Margolis and Walsh, 2003; Walsh, Weber and Margolis, 2003). Perrow (2000) has argued that organization theory could be reenergized by concepts and perspectives from economic sociology and social movement theory. We believe that SE is relevant to both of these arguments. SE certainly answers the call for more social issues-related research. There are real phenomena to investigate and the stakes are high (Wood, 1991a; 1991b).

Our efforts in convening the first International Social Entrepreneurship Research Conference have moved the field forward by demonstrating that rigorous research can be done in this field. Beyond this volume, we are confident that there are many more questions to be asked and answered by scholars from a variety of backgrounds. We offer both contextual and topical ideas for future research below.

Contexts

1. *Early stage* – the new social venture creation process, the challenges faced by the startup and the sustainability of the social venture.
2. *Growth and scale* – the growth and scaling of social ventures.
3. *International ventures* – the social venture across different national and institutional contexts; social ventures that operate in several nations.

Topics

1. *Innovation* – What types of social impact innovations are developed in social ventures? Where do they come from? How are they implemented?
2. *Performance metrics* – How do social entrepreneurs understand success and which measures do they use to assess their performance? What are the possibilities and limits of approaches such as the social return on investment (SROI) analysis?
3. *Social venture capital markets* – Are the financing mechanisms and criteria for social venture capital different from those from traditional venture capital? What theories might explain the underdevelopment of the social venture capital markets?
4. *Demographics* – What are the typical sectors social ventures emerge in? Are there differences by country? What is the typical size, growth and ownership structure?
5. *Networks* – Can the characteristics of social networks influence the sustainability of social entrepreneurial ventures?
6. *Public policy* – In what way would policy measures differ, if at all, for facilitating the sustainability of social entrepreneurial ventures?
7. *Values* – What role can values (ethical or moral) play in ensuring the sustainability of newly formed ventures?
8. *Strategic considerations* – How do social ventures establish their value net? Do social ventures require specific resource strategies?
9. *Organizational development* – What role do systems and processes play in ensuring the sustainability of the social venture?
10. *Governance* – What role do governance mechanisms play in ensuring the sustainability of the social entrepreneurial venture over time?
11. *Exit* – What are typical exit strategies for social ventures? How do these differ from traditional ventures? How can social ventures maintain their mission beyond the exit of the founding team?
12. *Sustainable development* – How can SE play a role in sustainable development?

What is required to move the field forward is a greater number of scholars who wish to engage in the activity of building up SE as a field of study. We admire our colleagues in strategic management who, 30 years ago, were part of a vanguard of researchers establishing a new perspective for the study of business organizations. As we look forward to the second International Social Entrepreneurship Research Conference at

New York University, we are pleased to know that there are others who are willing to take this path with us and look forward to the journey ahead.

References

Hinnings, C. R. and Greenwood, R. 2002. Disconnects and consequences in Organization Theory? *Administrative Science Quarterly*, 47(3): 411–21.

Hirsch, P. M. and Levin, D. Z. 1999. Umbrella advocates versus validity police: A life-cycle model. *Organization Science*, 10(2): 199–212.

Margolis, J. D. and Walsh, J. P. 2003. Misery loves companies: Rethinking social initiatives by business. *Administrative Science Quarterly*, 28: 268–305.

Perrow, C. 2000. An organizational analysis of Organization Theory. *Contemporary Sociology*, 29(3): 469–77.

Walsh, J. P., Weber, K. and Margolis, J. D. 2003. Social issues and management: Our lost cause found. *Journal of Management*, 29(6): 859–81.

Wood, D. J. 1991a. Corporate social performance revisited. *Academy of Management Review*, 16(4): 691–718.

Wood, D. J. 1991b. Social issues in management: Theory and research in corporate social performance. *Journal of Management*, 17(2): 383–406.

Part I

Perspectives and Agenda for Research

2
Introduction to Part I – Setting a Research Agenda for an Emerging Field

Ignasí Martí

Social entrepreneurship (SE) broadly understood as a practice that aims at social change has a long heritage; however it has only recently attracted the interest of researchers. Consequently, many of the issues arising in this book – and in Part I in particular – are typical of any emerging field of inquiry: the need to draw boundaries so as to delimit scope and clarify whether it is an independent field of research; and the need to identify the different levels of analysis, disciplines, theoretical lenses and methods for studying the phenomenon.

A common feature of emerging fields of research is the absence of clear theoretical boundaries and the need to coalesce thinking from other disciplines. Notwithstanding that most of the existing research on SE has built on business entrepreneurship approaches and constructs, an increasing number of scholars are making efforts to bridge this literature with other streams of research such as social movements theory (Alvord, Brown and Letts, 2004), sustainable development (Seelos and Mair, 2005) or institutional entrepreneurship (Dorado, 2005), just to mention some examples. In this vein, the authors of two of the chapters in Part I – James E. Austin, and Francesco Perrini and Clodia Vurro – conclude by calling for more interdisciplinary research. The author of the fourth chapter Albert H. Cho, puts that call into practice through a critical analysis of the same concept of SE, but also building on political science, political philosophy and sociology literatures. The variegated nature and multiple expressions of SE make it a fascinating playground for different perspectives and literatures (Mair and Martí, 2005).

Interestingly, one of the aspects highlighted by all three of the authors of papers in Part I is the need to resist premature definitional closure on major SE concepts. By providing purposely broad definitions of the phenomenon they aim to avoid errors of exclusion that may

17

constrain future avenues of research. Preventing premature termino-logical closure and accepting fuzzy boundaries to other fields of study invites richer and more interdisciplinary discussions. It is our belief that this will contribute to the advancement of knowledge not only on SE, but also on social and institutional change, on social and economic wealth creation, and on social and economic development. In other words, it offers an opportunity for researchers from different fields and disciplines to challenge and rethink some of their central concepts and assumptions.

The three papers of Part I offer a broad picture of the current state of the discipline and pinpoint, either implicitly or explicitly, some of the most intriguing questions that the emergence of SE as a field of research has opened. The next paragraphs provide a short summary of their main arguments.

Austin

Austin creates a working definition of SE around three key elements – innovation, social value creation, and loci – which becomes the starting point of the first chapter in Part I. The main objective is to set a broad research agenda for SE. Building on the existing research, which in turn, has generally built on business entrepreneurship research, James E. Austin proposes three avenues for future research: the comparative, the corporate, and the collaborative avenues.

Comparative analysis along five possible dimensions of time, place, form, actor, and practice, points towards issues and questions such as:

- What are the scaling up processes and the different stages in the entrepreneurial process?
- How does context shape the entrepreneurial process and how may it foster or inhibit opportunity enactment or recognition?
- Do optimal organizational forms exist and if so; do they vary by institutional sector?
- What are the key attributes of social entrepreneurs compared to commercial entrepreneurs?
- Is it possible to find relevant psychological differences?
- What are the consequences of a certain financing choice?
- How can we quantify social impact, outcomes and returns?

The second proposed area for future research is the corporate avenue, conflating corporate entrepreneurship with SE research. Finally, the collaborative avenue calls for studies on collaborations and alliances within and across sectors. To conclude, Austin encourages interinstitutional research partnerships along with interdisciplinary research as an excellent path towards advancing our knowledge on SE.

Cho

In Chapter 4, Albert Cho argues for a much needed consideration of politics and values when researching SE. Departing from descriptions by Habermas (1989) of the public sphere and the lifeworld, and building on political theorists and sociologists such as Karl Marx and Isaiah Berlin, Cho critically analyzes existing definitions of SE and warns against conceptualizing it as a panacea for what ails society.

He argues that definitions of SE are both tautological and monological, and that recognizing these features unveils the always politic nature of SE.

As a consequence, objectives, interests and identities are constructed in political arenas. Hence, relying on SE as an unquestioned solution to fill the gaps left open by market failures or by the reduction of the traditional social welfare state, may avoid centering the discussion around more inclusive and integrated systemic solutions.

We consider this latter point of particular interest: what exactly the *social* in SE *is*, needs further clarification. The world cries out for repair and social entrepreneurs are called upon to play a central role in fighting against deep-seated problems of human misery (Margolis and Walsh, 2003). However, their activities, as well as the problems they combat, are value-laden and always political in nature. Thus, while researchers, consultants, and practitioners agree on the need to develop useful measures to capture the social impact of social entrepreneurial activities, the truth is that prevailing definitions generally fail to unpack the complex concept of the 'social'. The social element should not merely be understood as a qualifier denoting altruistic behavior or nonprofit activities. While this might be useful in setting boundaries with business entrepreneurship, it hides more than reveals. It fails and even prevents us from unveiling the core of SE.

Hannah Arendt (1971) concluded her analysis on the 'banality of evil' by arguing that the key to understanding its emergence lies in the fact that it is not necessary to be bad at heart to cause great evil. History is full of initiatives that, under the flag of the common good, have had more perverse consequences. Neglecting the political and value-laden character of social entrepreneurs' activities and goals, and of the problems they attempt to ameliorate, may not only make us fail to recognize the possible dark side of SE, but also may prevent it to fully realize its potential for positive social change.

Perrini and Vurro

Francesco Perrini and Clodia Vurro begin by asking: what is SE? Their examination of literature on the topic to date, together with the analysis of 35 socially entrepreneurial ventures, allow them to extract what they believe to be the four main elements of the social entrepreneurial process, namely: mission vision and organizational values; entrepreneurial opportunities and innovation; an entrepreneurial business model; and finally the social outcomes that may lead to more general social transformation.

These elements, according to Perrini and Vurro, in turn, help to identify the differences from what could be called 'business' entrepreneurship. Furthermore, they provide insights on how socially entrepreneurial ventures work and how they are managed, and also address the controversial issue of whether it is possible to single out attributes that make social entrepreneurs different from other entrepreneurs.

Perrini and Vurro's analysis of the 35 socially entrepreneurial ventures permits the mapping of commonalities among them to each of the aforementioned elements in order to produce a descriptive framework of the SE process. The authors conclude by offering two avenues for future research along with the framework developed. First, it is necessary to study each of the four elements of the process. Certainly it is these four elements upon which most empirical research efforts have been devoted – for example, opportunity, recognition, business models and so on. Second, a promising area of inquiry might be to explore how these elements are linked and interrelated. This would provide an opportunity to develop the deep analysis and theory building which can enrich the field of SE research.

To conclude, the contribution of the three chapters in this part of the volume lies in their refreshing and critical review and examination of the literature to date and in their ability to frame a research agenda for SE. It is our hope that the answers to these questions, and the further questions and answers to which they give rise, will help to consolidate SE as a legitimate field of research.

Acknowledgment

This introduction has greatly benefited from a dialogue with Marc Ventresca, lecturer in strategy and organization theory at Saïd Business School, Oxford University. Many thanks to Marc for his thoughts and input.

References

Alvord, S. H., Brown, L. D. and Letts, C. W. 2004. Social entrepreneurship and societal transformation. *Journal of Applied Behavioral Science*, 40(3): 260–82.

Arendt, H. 1971. Thinking and moral considerations: A lecture. *Social Research*, 38(3): 417–46.

Dorado, S. 2005. Institutional entrepreneurship, partaking, and convening. *Organization Studies*, 26(3): 385–414.

Habermas, J. 1989. *The structural transformation of the public sphere*. Cambridge: MIT Press.

Mair, J. and Martí, I. 2005. Social entrepreneurship research: A source of explanation, prediction, and delight. *Journal of World Business*: forthcoming.

Margolis, J. D. and Walsh, J. P. 2003. Misery loves companies: Rethinking social initiatives by business. *Administrative Science Quarterly*, 48(2): 268–306.

Seelos, C. and Mair, J. 2005. Entrepreneurs in service of the poor: Models for business contributions to sustainable development. *Business Horizons*, 48(3): 241–6.

3
Three Avenues for Social Entrepreneurship Research

James E. Austin

The research imperative

Social entrepreneurship (SE) is an emerging field of academic inquiry. As has always been the case for newcomers, they must generate important new knowledge and advance the frontiers of understanding if they are to gain intellectual legitimacy. Thus, vigorous, rigorous, and ambitious research is a key driver to the development of this field.

The core definition

A foundational step for such research is to set forth a definition of the phenomenon. I offer the following:

> Social entrepreneurship is innovative, social value creating activity that can occur within or across the nonprofit, business, and public sectors. (Austin, Stevenson and Wei-Skillern, 2006)

The first key element to stress is *innovation*. Entrepreneurship is a creative process that pursues an opportunity to produce something new. Replicating an existing organization, activity, or process is an important managerial activity, but unless it brings an important new dimension or element, it is not very entrepreneurial. The second key element is *social value creation*. This is the fundamental dimension differentiating SE from commercial entrepreneurship (Austin, Stevenson and Wei-Skillern, 2006). While both forms are socially valuable, generating social value is the explicit, central driving purpose and force for SE. The third key dimension is the *loci*. SE transcends sectors and organizational form. It can occur in all the sectors and their collaborative interactions.

While there are many possible definitions that have been set forth in the early literature, I believe that the foregoing has the fundamental virtue of creating a broad umbrella for the SE research agenda. It is important for an emerging field to have an ample scope of inquiry so as not to constrain unduly, avenues of investigation that may reveal important dimensions of the phenomenon. In fact, part of our collective research agenda should be examining and refining our definition as our explorations reveal critical dimensions that merit salient emphasis.

Three research perspectives

There is a plethora of research opportunities in SE. That is the exciting dimension of an emerging field and many pioneers have begun the journey along a multitude of important paths of inquiry. To capture their wisdom I consulted many colleagues, all of whom are intellectually committed to this field and engaged in serious research, as to what they deemed as high priority and rich areas for investigation. These colleagues, too many to single out, generously shared their perspectives and offered their wisdom to the larger research community. Others, who were not consulted, had already through their writings signaled relevant agenda items. Accordingly, what I offer in this chapter reflects a collective perspective, although the author remains responsible for interpreting these collegial offerings and for injecting his own perspective and priority research judgment.

Among many possibilities, I offer three avenues of inquiry that are not exhaustive but do reveal the ample opportunities for important knowledge generation:

- *Comparative.* A particularly important and powerful form of inquiry is comparative analysis. We need to study SE along five comparative dimensions: *time, place, form, actor, and practice.*
- *Corporate.* Our definition encompasses multiple sectors and a high priority should be placed on the increasingly effervescent social waters in the business world by examining *corporate SE.*
- *Collaborative.* Rather than just confining our examination to that of single organizations, it is important to recognize that *social purpose alliances* are an important form of SE.

I shall examine each of these avenues, with major emphasis on the comparative dimension, trying to delineate important dimensions and research questions meriting our attention. This effort is meant to open windows onto areas of inquiry and stimulate further reflection and elaboration. The indicated paths can produce greater understanding both for the elaboration of theory and for managerial application. SE research can and should be pursued productively and necessarily by different disciplines as well as by interdisciplinary approaches. Similarly, a variety of qualitative and quantitative methodologies can be fruitfully deployed to carry out the research.

The comparative avenue

I will examine in turn the five comparative dimensions of time, place, form, actor and practice.

Time

- *Dynamic vs static?*
  Temporal comparisons can focus on the dynamic process of SE – that is, on the changes – or the research can examine the process at a particular point in time. The first is analogous to taking a video, while the second is akin to a snapshot. Both are useful and complementary perspectives.
- *Retrospective vs prospective?*
  A related research approach is to examine SE retrospectively. This involves historical analysis at distinct points in time or along a traveled path. Much can be learned by careful probing of what has happened empirically. A somewhat more ambitious and scarcer approach is to undertake longitudinal research that follows the evolution of a social purpose undertaking as it unfolds over time. This approach might also involve some action research to add more applied value.
- *Are there stages in the entrepreneurial process?*
  One of the interesting research questions that emerges from the foregoing approaches as a target of inquiry is the phenomenon of stages. While there has been some speculation on this question, it merits deeper probing as to the existence, drivers, and managerial implications of both the genesis and subsequent evolution of SE processes.
- *Scaling up: How does the entrepreneurial task change?*
  A related issue is the phenomenon of growth, which has received growing attention (Bradach, 2003; Dees, Anderson and Wei-Skillern, 2004). Expansion is an entrepreneurial inclination but how it should be done and what distinctive demands are placed on the entrepre-

neur and on the social enterprise merit systematic analysis. Should growth focus on the greater scale of a single organization or should it foster the expansion of a larger social movement of many distinct organizations? What are the distinctive entrepreneurial skills required to expand a single organization vs creating a network of multiple organizations? Which entrepreneurial approach generates greater social value?

Place

- *Context matters: regions, countries, localities*
  The locational context shapes the entrepreneurial process. Consequently, it is illuminating to carry out systematic research that enables us to understand regional, national, or local contextual factors and their impact on the entrepreneurial process. Some enlightening research has been carried out based on international comparisons of the nonprofit sector in general (Salomon, 2004) and on entrepreneurial undertakings (Austin, Reficco et al., 2004) but much more is needed.
- *Which contextual elements (political, legal, economic, sociocultural, demographic, and so on) impose barriers or enable opportunities?*
  Such research could productively illuminate which are the major contextual factors and how they impede or facilitate the entrepreneurial pursuit of social value creating opportunities.
- *Which elements foster innovation and how?*
  Of particular interest would be to examine which factors and processes create an enabling environment for social innovation and how these differ across locales. Such research might delve into the realm of the sources of entrepreneurs and their creativity.
- *How can contextual forces be effectively exploited or managed?*
  While many contextual forces may be beyond the entrepreneur's control, others may indeed be subject to influence. Context can create opportunities as well as constraints, so understanding how their positive roles can be enhanced via policy measures and social incentives in different contexts could carry conceptual as well as practical value.

Form

- *What are the determinants of optimal organizational form?*
  The social entrepreneur's starting point should be the opportunity for innovatively addressing a particular societal problem. The operating challenge is to design the organizational form that will most

effectively mobilize and deploy the requisite resources to attack the problem. Organizational form is a derivative rather than a determinant of the entrepreneurial process. This means that the entrepreneur faces multiple organizing possibilities. The scope of our comparative analysis of organizational form should span the spectrum ranging from nonprofit to for-profit and private to public enterprises and hybrids and combinations along the way (Dees and Backman, 1994). A core entrepreneurial task is comparing these organizational options to determine which is optimal. A highly useful line of research would strive, through comparative analysis, to identify the key factors that shape optimality in conjunction with how and why.

- *Does optimal organizational form vary by institutional sector (business, civic or government)?*
  One of the related lines of inquiry is comparisons across the sectors. While one would logically be inclined to think that the form will be quite different, there may be significant similarities. Finding commonalities through comparative analysis can be as helpful as identifying distinctions.
- *Does this vary with the problem focus of a social enterprise (environment, advocacy, health, and so on)?*
  Another dimension for organizational comparison is the nature of the social problem being addressed. One can compare across problem areas to ascertain the extent of differences, or one could stay within a subsector and do comparisons across the organizations therein. While it is reasonable to assert that specific activities will call forth distinct organizational responses, it may be conceptually and managerially important to identify any cross-cutting commonalities.
- *Does it vary by place? By time?*
  Building on the previous sections, one can utilize multiple parameters to guide the comparison. Geography might influence organizational form because of distinctive contextual forces. Also, as a social undertaking evolves over time, the organization, too, is likely to undergo changes. How should that evolution take place to best enhance performance?

Actor

- *What are the key attributes of social entrepreneurs compared to commercial entrepreneurs?*
  One of the main lines of research in the field of commercial entrepreneurship examines the characteristics of the entrepreneurs such

as attitudes, motivations, capabilities, skills, perspectives, behaviors and origins. It would be logical to do the same for social entrepreneurs, and some incipient efforts along this line have occurred. It would be even more informative and relevant to advancing grounded theory formulation to compare the two categories in order to identify similarities and differences. Along this same line, one could explore if and how the social entrepreneur's characteristics change as the organizational form moves along the social enterprise spectrum from purely charitable to more commercially focused. Is there convergence?

- *How do these change over time?*
  Adding the temporal dimension would address the evolutionary dimension of the entrepreneurs. Do social and commercial entrepreneurs become more or less similar, and along which attributes? This has practical implications for entrepreneurial education.

Practice

There are three sets of managerial practice that merit comparative analysis: financial, measurement, and governance.

Financial

- *What are the comparative advantages and disadvantages of different revenue sources?*
  The social entrepreneur needs to sort out, among multiple possible sources, how to mobilize the financial resources needed to launch and grow the enterprise: individual donations, institutional grants, government funding, earned income.
- *How do you determine the optimal financing mix?*
  This is a portfolio design task. How does this mix vary by time, place and organizational form? How does the mix affect financial sustainability? (Anderson and Dees, 2006)
- *How does the financing choice interact with organizational culture, values, and mission as well as capabilities?*
  Some observers consider earned income as intrinsic to SE (Boschee and McClurg, 2003). There is anecdotal evidence of tensions being created when nonprofits undertake earned income activities in commercial marketplaces (Hughes and Luksetich, 2004). There is growing debate about the pros and cons of income generating social enterprise (Boschee et al., 2000; Foster and Bradach, 2005). Comparing how different organizations have dealt with this issue would be illuminating as to its seriousness and manageability.

- *What are the motivations, expectations and behavior of funders and social investors in different places?*
  On the capital supply side, it is important for social entrepreneurs to understand their potential and actual funders. The emergence of venture philanthropy in the United States has introduced an innovative form of funding that merits further study (Letts, Ryan and Grossman, 1997). To what extent are funders' characteristics and actions similar or distinct in different places and why?

Measurement

- *How can the entrepreneur demonstrate his or her value proposition to stakeholders?*
  The social entrepreneur has to communicate to funders, beneficiaries, and other key groups the value to be generated from the undertaking, which is a very challenging task (Sawhill and Williamson, 2001). Comparing how practitioners actually measure and communicate value would be valuable as a descriptive informational base.
- *How to quantify social outcomes and returns?*
  Demonstrating quantitatively outcomes of social interventions is a particularly complicated task because of the nature of social change. This is among the most difficult entrepreneurial tasks and has challenged scholars and practitioners for a long time (Kanter and Summers, 1987; Campbell, 2003). Another complication in the valuation task is the nature of many inputs that are donated. Measuring economic and social impact together in the form of 'blended returns', is emerging as a promising approach (Emerson and Bonini, 2004).
- *How do performance measurements get integrated into the management and incentive systems?*
  Too frequently, it appears that measurements are inadequately incorporated into the managerial processes. Comparing how different organizations address this challenge would contribute to making progress on this task (Kaplan, 2001).

Governance

- *What are the key capabilities and functions of governing entities and individuals for entrepreneurial social undertakings compared to commercial businesses?*
  While there is a large literature on the governance of nonprofit and for-profit enterprises, there is insufficient understanding of the governance process in the startup and early development phase of SE.

The corporate avenue

I now turn to our second avenue of investigation, which I address more briefly due to its sharper focus. My contention is that corporations should also be a locus of SE research. My reasoning stems from the evolution of entrepreneurship studies. From the study of basic entrepreneurship, for which there is an enormous body of literature, there emerged two branches during the 1990s. One was SE, which is what I have been discussing in the previous section. The other was corporate entrepreneurship, which focused on the need for companies to create entrepreneurial processes within the corporate organization as a way to stimulate innovation and the exploitation of new opportunities. A logical extension and blending of these two streams of research is what can be referred to as *Corporate Social Entrepreneurship (CSE)*, for which I offer the following definition:

> CSE is the process of extending the firm's domain of competence and corresponding opportunity set through innovative leveraging of resources, both within and outside its direct control, aimed at the simultaneous creation of economic and social value. (Austin, Reficco and Wei-Skillern, 2005).

Several important research questions that emerge in this area follow here.

Why should companies engage in CSE?

There is a need to understand the rationale and motivations for companies to engage in what might be considered a distinct and higher form of what some have labeled corporate social responsibility (CSR). Almost all major corporations practice some form of philanthropy and their interest and investments in CSR have grown exponentially in recent years (Epstein and Hanson, 2005). However, CSE is aimed at going beyond traditional philanthropy and CSR. It takes a much more strategic and innovative approach to push outward together, the frontiers of social and economic value generation. This is what requires entrepreneurship.

How can social value creation generate business value and vice versa?

One essential dimension of this new configuration is the integration of social and business value. CSE aims to capture the synergies between these two. Understanding conceptually and empirically the nature of these linkages, is very important (Grayson and Hodges, 2004).

How can CSE best be carried out in terms of strategy, organizational structure and management processes?

Because CSE is in its early stages, it is important to document the operational processes by which it is implemented. A search for smart practices that would enable lateral learning is called for.

Do companies have a comparative institutional advantage for generating social value?

While companies' basic operations of producing desired goods and services and providing employment and wealth creation are, of course, socially valuable, businesses have not been seen as key generators of social value beyond these basics. However, there are reasons to hold that companies may actually possess capabilities and resources that enable them to be highly productive generators of social value (Austin, 2000; Porter and Kramer, 2002). Probing this possibility is an important arena due to the multitude of managerial and public policy implications.

The collaborative avenue

I envision collaboration among different types of organizations as a form of SE if there is an embedded social purpose and innovation. I conclude my chapter with a quick glimpse down this interesting research path. When institutions come together and jointly deploy their resources, they are frequently able to create an innovative configuration that has the capability to generate greater social value than either organization by itself. Distinctive combinations of existing resources and organizations are a manifestation of Schumpeterian innovation. Thus, collaborations and strategic alliances can be considered a distinct organizational form that is becoming increasingly used within and across sectors. (Austin, 2000)

What are the barriers, enablers, benefits, and key success factors for:

- *Intra-sector alliances?*
- *Cross-sector alliances (business-nonprofit, business-government, government-nonprofit)?*
- *Tri-sector partnerships?*

This is an ample multidimensional and multisectorial research agenda. While we have considerable and growing knowledge on such collaborations, more would be desirable, particularly from a strategy perspective (McLaughlin, 1998; Boris and Steuerle, 1999; Austin, 2003; Wymer and Samu, 2003). Furthermore, there is an opportunity for comparing collaborations in different sectors in order to identify the extent that the drivers and processes of collaboration are similar or distinctive. Studying partnership dynamics is an important accompanying perspective. Are there identifiable stages in the evolution of these relationships?

How can one most effectively create, manage, and govern social purpose networks?

Beyond alliances, an increasingly important and understudied form of collaboration is networks. Understanding network dynamics may also require a study of how to most effectively manage stakeholder relations. While networks in general have been the subject of extensive scrutiny in the organizational behavior and sociology literature (Powell and Smith-Doerr, 1994; Ebers, 1997), our interest is to explore the extent to which social purpose networks among social enterprises are distinct (Weiner and Alexander, 1998; Dees, Anderson and Wei-Skillern, 2004).

How can one create maximum value through collaborations?

To be sustainable, collaborations must generate value for the partners and the larger society. Existing research suggests that the magnitude of value depends significantly on the type of resources deployed (Kanter, 1999; Austin, 2000) and the depth and breadth of alignment of partners' missions, values, and strategies. (Austin, Reficco et al., 2004). Deepening our understanding of the value creation process is important. Accompanying this is the inevitable need to focus on how to measure value.

Moving forward

I end these reflections by pointing to collaboration, not only as a subject of substantive scrutiny on our collective research agenda, but also as a highly desirable form for carrying out our inquiry. There is a need for different disciplines to engage in the study of SE for us to learn from one another through these different perspectives. More ambitiously, we could engage in interdisciplinary research which is explicitly integrative. Comparative analysis can be productively pursued internationally through interinstitutional research partnerships, such as the Social Enterprise Knowledge Network (SEKN).[1] As an emerging field, SE offers rich opportunities for researching collabora-tively. The more we learn together, the faster and more robustly the field will develop. This book is an encouraging manifestation of such a collective contribution to our shared intellectual journey.

Note

1. This network consists of nine business schools in Latin America, one in Spain, and one in the US and its mission is to advance the frontiers of knowledge and practice in social enterprise; see: http://www.sekn.org.

References

Anderson, B. B. and Dees, J. G. 2006. Rhetoric, reality, and research: Building a solid foundation for the practice of social entrepreneurship. In A. Nicholls (ed.), *Social entrepreneurship: New paradigms of sustainable social change*. Oxford: Oxford University Press.

Austin, J. E. 2000. *The collaboration challenge: How nonprofits and businesses succeed through strategic alliances*. Indianapolis: Jossey-Bass.

Austin, J. E. 2003. Strategic alliances: Managing the collaboration portfolio. *Stanford Social Innovation Review*, 1(2): 48–55.

Austin, J. E., Reficco, E. et al. 2004. *Social partnering in Latin America*. Boston: Harvard University Press.

Austin, J. E., Leonard, H., Reficco, E. and Wei-Skillern, J. 2005. Corporate social entrepreneurship: A new vision for CSR. In M. J. Epstein and K. O. Hanson (eds), *The accountable corporation*. Vol. 3. New York: Praeger Publishing.

Austin, J. E., Stevenson, H. and Wei-Skillern, J. 2006. Social entrepreneurship and commercial entrepreneurship: Same, different, or both. *Entrepreneurship Theory and Practice*, 30(1): forthcoming.

Boris, E. and Steuerle, C. E. 1999. *Nonprofits and government: Collaboration and conflict*. Washington: Urban Institute Press.

Boschee, J., Emerson, J., Sealey, K. and Sealy, W. 2000. *A reader in social enterprise*. Boston: Pearson Custom Publishers.

Boschee, J. and McClurg, J. 2003. Toward a better understand of social entrepre-neurship: Some important distinctions. Available: http://www.se-alliance.org.

Bradach, J. L. 2003. Going to scale. *Stanford Social Innovation Review*, 1(1): 18–25.

Campbell, D. 2003. Outcomes assessment and the paradox of nonprofit accountability. *Nonprofit Management and Leadership*, 12(3): 243–60.

Dees, J. G., Anderson, B. B. and Wei-Skillern, J. 2004. Scaling social impact. *Stanford Social Innovation Review*, 1(4): 24–32.

Dees, J. G. and Backman, E. 1994. *Social enterprise: Private initiatives for the common good*. Harvard Business School Note: 9-395-116.

Ebers, M. 1997. *The formation of inter-organizational networks*. Oxford: Oxford University Press.

Emerson, J. and Bonini, S. 2004. *The blended value map*. Available: http://www.blendedvalue.org.

Epstein, M. J. and Hanson, K. O. 2005. *The accountable corporation*. New York: Praeger Publishers.

Foster, W. and Bradach, J. L. 2005. Should nonprofits seek profits? *Harvard Business Review*, 83(2): 92–100.

Grayson, D. and Hodges, A. 2004. *Corporate social opportunity! 7 steps to make corporate social responsibility work for your business.* Sheffield, UK: Greenleaf Publishing.

Hughes, P. and Luksetich, W. 2004. Nonprofit arts organizations: Do funding sources influence spending patterns? *Nonprofit and Voluntary Sector Quarterly,* 33(2): 203–20.

Kanter, R. M. 1999. From spare change to real change: The social sector as beta site for business innovation. *Harvard Business Review,* 77(3): 121–32.

Kanter, R. M. and Summers, D. 1987. Doing well while doing good: Dilemmas of performance measurement in nonprofit organizations and the need for a multiple-constituency approach. In W. W. Powell (ed.), *The nonprofit sector: A research handbook:* 154–66. New Haven, CT: Yale University Press.

Kaplan, R. S. 2001. Strategic performance measurement and management in nonprofit organizations. *Nonprofit Management and Leadership,* 11(3): 353–71.

Letts, C.W., Ryan, W. and Grossman, A. 1997. Virtuous capital: What foundations can learn from venture capitalists. *Harvard Business Review,* 75(2): 1–7.

McLaughlin, T. A. 1998. *Nonprofit mergers and alliances.* New York: John Wiley and Sons.

Porter, M. E. and Kramer, M. R. 2002. The competitive advantage of corporate philanthropy. *Harvard Business Review,* 80(12): 56–8.

Powell, W. W. and Smith-Doerr, L. 1994. Networks and economic life. In N. Smelser and R. Swedberg (eds), *The handbook of economic sociology:* 368–402. Princeton, NJ: Princeton University Press.

Salomon, L. M. (ed.). S Wojciech Salomon, and Associates. 2004. *Global civil society: Dimensions of the nonprofit sector.* Vol. 2. Bloomfield, CT: Kumarian Press.

Sawhill, J. C. and Williamson. D. 2001. Mission impossible? Measuring success in nonprofit organizations. *Nonprofit Management and Leadership,* 11(3): 371–87.

Weiner, B. and Alexander, J. A. 1998. The challenges of governing public-private community health partnerships. *Health Care Management Review,* 23(2): 39–55.

Wymer Jr., W. W. and Samu, S. 2003. Dimensions of business and nonprofit collaborative relationships. *Journal of Nonprofit and Public Sector Marketing,* 11(1): 3.

4

Politics, Values and Social Entrepreneurship: A Critical Appraisal

Albert Hyunbae Cho

Introduction

Social entrepreneurship (SE) has many champions and a notable lack of detractors. Governments have embraced it, business schools have committed millions of dollars to study it, nonprofit organizations have been founded to incubate it, and creative individuals are rapidly evolving it into new and innovative forms. Like the concepts of the 'Third Way' and 'compassionate conservatism', SE's millennialist vision of harmony between private sector initiatives and public sector values appeals to a world tired of political economy's time-worn ideological battles. SE speaks a compelling language of pragmatism, cooperation, and hope.

Doubtlessly, SE has achieved impressive successes and will inspire even more. Yet the fact that it has attracted enthusiastic support from such an unusually broad group of stakeholders suggests cause for caution as well as hope: 'social' concepts that attract such unqualified support are usually vacant of normative content or require further examination to uncover the conflicts of interest that inevitably accompany discussions of the common good. This paper interrogates the concept and practice of SE by exploring the vision of the 'social' it implicitly invokes. It demonstrates that existing definitions of SE are both tautological and monological, and that these features reflect complicated questions about the relationship between SE, politics and values; questions that need to be resolved in order to understand the broader implications of the turn toward SE. In order to advance 'social' objectives more effectively, social entrepreneurs will need to grapple with fundamentally political questions about the normative content of their objectives and their relationship to broader social and deliberative processes.

Defining social entrepreneurship: tautology, monologue and politics

A recent literature review of research on SE notes that 'defining what social entrepreneurship is, and what its conceptual boundaries are, is not an easy task... in part because the concept is inherently complex, and in part because the literature in the area is so new that little consensus has emerged on the topic'. (Johnson, 2000) Nevertheless, a few key definitions have emerged. Schuyler (1998) describes social entrepreneurs as 'individuals who have a vision for social change and who have the financial resources to support their ideas'. Thompson, Alvy and Lees (2000) describe social entrepreneurs as 'people who realize where there is an opportunity to satisfy some unmet need that the state welfare system will not or cannot meet, and who gather together the necessary resources (generally people, often volunteers, money and premises) and use these to "make a difference"'. One of the most frequently cited definitions of SE comes from J. Gregory Dees who defines social entrepreneurs as people who:

> ...play the role of change agents in the social sector, by:
> * Adopting a mission to create and sustain social value (not just private value),
> * Recognizing and relentlessly pursuing new opportunities to serve that mission,
> * Engaging in a process of continuous innovation, adaptation and learning,
> * Acting boldly without being limited by resources currently in hand, and
> * Exhibiting heightened accountability to the constituencies served and for the outcomes created. (Dees, 2001: 4)

Two problems emerge from these definitions: first, that they are tautological, and second, that they are monological. Initially, most definitions of SE clarify the components of 'entrepreneurship' but leave 'social' undefined, a surprising lapse given that the social dimension of SE is, in large part, responsible for the concept's inherent complexity. Second, definitions tend to emphasize a monological (as opposed to dialogical) approach to the definition and pursuit of putatively 'social' ends. Entrepreneurs have a vision for social change and mobilize resources to pursue this vision; they are ambitious, independent, and focused on achieving ends. While this vision may come from deliberative processes, entrepreneurship nevertheless takes a subject-centered approach to engaging with the world, from the individual articulation of a 'social' vision to the autonomous execution of projects and programs. This 'monological' approach may neglect competing visions and supplant important political processes of dialogue, negotiation, and social integration.

Many definitions of SE, then, seem inadequate to deal with the central theoretical and normative issues that arise from the concept's juxtaposition of 'social' objectives and the instruments of private enterprise. The issues of tautology and monologue are not innocent lapses; rather, they reflect a gap in the way we think about SE and its relationship to politics. Initially, SE distinguishes itself from its private cousin on the basis of its pursuit of 'social' ends. If this distinction is to be meaningful, 'social' requires definition. Yet the act of defining the domain of the social inevitably requires exclusionary and ultimately political choices about which concerns can claim to be in society's 'true' interest. These choices reveal that, despite its protestations to the contrary, SE *by its very nature* is always already a political phenomenon. In the next section, this paper argues that social entrepreneurs and their stakeholders must come explicitly to terms with the substantive and political values embedded in their actions.

Furthermore, if entrepreneurship is inherently monological, SE raises important questions about political ends and the processes appropriate to pursue them. Within social contexts, the pursuit of subjective values requires negotiation and public deliberation. Where these processes are situated within democratic social institutions, the discourse of entrepreneurship may sidestep or supplant important deliberative political practices. As the state lottery example later in this chapter suggests, the discourse of entrepreneurship may even undermine the achievement of social objectives. Both conclusions suggest that social entrepreneurs need to achieve a critical understanding of the 'values' dimension of their work in order to ensure that their actions are ultimately consistent with 'social' objectives.

Because this paper explores basic principles, it uses a quite general working definition of SE: a set of institutional practices combining the pursuit of financial objectives with the pursuit and promotion of substantive and terminal values. This definition, though open-ended, has two advantages. First, it permits discussion of a wide range of practices from which to extract an understanding of broader trends. Second, it minimizes the risk of selectivity bias. Restrictive definitions of SE seem to cause more problems than they solve, not least because the research community continues to explore new forms and avenues for SE. Given our nascent understanding of SE, Type II errors of exclusion are likely to be more serious than Type I errors of inclusion.[1] Given the potential breadth of different kinds of socially entrepreneurial behavior, our analysis will purposely err on the side of generality to focus attention on the conceptually interesting features that arise from the juxtaposition of the terms 'social' and 'entrepreneurship'.

Breaking the tautology: exploring the 'social' in social entrepreneurship

By defining itself in opposition to regular entrepreneurship, the term 'social entrepreneurship' implicitly advances a sociological, sui generis vision of the 'social' good, one irreducible to and greater than the sum total of individual welfare functions. Where economic theorists such as Milton Friedman conflate the social good with the welfare optimum resulting from the free operation of market forces, the move to distinguish SE from private enterprise already suggests that social objectives stand distinct from the interplay of individual pursuits. In its very etymology, SE proclaims the existence of a distinct sphere of common processes, values and concerns. Its conceptual coherence therefore depends upon a substantive vision of the 'social' good that is qualitatively different from and irreducible to the aggregate of private interests and objectives. By aligning themselves with 'social' objectives, social entrepreneurs implicitly commit to this vision of the distinctly *social* welfare optimum.

But what are the contents and details of this implicitly 'social' vision? Elaborating the substantive and normative content of the 'social' good proves to be a complex challenge that existing definitions do not help to resolve. The prevailing definitions in the field generally fail to explain or investigate the concept of the 'social', treating it as a predetermined and exogenous concept, or one so patently obvious as to require no further explanation. Some of these definitions are procedural, focusing primarily on the nature of the behaviors that make the pursuit of social ends entrepreneurial. Others attempt to be substantive, but do not provide a comprehensive framework for understanding the normative content of the 'social.' Yet without closely examining what 'social' means and how it comes to take that meaning, SE is left mired in tautology and subject to misunderstanding, misinterpretation and manipulation. Clarifying the values embedded in SE is an important exercise because the concept of the 'social' turns out to be quite complicated. This section of the paper explores theoretical perspectives on the 'social' and demonstrates that the conflicts intrinsic to social existence render SE an inherently political enterprise.

Thompson (2002) provides a point of departure in his description of organizations that fall within the category of the 'social':

> Organizations are 'social' when they are not owned by identifiable shareholders and profit is not the driving objective. Moreover, they 'belong' to society, rather than, say, to the state. (Thompson, 2002)

Thompson's definition raises several important distinctions. Initially, it establishes the 'social' as a domain purposively separate from the world of private ownership. Second, the definition distinguishes 'society' from the 'state', establishing the 'social' as a domain separate from the formal apparatus of public authority. Social organizations are therefore neither fully private nor fully public; they operate somewhere in the space between state and market.

This description of the social sector will sound familiar to anyone familiar with the work of Jürgen Habermas, who has written extensively on the concept of the public sphere. In *The structural transformation of the public sphere*, Habermas discusses features of bourgeois society that developed during the late seventeenth and eighteenth century in Europe. According to Habermas (1989: 27), this sphere:

> ...may be conceived above all as the sphere of private people come together as a public; they soon claimed the public sphere regulated from above against the public authorities themselves, to engage them in a debate over the general rules governing relations in the basically privatized but publicly relevant sphere of commodity exchange and social labor. The medium of this political confrontation was peculiar and without historical precedent: people's public use of their reason.

The public sphere gave birth to an historically new atmosphere of free and rational debate symbolized by the Parisian salons of the eighteenth century, sites of political discourse that eventually led to an 'idea of society separate from the ruler (or the state) and of a private realm separate from the public' (Calhoun, 1992). Forged from the spreading flames of the Enlightenment, the public sphere gave birth to the idea of a 'civil society' set apart from the market and the state, spheres of interaction that coordinate behavior, not through the communicative

practice of discourse, but through the nonlinguistic 'steering mechanisms' of money and power (Habermas, 1997). Indeed, in complex
societies, 'the public sphere consists of an intermediary structure
between the political system, on the one hand, and the private sectors
of the lifeworld and functional systems' (Habermas 1996: 373). It is to
this concept of the bourgeois public sphere that definitions of society
like Thompson's trace their ancestry.

To the extent that SE is invested in these images of civil society, it
is also tied to the concept of a discursively achievable consensus
over what 'society' wants. In the idealized vision of the public
sphere, status differences are 'bracketed' and left at the door, and
the power of intersubjective discourse produces consensus around
major issues of social concern. In the public sphere, we can collectively identify 'society's' interests through the exercise of dialogical
reason. Because we can identify 'social' aims and objectives, we can
therefore agree upon how to distinguish 'social' entrepreneurship
from its private cousin. The assumption of a unitary social agenda is
consistent both with the hegemonic view of reason advanced by
the Enlightenment thinkers – and with Habermas' subsequent
attempt to rehabilitate their claims with the concept of public and
communicative action.

If Habermas is right, and consensus around values can be achieved in
the social arena, then the normative objectives of SE are incontestably
consistent with 'society's' best interests. But not all theorists are so san-
guine about the possibility of mutually compatible social interests. Karl
Marx's sociological work, upon which Habermas drew extensively in
his early writings, suggests that defining a 'social' agenda may not be a
simple matter because individuals advance competing and conflicting
identities and interests in the social arena. While Thompson defines
'social' as the residual category left after subtracting the 'public' and
the 'private' from the sum total of institutional and intersubjective
interactions, Marx observes that this formulation virtually ensures an
irreconcilable heterogeneity of preferences. In *On the Jewish Question*,
Marx (1978) suggested that:

Man, as the adherent of a particular religion, finds himself in
conflict with his citizenship and with other men as members of the
community. This conflict reduces itself to the *secular* division
between the *political* state and *civil* society. For man as a bourgeois,
'life in the state' is 'only a semblance or a temporary exception to
the essential and the rule'... The difference between the merchant

and the citizen, between the day-laborer and the citizen, between the landowner and the citizen, between the *living individual* and the *citizen*. The contradiction in which the religious man finds himself with the political man is the same contradiction in which the bourgeois finds himself with the *citoyen*, and the member of civil society with his political lion's skin.

Though Marx's analysis may exaggerate the distinction between private life and public citizenship in the service of his larger theoretical project, he insightfully demonstrates that 'civil society' contains sectarian and subjective interests incapable of encapsulation within a unitary view of 'social' needs. To the extent that dissimilar identities and interests divide and distinguish the body politic, the realm of the social is riven by conflicts that may not be easily reconcilable through communicative action.

At a broader level of abstraction, Isaiah Berlin identifies conflicts not only between divergent interests, but also between incompatible terminal values. Berlin, not a Marxist theorist by any means, sharply criticized what he called the 'Ionian fallacy' of worldviews that presume the possibility of mutually consistent ends. 'Ionians' fallaciously contend that:

> ...all genuine questions must have one true answer and one only, all the rest being necessarily errors; in the second place, that there must be a dependable path toward the discovery of these truths; in the third place, that the true answers, when found, must necessarily be compatible with one another and form a single whole, for one truth cannot be incompatible with another – this we know *a priori*. (Berlin, 1997: 5)

Yet such a priori assumptions appear to depart quite sharply from the empirical reality of dissensus over social goals. In his essay entitled *Does political theory still exist?* Berlin argued that political theory is possible 'only in a world where ends collide' (Berlin, 1997) – and that we live in just such a world. Berlin suggests that:

> The notion of a perfect whole, the ultimate solution, in which all good things coexist, seems to me to be not merely unattainable – that is a truism – but conceptually incoherent; I do not know what is meant by a harmony of this kind. Some among the Great Goods cannot live together. (Berlin, 1997: 13)

Marx argues that private identities and interests create social conflicts that cannot be eliminated by fiat, and Berlin suggests that fundamentally different worldviews may prevail even among similarly situated people. Both narratives suggest that there are limits to the implicit community of interests upon which the idea of 'social' needs depends. Indeed, even Habermas' intellectual descendants concede that the structural transformation of the public sphere to which he refers is ultimately a narrative of collapse because interpenetration of the public and private spheres hampers the public sphere's ability to mediate conflicting claims through discourse. According to Calhoun (1992: 21):

> The blurring of relations between private and public involved centrally the loss of the notion that private life created autonomous, relatively equal persons who in public discourse might address the general or public interest. First, the inequalities always present in civil society ceased to be 'bracketed' and became instead the basis of discussion and action. This happened both because these inequalities grew greater and because the inclusion of more people in the public sphere made it impossible to escape addressing the class divisions of civil society.

The gradual intrusion of distortions generated by inequalities of wealth and power sharply limit social integration in practice, destabilizing the public sphere.

Nancy Fraser (1992) extends this criticism by developing the notion of *inter*public heterogeneity. Fraser suggests that there have always been 'subaltern counter-publics' that operate in the shadow of dominant groups. Subaltern counter-publics constitute their own discursive communities, share distinct sets of normative commitments, and formulate 'oppositional interpretations of their identities, interests and needs'. Fraser's critiques of a hegemonic view of the 'public' or 'social' are important because the communicative distortions generated by wealth and power '... will be exacerbated where there is only a single, comprehensive public sphere'. In that case, members of subordinated groups would have no arenas for deliberation among themselves about their needs, objectives and strategies. They would have no venues in which to undertake communicative processes that were not, as it were, under the supervision of dominant groups. In this situation they would be less likely than otherwise to 'find the right voice or words to express their thoughts' and more likely than otherwise 'to keep their wants inchoate'. This would render them less able than otherwise to articulate and defend their interests in the comprehensive public sphere. They would be less able than otherwise to expose modes of deliberation that mask domination by, in Mansbridge's words, 'absorbing the less powerful into a false "we" that reflects the more powerful.' (Fraser, 1992: 123)

These arguments bear directly upon the definition of SE by asking the question: does the 'social' in SE also postulate and impose a 'false we'? If there exist multiple conflicting interests, values, and discursive communities that possess oppositional worldviews and social projects within the public sphere, then to speak of 'the' social good may be to engage in an act of discursive marginalization. If heterogeneity, counter-narrative and dissent are indeed important elements of 'society', then the social is inherently political – and what we think of as 'social' entrepreneurship is always already invested in political agendas and struggles. When entrepreneurs organize their actions around values they have identified as 'social', they have already made demanding epistemological and political claims about their ability and entitlement to articulate what lies in the public's interest.

A distinct but related issue is defining the spatial and temporal limits of 'society' itself. Even as Fraser correctly identifies the presence of subaltern counter-publics within the public sphere, it is also true that the public sphere has, since the birth of the nation-state, been inscribed within the geographical and social boundaries of the nation. Yet there are compelling arguments for thinking about social needs beyond borders by taking a cosmopolitan perspective. However, as a number of contemporary debates suggest, what is good from a global perspective may not be desirable or politically feasible from a national or regional perspective. Conflicts over outsourcing white-collar jobs are fueled by difficult concerns about the distribution of welfare gains, concerns that have both 'social' and political elements. Likewise, the mass migration of skilled medical personnel from the countries of subSaharan Africa to the industrialized countries raises ethically complicated questions about 'social' benefits and where they accrue.

A related point has to do with society's temporal dimension. If our societies include only existing generations, then our priorities and values are likely to be different than if we consider our societies to include future, unborn generations. Trade-offs between present and future societies are particularly salient in conflicts between economic development and environmental conservation practices. Although the discourse of 'sustainable development' attempts to resolve these conflicts, the rapid pace of environmental change suggests that our behaviors currently privilege the interests of the present over the future. Whenever we talk about 'social' objectives, different views of the geographical, cultural, political, economic and temporal boundaries of 'society' can produce widely divergent conclusions about the social good and the interventions needed to achieve it.

These issues are central to the SE research agenda, which has to date focused primarily on questions of performance, efficiency and best practices. Yet performance, efficiency and best practices are operational benchmarks that are only sensible in the context of specific and well-defined terminal 'social' objectives. If we want to think rigorously about how to evaluate and understand SE, then we also have to think critically about what SE *is* and what it ought to include. One set of questions might ask: if one of the principal characteristics of SE is the application of 'market-based approaches' to 'social' questions, then social service delivery probably does not represent the full range of eligible activities. Indeed, if 'society' is more fragmented and conflictual than the notion of a discursively achievable consensus suggests, SE might also include initiatives that divide rather than integrate. Consider the following examples:

- A nonprofit organization that raises money for poor girls to have abortions
- The National Rifle Association running a for-profit shooting range to finance its nonprofit advocacy activities
- A business that seeks to bring nurses from abroad to serve underprivileged communities in the US despite the human resource crisis in many developing country health systems
- A church organization that provides housing to the homeless, to whom volunteers proselytize in an attempt to convert
- An organization that pays runaway gay and lesbian teenagers to conduct educational 'outreach' events to other community groups
- Ecotourism (discussed below), which generates incomes and advances certain conservation objectives while simultaneously influencing culture and changing patterns of access to natural resources

These examples suggest that the line between what is traditionally seen as 'social entrepreneurship' and more controversial forms of social engagement may be difficult to draw with precision. At issue here, as in the work of Berlin, Fraser and Marx, is the multiplicity of potentially incompatible visions at play in the 'social' field. If all of these enterprises qualify as 'social' entrepreneurship despite their embrace of divisive social visions, then we have moved quite a distance away from the comfortable position of knowing what is in the public interest, and what values 'social entrepreneurs' can legitimately elect to pursue. Though many social entrepreneurs are likely to advance causes that many, if not all of us agree are worthwhile, the theoretical framework explored above suggests that these initiatives are simply the limiting case in a continuum of contentious political visions regarding social change.

Box 4.1   Ecotourism

Ecotourism is a popular example of SE's contribution to the objectives of sustainable development. Ecotourism is one of the fastest growing segments of tourism, itself one the world's largest and fastest growing industries. While accurate global figures for the economic impact of ecotourism are difficult to obtain, the sector has had obvious economic impacts in specific countries. In Costa Rica, for example, the number of foreign visitors to national parks increased from 65,000 in 1982 to over 400,000 in 1998 (UNEP, 2001).

The benefits of ecotourism are well known. Ecotourism generates much-needed revenues that can be used to support local communities and the conservation of natural resources. It creates jobs and opportunities for the acquisition and productive use of new skills. Community-based tourism can increase pride in local culture and make resources available for maintaining cultural assets and heritage sites (UNEP, 2001). Ecotourism has the potential to bring the frequently conflicting objectives of poverty reduction and conservation into alignment.

But ecotourism is not a uniformly positive phenomenon; it poses both contingent and intrinsic risks. If managed poorly, ecotourism can have serious negative environmental consequences, damaging the ecosystems around which it is organized. Critics of ecotourism note that the practice is an 'instigator of change' that 'can be very demanding' and 'has the potential to be environmentally destructive' (Wall, 1997). But there are deeper problems with the distributional impacts of ecotourism. Many models of ecotourism involve land privatization and forcible exclusion of indigenous peoples; benefits are concentrated in a limited number of hands. Traditional rights of access to the environment and the services it provides are lost as modern property rights trump these sometimes poorly defined claims, potentially intensifying poverty among specific groups.

Box 4.1   Ecotourism – *continued*

In the Philippines, hundreds of people were evicted and their houses razed by authorities clearing the area for an ecotourism venture, and in the Moulvibaza district of Bangladesh, over 1000 indigenous families face eviction from ancestral lands for the development of a 1500 acre ecopark (Wheat, 2002). In Costa Rica, the designation of Tortuguero National Park disadvantaged local residents who had previously used the land for hunting and gathering activities (Place, 1991; Wall, 1997). In Surinam, one ecotourist business focused around a turtle reserve, benefited the reserve and one indigenous community, but provided no income for the larger community that was impacted by its operations. These inequalities created hostility, disinterest in conservation and social divides (Lindsay, 2003). Social systems are reoriented toward tourism and hospitality, a phenomenon responsible for altering traditional cultures and modes of existence. Ecotourism may drive population inflows, price inflation, and other socio-economic changes that destabilize communities and cultures. In Mexico, ecotourism oriented around the migratory patterns of the monarch butterfly led effectively to the coercive appropriation of indigenous lands (Barkin, 1996). Ecotourism creates political benefits and trade-offs while strategies to promote it implicitly privilege the needs of certain groups and values above others.

Ecotourism illustrates some of the central normative issues raised by SE. Defining the 'social' dimension of ecotourism is difficult because both its proponents and critics couch their arguments in the language of 'social' objectives. At issue are competing visions of the social good, both at the level of interests (protecting local people versus tourism developers generating economic growth), and values (environmental conservation versus economic development). Developers of ecotourist ventures can legitimately claim to be advancing social objectives because they may indeed be protecting resources and generating revenues. But ecotourism may 'crowd out' other kinds of initiatives that might be in the public interest, such as national conservation strategies or access rights for indigenous communities. While many of these potentially negative impacts can be mitigated by well-designed plans, limited regulatory capacity in many countries leaves environmental management in the hands of entrepreneurs whose social vision may not be consistent with the objectives of various social groups. Though ecotourism generates significant advantages for some communities and some benefits for society at large, it also produces political challenges that require political solutions.

Monologue, entrepreneurship and the colonization of the lifeworld

If society, as the forgoing analysis suggests, is a heterogeneous pool of conflicting social objectives, then how are we to negotiate between these competing visions? This dilemma is one of the fundamental problems of political theory, and it is beyond the scope of this paper to offer a complete answer. However, a recent strand of thought articulated in the work of Iris Marion Young (2000), suggests that deliberation, debate and discussion are critical to reconcile fundamentally different social points of view. In a democracy, people have different values and worldviews, but at the end of the day they still inhabit a single polity governed by common rules. They have to broker compromises in order to survive as a community. Notwithstanding the criticisms of the 'public sphere' advanced above, principles of discourse, equal participation, and reasoned argumentation are certainly better arbiters of value than authoritarian or strictly market-based outcomes that reinforce the ability of the wealthy or powerful to impose their choices upon others. When we think or speak about the elements of 'good governance', we usually include individual rights to free expression and political participation – precisely because these provisions are critical to empower people to speak and negotiate on behalf of their deeply held values.

Collective deliberation and participation, then, are the instruments by which polities fashion a synthetic vision of the 'social' from the fractious and dissonant value claims advanced by private individuals. These elements of governance underscore the importance of dialogue – and raise concerns about the monological dimensions of SE. The distinction between 'monological' and 'dialogical' reason is well-developed in social theory; in basic terms, it involves a distinction between subject-centered and intersubjective modes of interaction. The former category, advanced by theorists such as Adam Smith, begins with the conceptual building block of the atomistic individual exercising reason to form judgments and pursue projects in alignment with his or her preferences and perceptions. It is sometimes claimed that the uncoordinated individual pursuit of welfare maximization produces socially optimal outcomes. The latter category, represented by theorists such as Iris Marion Young or Jürgen Habermas, suggests that deliberative, political processes are needed to steer intersubjective interactions fairly, justly – and optimally.

Private enterprise is clearly monological, as it involves unitary and independent actors maximizing individual welfare – a calculus flexible enough to include the agent's subjective and normative objectives. The vision of SE most commonly advanced in the literature is no less monological. Dees (2001), for example, describes social entrepreneurs as 'reformers and revolutionaries' whose 'visions are bold', who 'break new ground, develop new models, and pioneer new approaches'. Social entrepreneurs have their own, divergent, subjective visions for the rest of society and rationally mobilize resources in order to enact their agendas.

This monological stance is simultaneously SE's greatest asset and its greatest challenge. Entrepreneurial ambition accounts for the extraordinary dynamism and many admirable achievements of social enterprise. The development of microfinance, community health systems, and worker training programs by social entrepreneurs is an irreproachably positive achievement. Nevertheless, embedded within the monological frame lies a troubling conceptual difficulty: the possibility of disjuncture between entrepreneurial objectives and processes and the need to engage in participatory deliberation to negotiate between conflicting visions for social transformation. If the model of social conflict over values advanced in the previous section is descriptively accurate, SE could be potentially coercive in its use of entrepreneurial means to promulgate political objectives.

But there is a deeper point here: even if we bracket the assumption of divergent ends and posit consensus around particular social objectives, the actions of well-intentioned monological actors might nevertheless displace social processes and strategies more appropriately positioned to achieve discursively negotiable common objectives. According to Dees, social entrepreneurs 'attack the underlying causes of problems, rather than simply treating symptoms' (Dees, 2001). Yet by construction this appears to be untrue in cases where problems are rooted in politics, not market failure. Returning to Thompson, Alvy and Lee's description of social entrepreneurs as 'people who realize where there is an opportunity to satisfy some unmet need that the state welfare system will not or cannot meet, and who gather together the necessary resources (generally people, often volunteers, money and premises) and use these to "make a difference"'(Thompson, Alvy and Lees, 2000), one might reasonably argue that social entrepreneurs are asking the wrong question.

Faced with evidence of state incapacity to resolve pressing social problems, the social entrepreneurs of Thompson, Alvy and Lee's definition ask: 'How can I mobilize resources to solve this issue?' rather than 'Why does this issue exist; why is it that the state welfare system can't or won't meet this need?' Where problems derive from politics rather than from market failures, SE may well end up addressing symptoms rather than root causes.

State lottery systems illustrate elements of this tension. In an effort to diversify funding revenues after the Reagan governments of the 1980s drastically cut federal aid to the states, many state governments implemented lotteries to fund social projects and programs. Many states built political support for lotteries by promising to fund university scholarships, parks, and other amenities, and indeed, lotteries have generated profits of around 33 per cent per ticket sold by the states (Clotfelter, 2000). Besides the fact that they are operated by the state, lotteries seem to be a perfect example of SE. They use market-based approaches to generate income by selling products that people want; in this case, contingent claims to a sizable jackpot. The lotteries generate funds that can be channeled in socially meaningful directions, including the advancement of education, environmental conservation and health programs.

Yet lotteries are also a problematic source of income because they are fundamentally a regressive tax on the poor. Sociological research has demonstrated that poor people spend as much as four times more as a proportion of income than rich people do on lottery tickets (South Carolina Policy Council, 1999). Lotteries have relentlessly marketed tickets to underprivileged populations. An Ohio Lottery marketing plan advised officials to advertise early each month to coincide with government benefits and Social Security payments (Clotfelter and Cook, 1989). One particularly perverse Illinois campaign targeted a poor Chicago neighborhood with posters reading, 'This could be your ticket out'. In many states, lottery outlets are more concentrated in impoverished neighborhoods than in wealthy ones. It should be no surprise that, in Colorado, for example, the 32 counties with the highest per capita lottery sales all have per capita incomes less than the state average; or that those living in the most impoverished areas of New York spent eight times more from their incomes on lottery tickets than those living in affluent sections (South Carolina Policy Council, 1999).

The lottery system collects a disproportionate amount of its revenues from poor neighborhoods, but it spends many of the profits on programs that benefit richer portions of society. In Georgia's lottery system, which is used to fund a state-wide college scholarship program, students in the poorest neighborhoods received seven cents per dollar spent on the state lottery. Students in the ten richest neighborhoods, by contrast, received twenty cents in scholarship aid (Hill and Palmer, 2002). In effect, the lottery system represented a transfer of income from the very poor to the relatively well-off.

The lottery example raises relevant questions about the appropriateness of instruments to achieve social ends. Lotteries mobilize resources in the private market in order to pursue a 'social' mission, including support for public goods such as schools and parks. But at the same time, they are a decidedly suboptimal palliative measure for an inadequate system of public goods provision. The cash flow from lotteries defers closer scrutiny and debate over the distributional impacts of fiscal policies, perpetuating an ethically perverse financing structure for public goods. Though their visible effect is to generate social benefits in a self-financing and theoretically noncoercive manner, their ultimate impacts are socially negative. Lotteries appear to benefit society by paying for public goods; indeed, their public finance advantages are routinely touted in campaigns to expand their reach. Yet the distributive impacts of lotteries suggest that they may actually be detrimental to the poor, a consequence that many people would find objectionable and contrary to their conception of the 'public interest'.

SE is a means to an end; it is not itself capable of defining social needs or assessing whether the burdens of meeting these needs are being shared equitably. These are fundamentally political questions. As Iris Marion Young notes, 'reasonable people disagree about what values and priorities come under the umbrella of social justice. They disagree as well about what policies are most efficient and effective for promoting the well-being of citizens, and require the fewest tradeoffs with other values' (Young, 2000: 187). By trying to apply private strategies to meet 'social' needs, however defined, SE can ignore the political nature of the common good, bypassing political processes in favor of a subject-centered, sometimes market-oriented approach to the definition and achievement of 'social' objectives.

SE's subtle revision of the structure of society's relationship to the state and market raises important questions about the functional roles of these institutions. While few people believe that SE could ever supplant the integrative functions of the state, some proponents nonetheless betray a hopelessly fatalistic attitude toward the state's lumbering bureaucratic apparatus. In America, this attitude manifests itself in the discourse of 'reinventing government' (Ryan, 1999). In many countries, it has also taken the form of deep pessimism toward the state's perceived inefficiency and corruption. Donor agencies and foundations around the world have embraced SE, hoping to cultivate active social networks and a thriving civil society that they hope will discipline the state (Alter, 2003). The discourse of SE as redeemer of the failed state heralds the arrival of new, flexible, dynamic methods of meeting social needs with innovation and sustainable sources of finance.

A heroic image; but seen in another light, this characterization bears an uneasy resemblance to Habermas' (1987) dystopian narrative of the system's colonization of the lifeworld. Habermas' theory of social integration posits two models for action coordination: the lifeworld and the system, which correspond roughly to dialogical and monological behavioral models, respectively. The lifeworld represents a shared realm of meaning structured by intersubjective discourse; it is 'the horizon within which communicative actions are "always already" moving' (Habermas, 1987). Participation in the public sphere, then, is roughly equivalent to coexistence within a 'lifeworld', where individuals coordinate 'action orientations' to achieve a 'communicatively achieved consensus'. The lifeworld is a realm of discourse, of mutual adjustment and joint deliberation, the outcome of which is social integration. The system, on the other hand, is a path of integration that organizes society on the basis of 'delinguistified steering media' like money in the economy or power in the bureaucracy. The system 'stabilizes nonintended interconnections of action by way of functionally intermeshing action consequences' – precisely as Adam Smith describes in his analysis of the social optimality of capitalism. Habermas suggests that modern society displays an unerring tendency for systemic forces to 'colonize the lifeworld', a process in which 'normatively embedded interactions are turned into success-oriented transactions'. Socially embedded processes of interaction 'crystallize around interchange relations' of contract and 'system integration'.

Some degree of system integration is inevitable and positive, as it corresponds to the development, rationalization, and differentiation of social functions. Yet taken to an extreme, system integration vitiates public discourse, collapsing the realm of the 'social' into a discursively inert shell. Intersubjective processes of negotiation and deliberation give way to the pursuit of individual projects, organized around subjective preferences that are advanced according to their ability to access the steering media of money and power. Eclipsed by the rise of monological rationality, social integration weakens. Social performance is equated with technical efficiency, sharply reducing the capacity for critical discourse about the normative consequences of rationalization (Marcuse, 1988).

The market analogy implicit in SE invites comparison to the colonization of the lifeworld. SE embeds itself in the 'social capital market', encouraging competitive entrepreneurs to seek new and innovative, potentially disruptive solutions to specific 'social' problems. Its erosion of boundaries between society, market and state reduces the capacity for critique to the subject-centered desire to solve perceived social problems. Meanwhile, the burden of identifying and solving 'social' problems falls to independent subjects who form local judgments about needs, objectives, methods and outcomes. For these individuals, changing society consists in addressing specific 'gaps' or pathologies. But if these gaps are actually symptoms of macrolevel political problems, SE may alleviate the patient's immediate discomfort without solving deeper problems, becoming a palliative, not a curative measure. The entrepreneurial turn is therefore substantively different from an approach that attempts to preserve the autonomy of 'civil society' to participate in concerted, critical evaluation of the operations of the 'system'; to assemble and integrate information holistically for collective evaluation and action.

Granted, poor governance, limited public sector capacity and political intransigence are all binding constraints that have bred serious social problems. Yet the implicit treatment of SE as a substitute for, rather than a complement to, concerted public action raises troubling issues related to the distribution of burdens. Social enterprises identify service gaps and efficiently mobilize resources to fill them. In doing so, however, they may privilege addressing symptoms over resolving more fundamental root causes, such as social inequality, political exclusion, and cultural marginalization.

As the lottery example suggests, SE, born in response to the 'responsiveness gap' of public authority, may ultimately sustain this gap by providing cosmetically satisfying solutions. By assuming the responsibility to alleviate the most perverse symptoms of public sector failures, SE may blunt civil society's critical capacity to assess the root causes of social objectives. Rather than interrogating institutional arrangements that produce perverse outcomes, the discourse of social enterprise as redeemer of the failed state saddles civil society with the responsibility for managing the consequences of market and policy failures. The public sphere ceases to be the pilot of society's steering mechanisms; instead, civil society begins to take its direction from the mechanistic operations and failures of markets and states. This reversal of agency lies at the heart of the theoretical problem with SE.

The spread of SE will undoubtedly inspire entrepreneurial souls to invent new ways of meeting social needs and financial objectives. This is an unambiguously positive effect. However, by promulgating a vocabulary of win-win situations and self-sustaining earned income, SE may divert attention from the possibility that more basic structural reforms might be necessary to address social problems, particularly where governance is weak or exclusionary. The sight of successful self-sustaining community programs, like the vision of lotteries funding scholarships at no cost to the state, may focus dialogue on the joy of alleviating symptoms rather than upon the difficult process of resolving the social pathologies that produced them.

The social entrepreneur's answer to this critique is obvious and powerful. It is easy to argue that society needs consensus around major structural changes rather than entrepreneurial solutions to pathological symptoms. But when markets and states are unresponsive to 'social' considerations, then surely it is better to intervene and assist those in need rather than to sacrifice them for the sake of attracting attention to the need for social change. This is an important and valid critique, and it is beyond the scope of this paper to resolve the debate.

Integration and conclusions

SE has captured well-deserved attention because of its potential for rapidly improving human lives and livelihoods. SE unleashes innovation and mobilizes new resources to deal with important issues that affect many, often underserved, groups of people. Yet at best, SE is only an instrument; its importance is inextricably linked to the terminal objectives it promotes. Understanding the normative content of these objectives is an essential part of understanding what SE is and what it ought to be.

Heterogeneity of identities, interests, cultures and values characterizes modern society, and it complicates efforts to identify or understand the nature of 'social' objectives. Social enterprises have both financial and mission-related goals, and the definition of the latter entails specific normative and political commitments. In the context of persistent conflict over values and ends, SE needs to give an account of the 'social' that it has heretofore neglected to provide. Operationally, this entails defining how social entrepreneurs interpret 'social' objectives to enable the rational pursuit of values and objectives. On a broader scale, the politics of SE require a reconsideration of how we define the sector and its practices. If SE is indeed always political, then the line between SE and political advocacy inevitably blurs, as perhaps it ought.

At the same time, linkages between SE and politics raise an important set of questions about approaches to issues with deep political and institutional roots. Social heterogeneity and conflicts between values and approaches can create normative impasses, and inclusive institutional practices are needed in order to arbitrate between competing objectives. These political processes of negotiation are both formal and informal, and they represent the best hope of achieving a discursively mediated compromise around what constitutes the common good. SE may, however, sidestep these processes in a monological effort to circumvent grid-locked institutional processes of negotiation.

Monological approaches pose two principal threats: they may coercively impose entrepreneurs' visions of terminal objectives and the means appropriate to achieve them, and they may yield incomplete, even perverse solutions that ignore fundamental drivers of social problems. As Iris Marion Young notes:

> Ensuring investment in needs, infrastructure, and education and training enough to support self-development for everyone and the organization of the work of society so that everyone who is able does meaningful work requires much society-wide decision-making and coordinated action. Precisely the virtues of civil society, however – voluntary association, decentralization, freedom to start new and unusual things – mitigate against such coordination. Indeed, the activities of civil society may exacerbate problems of inequality, marginalization, and inhibition of the development of capabilities. For persons and groups with greater material and organizational resources are liable to maintain and even enlarge their social advantages through their associational activity. Especially to the extent that their associational life is private as distinct from civicly oriented, their associational activities often reinforce unequal opportunities for developing capabilities. Associations of civil society, moreover, cannot mobilize the amount of resources necessary to support conditions for the self-development of everyone. (Young, 2000: 186)

As a subset of 'civil society' that pursues putatively common objectives, SE should heed Young's admonitions. First, while SE may produce immediate and impressive gains, it cannot replace sustained public engagement with questions of social importance. Second, as the lottery example suggests, relying on SE to fill these gaps raises the possibility of generating unexpectedly perverse outcomes that may disempower its intended beneficiaries. Third, while SE addresses local symptoms of deeper political and institutional malaise – poverty, exclusion, marginalization, environmental degradation – it may also avoid discursively mediated processes that could produce more inclusive and integrative systemic solutions. Social entrepreneurs, then, may need to adjust their optical depth of field to include the background institutional processes that generate the pathologies that motivate their existence, and realign their behavior accordingly.

The analysis of SE's political dimension suggests a number of guiding principles for social entrepreneurs. Initially, SE is a promising tool for resolving specific problems, but it must be seen as a complement to, rather than a substitute for, processes of governance and deliberation. Social entrepreneurs must not underestimate the importance of participation in processes intended to broker and articulate social compromises. They should approach the public sector as a potential partner rather than a competitor in the delivery of key services. In places where governance is weak, this may entail supporting movements designed to improve and rehabilitate the capacity of the public sector to define and meet social needs. If social entrepreneurs are truly committed to the advancement of broader social objectives, they cannot afford to isolate themselves from other key actors, but must actively search for opportunities to cooperate with and actively support their partners.

To avoid the adverse consequences of monologue, the social entrepreneur can attempt to supplant monologue with dialogue. Dialogical action is not subjective, but intersubjective; it treats others as interlocutors whose needs and ideas should be respected, rather than as objects to be manipulated or inferiors to be taught, enlightened or instructed. Approaching SE through the spirit of dialogue entails both a shift in frame and a shift in action. Initially, it involves moving toward an understanding that others might have valid views and objectives very different from one's own; what Laible (2000) calls a 'loving epistemology'. Second, it means putting dialogue in practice, through partnerships and networks that include affected stakeholders in the articulation and assessment of needs, as well as in relevant deliberative processes. Partnerships and networks help organizations expand the scope of their inquiries and provide a discursive forum for social entrepreneurs to test hypotheses about their interpretations of social needs. But if they are to be substantively valuable and not perfunctory exercises, dissenting views need to be taken seriously and incorporated into decision-making processes and outcomes.

SE is unquestionably a very promising avenue for effecting social change. But the very efficiency that is its hallmark is also a critical cause for concern. History is littered with examples of individuals who have attempted to advance their view of the world to the exclusion of competing perspectives, and results have been decidedly mixed. Given the shifting and deeply contested nature of the 'social' good, attention to politics and values will be critical if SE is to fulfill its potential as a driving force for positive social change.

Note

1. 'Type I' errors are 'false alarms', for example, including in SE something that should not be. Type II errors are 'failed alarms', which omit relevant cases from the sample.

References

Alter, K. 2003. *Social enterprise: A typology of the field in Latin America.* Inter-American Development Bank.

Barkin, D. 1996. Ecotourism: A tool for sustainable development in an era of international integration? In J. Miller (ed.), *The ecotourism equation: Measuring the impacts.* Yale School of Forestry and Environmental Studies Bulletin No. 99.

Berlin, I. 1997. Does political theory still exist? In H. Hardy and R. Hausheer (eds), *The proper study of mankind: An anthology of essays.* New York: Farrar, Straus and Giroux.

Calhoun, C. 1992. Habermas and the public sphere. In C. Calhoun (ed.), *Habermas and the public sphere.* Cambridge, MA: MIT Press.

Clotfelter, C. 2000. Do lotteries hurt the poor? Well, yes and no. Summary of testimony given to a House Select Committee on a State Lottery, 19 April 2000. Available: http://www.pubpol.duke.edu/people/faculty/clotfelter/lottsum.pdf. Posted 28 April 2000.

Clotfelter, C. and Cook, P. J. 1989. *Selling hope: State lotteries in America.* Cambridge, MA: Harvard University Press.

Dees, J. G. 1998. The meaning of social entrepreneurship. Paper, Center for the Advancement of Social Entrepreneurship, Fuqua School of Business, Duke University, Durham. Available: http://www.fuqua.duke.edu/centers/case/documents/dees_SE.pdf. Accessed: 8 August 2005.

Fraser, N. 1992. Rethinking the public sphere: A contribution to the critique of actually existing democracy. In C. Calhoun (ed.), *Habermas and the public sphere.* Cambridge, MA: MIT Press.

Habermas, J. 1987. *The theory of communicative action. Vol. 2: Lifeworld and system: A critique of functionalist reason.* Boston: Beacon Press.

Habermas, J. 1989. *The structural transformation of the public sphere.* Cambridge, MA: MIT Press.

Habermas, J. 1996. *Between facts and norms.* Cambridge, MA: MIT Press.

Habermas, J. 1997. *The philosophical discourse of modernity.* Oxford: Blackwell Publishing.

Hill, J. R. and Palmer, G. 2002. Going for broke: The economic and social impact of a South Carolina lottery. South Carolina Policy Council Education Foundation, 1 March 2002. Available: http://www.scpolicycouncil.com/Going%20for%20Broke.htm. Accessed 20 August 2004.

Johnson, S. 2000. Literature review on social entrepreneurship. Canadian Centre for Social Entrepreneurship, University of Alberta School of Business, Canada. Available: http://www.bus.ualberta.ca/ccse/Publications. Accessed 10 December 2004.

Laible, J. 2000. A loving epistemology: What I hold critical in my life, faith and profession. *Qualitative Studies in Education*, 13 (6).

Lindsay, H. 2003. Ecotourism: The promise and perils of environmentally-oriented travel. *Cambridge Scientific Abstracts feature*, February 2003. Available: http://www.csa.com/hottopics/ecotour1/overview.html. Accessed 30 December 2004.

Marcuse, H. 1988. Some social implications of modern technology. In A. Arato and E. Gebhardt (eds), *The Essential Frankfurt School Reader*. New York: Continuum.

Marx, K. 1978. On the Jewish Question. In R. C. Tucker (ed.), *The Marx-Engels Reader*, Second edn. Boston: W. W. Norton and Company.

Place, S. E. 1991. Nature tourism and rural development in Tortuguero, Costa Rica. *Annals of Tourism Research*, 18.

Ryan, W. 1999. The new landscape for nonprofits. *Harvard Business Review*, January–February.

Schuyler, G. 1998. Social entrepreneurship: Profit as a means, not an end. CELCEE, Kauffman Centre for Entrepreneurial Leadership Clearing House on Entrepreneurial Education. *Digest 98*, **Vol. 7.** Available: http://www.celcee.edu/publications/digest/Dig98-7.html. Posted 30 November 1998.

South Carolina Policy Council. 1999. The economic facts of state-run lotteries: Windfall or hoax? Available: http://www.scpolicycouncil.com/index.asp?CONTENT=lottery. Accessed 9 August 2005.

Thompson, J. 2002. The world of the social entrepreneur. *International Journal of Public Sector Management*, 15(5): 412–31.

Thompson, J., Alvy, G. and Lees, A. 2000. Social entrepreneurship: A new look at the people and the potential. *Management Decision*, 38(5): 328–38.

United Nations Environment Program (UNEP). 2001. Ecotourism: Facts and Figures. *Industry and Environment*, 24 (3–4): 5–9.

Wall, G. 1997. Is ecotourism sustainable? *Environmental Management*, 21(4).

Wheat, S. 2002. Sold out: A rapid growth in ecotourism has been at the expense of indigenous peoples. *The Guardian* (UK), 22 May 2002.

Young, I. M. 2000. *Democracy and Inclusion*. Oxford: Oxford University Press.

5

Social Entrepreneurship: Innovation and Social Change Across Theory and Practice

Francesco Perrini and Clodia Vurro

Introduction

Companies and nonprofits, regardless of the sector they belong to, their dimension or their geographical location, are increasingly asked to provide innovative solutions to manage complex social problems: from community development to social exclusion and poverty reduction (Margolis and Walsh, 2003). Social entrepreneurship (SE), an unusual contact point among entrepreneurship, innovation and social change, has been increasingly catalyzing the interest of academics, companies, and the business debate for about a decade. Attention is expanding exponentially with a multiplicity of publications, MBA core and elective courses and academic research centers explicitly focused on deep analysis of the SE phenomenon. There are also numerous innovative and supportive actors such as specialized consulting groups, social venture capitalists, social angels and so on.

In this context, therefore, it becomes critical to identify how SE protagonists – 'socially entrepreneurial ventures' (SEVs) and 'socially innovative entrepreneurs' – feel about and act on social change in terms of the altered performance capacity of society (Bornstein, 2004).

It is not by chance that in this chapter we will speak about SEVs (Waddock and Post, 1991; Kanter, 1999; Henton, Melville and Walesh, 1997; Dorado and Haettich, 2004) or alternatively about 'innovative social purpose business enterprises' (Campbell, 1998; Foryt, 2002; Larson, 2000; Mair and Noboa, 2003a; Schaltegger, 2002; Volery, 2002). These alternative expressions have been introduced in an attempt to give the same weight to the different components of the SE construct (that is, entrepreneurship, innovation and social issues), as well as to avoid misunderstandings when assigning a typical nonprofit nomenclature (such as 'social enterprise') to organizations consistent with the SE paradigm.

Starting from these premises, the present contribution aims at an assessment of how SEVs are actually responding to this tension over entrepreneurial involvement in filling wider social gaps. In so doing, we first identify the drivers of SE affirmation and emergence. Second, we reframe current SE literature in order to answer three main questions: (i) what does SE mean?; (ii) how do SEVs work and how are they managed?; and (iii) who are these socially innovative entrepreneurs? Third, we shift from theory to practice and analyze the behavior of 35 acknowledged SEVs in order to uncover consistency in their aptitude towards social change and wealth creation. In this section, we focus on four areas: (I) mission, vision and organizational values; (II) entrepreneurial opportunities and innovation; (III) entrepreneurial model; and (IV) social welfare impact. Fourth, we conclude with brief reflections on the correspondence between theory and practice in order to obtain a preliminary descriptive framework of the SE process. Ultimately, we draw attention to some empirical questions and implications for future research.

Before going on a clarification is due: the number of SEVs analyzed is not to be considered as comprehensive or perfectly proportionate to the current range of social entrepreneurial initiatives around the world. Organizations were at first chosen with reference to the availability of structured data and information on their explicitly socially entrepreneurial nature and later with reference to their own awareness of being part of the SE movement. In so doing we have attempted an assessment of behavioral descriptions starting from well-established experiences and recognized best practices.

Where does SE come from?

SE is a composite phenomenon and can initially be explained by the strengthening requests from various stakeholders to the nonprofit sector to enhance its economic efficiency and effectiveness, as well as to the for-profit sector to encourage the adoption of socially responsible behavior.

Therefore, even if the idea of social enterprise is certainly not new, (examples of business companies with a prevalent social mission can be found from the nineteenth century), the phrase 'social entrepreneurship' was coined only in the late 1990s in the US, emerging from business practice and then being translated in the academic debate (Johnson, 2000).

As a consequence of the extreme newness that characterizes this research field, a palpable lack of common frameworks at each level of analysis is noticeable – from theoretical explanation to current practices. This situation makes it difficult to establish a shared reading grid and to clearly distinguish distinctive boundaries. For example, can nonprofit organizations be defined as SEVs if they engage in for-profit activities in order to sustain their social mission? On the other hand, what is the link between SE and corporate social responsibility? Can active socially responsible enterprises be included in the field of SE if they publish a social or sustainability report or have a social or environmental certification? Referring to what school of thought can 'social entrepreneurialism' be conceptualized? And so on.

Notwithstanding the many uncertainties and unsettled research questions, a preliminary attempt, aimed to at least discern those entrepreneurial behaviors consistent with SE, can be made by starting with the entrepreneurial quality and leaving aside sectorial considerations and judgments about organizations' formal legal status. In this sense, even if it is surely praiseworthy that more and more companies assign growing resources to philanthropy and social giving, this activity can be conducted in an entrepreneurial way but it is certainly not entrepreneurial per se (Mair and Martí, 2004). Similarly, the adoption of managerial techniques on the part of nonprofits is not enough to call them social entrepreneurial actors.

As a result, it can at first be assumed that SE emerges as anything but a 'one-way phenomenon' exclusive to the nonprofit sector, rather it implies an intersectorial dynamic: SE initiatives ideally break up boundary lines among organizational clusters, configuring themselves as hybrid organizational forms (Mair and Noboa, 2003b). These are characterized by altered and mixed behavior, a strong entrepreneurial orientation and above all, an unquestionable accent on social innovation.

Although sharing the entrepreneurial soul with business entrepreneurship theories, these new social players differentiate themselves from their business counterparts in terms of the final objective toward which the entrepreneurial process is addressed. This is an explicit social objective – for example, the creation of social welfare, the enhancement of social inclusion and cohesion, wide access to knowledge and information, community development, and so on – to which wealth creation becomes

subordinated. Profit maximization and wealth creation – the two generalized company final objectives in classical economic theory – become
the means through which socially entrepreneurial innovators pursue
their social mission.

Most existing academic contributions to this field agree to recognize
two main macrodynamics as decisive in the emergence of SEVs: the
crisis of the traditional welfare state (Johnson, 2000; Cook, Dodds and
Mitchell, 2001; Borzaga and Defourny, 2004), and the increase in competitive pressure within the nonprofit sector (Dees, 1998b; Reis, 1999).

With the generalized slowdown of national economic growth rates
and increases in unemployment, the first phenomenon has been
accompanied by a deep rethink of social strategies at every level with
specific regard to the supply of social services. Those waves of privatiza-
tions and decentralizations so common in the public policies of the
1980s are the main effect of this trend. As a result, a progressively
increasing number of social needs has been left unsatisfied thus giving
rise to a growing demand for private providers of social services able to
match socially relevant goals with efficient and effective management
practices (Dees, 1998b).

Partially linked to the first dynamic, cuts in the number and value of
public grants addressed to nonprofits, have caused an unprecedented
and increased rivalry in the field of social services supply in conjunction
with a global demand which is certainly not in decline (Reis, 1999). In
such a situation, nonprofits have been compelled to 'reinvent' themselves and their traditional modus vivendi. As a consequence of 'rising
costs, more competition for fewer donations and grants, and increased
rivalry from for-profit companies entering the social sector' (Reis, 1999:
5), nonprofit organizations have been enlarging their range of possibility, experimenting with management practices, for-profit sector tools
and, more evidently, new funding strategies. In other words, nonprofits
are now shifting from a traditional philanthropic dependency, in which
profits are considered mere gifts devoted to a good cause, to a focus
on the measurability of results and the identification of all potential
commercial sources of revenue.

With specific reference to the European case, an empirical research
work (Borzaga and Defourny, 2004) promoted by EMES – European
Network Research and aimed at analyzing the current state of the
industry in the third sector, has demonstrated the existence of a proportional relationship between national economic and social development, and the emergence of SEVs and social enterprises. In those
countries characterized by a relatively low development level, the per-

ceived need for social services is modest and social needs satisfaction is generally 'delegated' to the informal, family-based system. In these cases, SE is mainly confined to the field of *work-integration*. In the meantime, competing in the same action field with public sector and traditional nonprofit organizations but as *latecomers*, the strength of SEVs is strictly related to the strength of the other competitors. For example, in Northern European countries characterized by a well-developed welfare state and an orientation towards the minimization of the population's social risks, SEVs are confined to underserved market niches, benefiting largely from public subsidies. On the contrary, in those countries with a well-developed welfare state but without direct provision for public services (Germany and Belgium, for example), SEVs will strongly compete with traditional nonprofits and will succeed with regard to a reciprocal development level. Finally, Borzaga and Defourny identify the existence of a strong relationship between the emergence of SEVs and the characteristics of the legal system. The degree of autonomy and the relative ease to carry out productive activities are positively related to the emergence of innovative social-purpose business enterprises.

This description of the drivers at the bottom of SE phenomenon allows us to think about the functions that SEVs will cover in the short term. First of all, they will support state action: an innovative way to obtain a distribution of resources nearer to the real needs of communities. SEVs will reintegrate the overall social services supply and contribute to the public expense cutting process. The link between SEVs' innovative power and the possibility to enhance or maintain the qualitative level of social services cannot be underestimated.

However SE cannot solely be considered a mere public sector surrogate which has emerged as a result of the failure of the welfare state and as a consequence of low efficiency in the third sector.

SE goes further, proactively contributing to social change and innovation within several action fields (Walsh, Weber and Margolis, 2003): from social inclusiveness to work creation; and development and poverty reduction, both locally and with a global-oriented perspective.

Reframing the literature: a theoretical basis for SE

Even if there is generally agreement with regard to the drivers of the emergence and spread of SE, the existing academic contributions to a definition of SE and its points of reference, are still extremely heterogeneous.

The first contributions specifically devoted to the topic barely go back to the last decade, blurring on the one side with literature on the enterprising and commercializing of traditional nonprofit organizations (Letts, Ryan and Grossman, 1999; Dees, Emerson and Economy, 2001; 2002; Paton, 2003) and on the other side with literature focused on corporate social responsibility (CSR) and socially responsible corporate behavior.

In order to overcome this apparent ambiguity, in this chapter we do not focus on literature regarding profit-seeking businesses' active contributions to social welfare, but on studies and research specifically focused on organizations 'whose primary objective is the creation of social welfare' (Hockerts, 2004: 7) through the adoption of an innovative mix of profitable practices and social outcomes.

Given these premises, one can recognize three main research questions which lead back to existing academic contributions:

- What does SE mean?
- How do SEVs work and how are they managed?
- Who are socially innovative entrepreneurs?

What does SE mean?

At a glance, literature on the cornerstones of SE can be grouped into two main schools of thought: one that considers SE as belonging to nonprofit theory and one that looks at SE as a new intersectorial domain.

On the one extreme, some authors (McLeod, 1997; Boschee, 1998; Dees and Elias, 1998; Reis, 1999; Cannon, 2000; Boschee and McClurg, 2003; Dart, 2004) place SE in the nonprofit research field, supporting the belief that the SE concept can be explained as a sort of 'recent innovation' in the field of social enterprise functioning (Dart, 2004) and then substantiated in the shift towards managerial competencies and market-based attitudes of nonprofit actors in order to improve their operational efficiency and effectiveness.

In this sense, social enterprise and SE are viewed as a kind of 'encompassing set of strategic responses to many of the varieties of environmental turbulence and situational challenges that nonprofit organizations face today' (Dart, 2004: 413).

In slightly different words, SE emerges as the rational and strategically better third sector (or nonprofit sector) response to a changed and challenged macrosituation: a situation comprised of the perceived breakdown of the welfare system (Cook, Dodds and

Mitchell, 2001), increased financial pressure on social-purpose organizations, increased costs in many areas of the social sector, and a decrease in public and private grants and donations (Dees and Elias, 1998; Boschee and McClurg, 2003). According to these positions, the innovation, intrinsically tied to the term entrepreneurship (Bruyat and Julien, 2000), is defined as the ability of third sector actors to reinvent themselves through a process of nonprofit expertizing.

On the opposite extreme, it is possible to single out the upholders of a widened SE theory: these authors (see Henton, Melville and Walesh, 1997; Dees, 1998a; Johnson, 2000; Thompson, Alvy and Lees, 2000; Grenier, 2002; Hockerts, 2004; Mair and Martí, 2004) believe that the phenomenon can be considered as a new and independent (Dorado and Haettich, 2004) and extremely intersectorial (Johnson, 2000; Mair and Martí, 2004) domain of research. They stress the social content of entrepreneurial initiatives, as founding the field. In this sense, they define the social entrepreneur as only that innovator able to actively contribute to social change with the creativeness and innovative-orientation typical of the classical entrepreneurial process. The juridical form of these organizations and their sectorial belonging fade into the background, subordinated to the social change purpose.

To date, this second point of view seems to fit the SE phrase better than others. In fact, besides the possibility of giving autonomy to the overall discipline, it explains the series of initiatives hardly ascribable to the third sector, even if characterized by a prominent social mission and social-purpose soul. For example, all the activities catering to the bottom of the world economic pyramid and aimed at converting poverty into an entrepreneurial and profitable opportunity would be left aside. Even though most of these are traditional for-profit companies, their contribution to the enhancement of community social, cultural and economic conditions has been proved to be relevant (Prahalad and Hart, 1999; Prahalad and Hammond, 2002; Prahalad, 2004).

Additionally, if SE was considered a mere innovation within the nonprofit sector, it would lose that character of innovativeness in dealing with complex social problems (Johnson, 2000; Grenier, 2002) and would simply qualify as a tool in the service of the process of nonprofit enterprising.

Going into detail: what are, at this point, the specific features of the pure SE concept and the commonalities among existing definitions? How can SEVs be distinguished among other more or less social and more or less entrepreneurial organizations? Starting from the firm conviction that SEVs today are much more than the result of the natural reshaping of the nonprofit sector, the most logical and direct way to clarify these doubts is by making distinctions.

At the first level, it is important to understand what the phrase *SE* implies, what its roots are and how it differs from business entrepreneurship.

All contributions to the field seem to be in agreement in recognizing that the key to understanding the concept lies in the field of business entrepreneurship and the consequent Schumpeterian foundation of the SE theories (Dees, 1998a; Mort, Weerawardena and Carnegie, 2002; Dorado and Haettich, 2004). SE shares its business counterpart's strong tension toward innovation through an ongoing change-friendly orientation (Dorado and Haettich, 2004: 6) and the ability to discover unmet needs and entrepreneurial opportunities (Casson, 1982; Leadbeater, 1997; Shane, 2000). In other words, SEVs are mainly innovators and, like their business counterparts, change agents and propellers of social and economic progress (Leadbeater, 1997; Dees, 1998a; Johnson, 2000) with strong analytical capacity and problem solving orientation.

On the other side, SE has its own distinguishing marks, which substantiate it in a different long term objective: the enhancement of global or local social conditions. At this point, one could argue that every business company, in particular those expressly socially responsible, has a social mission. This is certainly true, but SEVs go further: as business companies they create economic value but this is only a useful tool to achieve their social mission.

In particular, SEVs share with their nonprofit counterparts a preference for serving members and the community rather than workers or stakeholders. They also share a democratic/participatory decision-making process and place the interests of all stakeholders above investors and profit distribution (Laville and Nyssens, 2004). In contrast to the functioning of nonprofits, SEVs lose that typical 'charity label', focusing their processes on the efficient and effective production of goods and services. Additionally, SEVs cannot be confused with traditional nonprofit organizations because of a further characteristic: the nondistribution of profit, in fact, is not considered a constraint but an essential proxy of the pursuit of the social mission (Dees, 1998a).

How do social entrepreneurial ventures work and how are they managed?

The contributions specifically devoted to explaining how SEVs work and are managed are naturally scanty. Notwithstanding, most of the current literature focuses itself on a preliminary 'definer level'; the most recent contributions that consider SE as a totally new field of study, show the emergence of a firm interest regarding the SE process, the establishment and running of an innovative SEV, the functions of socially innovative enterprises, and so on. In particular, Guclu, Dees and Battle Anderson (2002), Dorado and Haettich (2004) and Hockerts (2004) begin to view SE as a process made of different phases and SE theory as an evolutionary one.

Current literature is also in agreement in recognizing three main steps which, although typical of business entrepreneurship, take on a new value and therefore become useful in the overall comprehension of the SE phenomenon. They are:

(i)   Opportunity definition
(ii)   Organizational launch and functioning
(iii) Financial resource collection and leveraging

These phases are not temporally consequent but can both follow one another in a totally different order as well as be concomitant.

Opportunity definition

The first step of the SE process comprises opportunity definition: 'the cognitive process followed by entrepreneurs as they intentionally identify a solution to a specific problem or need because of diverse motivations, including financial rewards' (Dorado and Haettich, 2004: 6). Surprisingly, at the moment, social entrepreneurial opportunity is the aspect of SE most explored by scholars. Mair and Martí (2004: 3) consider entrepreneurial opportunities as 'opportunities to bring into existence new goods, services, raw materials, and organizing methods that allow outputs to be sold at more than their cost of production' and affirm that a central way to differentiate between traditional business entrepreneurship and SE is by looking at the identification of opportunities. In this sense, even if social opportunities share the same source as their business counterparts, that is, arising from unsatisfied needs whether they are social or not, in SE process the interest is centered on the possibility to 'meet a social need in a sustainable matter, and thus to (partially) alleviate social problems' (Mair and Martí, 2004: 3).

With regard to social entrepreneurial opportunities, Hockerts (2004: 11) goes further, affirming how the exploitation of opportunities is substantiated on the possibility to 'generate simultaneously, economical rents and social benefits'. He considers the discovery process as the sole opportunity for SEVs to survive 'in the limbo between social welfare and the profit maximization motive' (Hockerts, 2004: 11). Starting from these premises, Hockerts identifies, in activism, self-help, and philanthropy, the three main sources of social entrepreneurial opportunities.

Instead of focusing only on external drivers, Guclu, Dees and Battle Anderson (2002: 3) see at the base of the opportunity exploitation, the concurrence of internal and external factors. In particular, an entrepreneur's previous personal experience combines with social needs, 'gaps between socially desirable conditions and the existing reality', social assets, and change to stimulate entrepreneurial ideas or innovations for social impact. Studying seven accredited SEVs, Alvord, Brown and Letts (2002: 5) formulate some hypotheses on the characteristics of social entrepreneurial innovation, focusing on the capacity to reconfigure 'existing resources or services for more effective or wider delivery'. They identify three major types of social innovation. The first, *building local capacity*, refers to the possibility of enhancing local conditions by giving power to underused local capacities: 'Local actors may solve many of their own problems given increases in local capacities' (Alvord, Brown and Letts, 2002: 10). The second consists of *disseminating a package of innovations* through the reconfiguration of products, resources and management practices into forms that fit better with local specificities. Thirdly, Alvord, Brown and Letts identify as socially innovative, the possibility to contribute in *building a movement*, giving voice to marginalized groups.

Organizational launch and functioning

The circle is closed only when, by adopting an opportunity-oriented mindset, SEVs transform a viable idea into a functioning organization. This leads us towards the next step of the SE process: organizational launch and functioning. To become concrete, a social innovation needs a social impact theory, a specific business model and a composite social strategy (Guclu, Dees and Battle Anderson, 2002).

On this point current research becomes much more exiguous, mingling with literature on nonprofit management and enterprising (Letts,

Ryan and Grossman, 1999; Brinckerhoff, 2000; Dees, Emerson and Economy, 2001; 2002; Paton, 2003). However, it is possible to list some preliminary features that have been claimed as typical and specific of SEV functioning:

- The production of goods and services is made by SEVs on an ongoing basis, with a firm orientation towards problem solving and emphasis on the ability to obtain measurable results
- SEVs are characterized by a low dependence level and, therefore, a high level of autonomy: they may receive public grants but they are not managed directly or indirectly by public actors
- In the management of SEVs, decisional power is not dependent on capital shares; individual behavior aimed at profit maximization and company rights is generally excluded within SEVs; powers are widened and shared by all stakeholders (Borzaga and Solari, 2004)
- Operations within SEVs are based on a complex mix of monetary and nonmonetary resources (for example, volunteers) and are oriented towards a collaborative and participatory spirit (Grenier, 2002)
- Partially tied to the former point, training and capacity building is crucial in all the phases of the SE process, because of both the difficulty to achieve skill replication and the consequent necessity to build an organizational environment in which competencies and skills can easily flow around (Johnson, 2000)
- In general, practice shows how regularities in building organizational capacity are still not present. Even if SE initiatives vary considerably, the larger the organizational size, the more sophisticated are the organizational systems and arrangements (Alvord, Brown and Letts, 2002). In any case, at the moment, the organizational form does not seem to be the driver of social entrepreneurial character (Mair and Martí, 2004). On the contrary, the focus remains on the nexus among entrepreneurial aptitude, innovation, and social change and its results.

Financial resource collection and leveraging

The third major step of the SE process refers to the collecting and leveraging of financial resources. In parallel with analysis of the SE concept and features of SEVs, research on the financial aspects of SE and, in particular, on the innovative sources of such financing, are becoming widespread. Among others, the most quoted source of financing is a particular kind of patient capital (Bank of England, 2003): social venture capital or venture philanthropy (VP).

In more detail, VP has established itself since the 1990s as an alterative form of charitable giving based on the application of venture capital principles to the first SEVs (Reis, 1999). In the VP model a private, or alternatively, a corporate foundation decides to develop a financing relationship with a social organization that has been able to distinguish itself by its innovative spirit and high growth potential as well as its impact in contributing to social change.

In this sense, VP would seem an innovative expression of the classical financing relationship between foundations and nonprofits. In reality, the premise changes radically. In fact, venture philanthropists stop paying attention to the abstract social effectiveness of social projects, thus enriching the evaluation process (the deal flow) of a further new dimension: an assessment of the concrete SEV's ability to implement its social mission through an economically sustainable business model.

In brief, VP is characterized by a permanent attention to SEV's capacity building, the development of organizational and managerial skills: from the building of a solid organizational infrastructure to the hiring of qualified personnel; and from the achievement of clear task definitions to the development of a problem solving orientation and a functioning business strategy. Additionally, VP is based on conceiving and implementing ad hoc measurement instruments able to evaluate the degree of attainment of both economic and social objectives, and the soundness of a firm's performance through specific indicators and tools (for example, the Balanced Scorecard). VP is also settled on a partnership approach to relationship management and characterized by a collaborative exit strategy, aimed at evaluating and sustaining the ability of SEVs to survive in the long term.

For the purposes of this chapter it would be misleading to go into details of actual financing practices and theories. It is enough to underline this aspect as crucial in SE theorization and overall comprehension.

Who are socially innovative entrepreneurs?

A large part of the current literature goes into detail in outlining the attributes that make social entrepreneurs different from other entrepreneurs. As for the SE concept, it is possible to identify two main areas of analysis: one focused on what social entrepreneurs share with their business counterparts and the other focused on the differences between the two.

With reference to the first stream of research, the literature stresses entrepreneurial aptitude more than social orientation (Johnson, 2000).

For example, social entrepreneurs are not limited by the initial lack or scarcity of resources, instead they look for more innovative sources (McLeod, 1997); at the same time they also present a certain risk-tolerance and a strong desire to control the surrounding environment (Prabhu, 1999). But social entrepreneurs also represent a breaking point in the entrepreneurship panorama, possessing specific aptitudes and qualities and above all, a founding orientation. Even when an SEV is established within the for-profit sector, profit is considered as an instrumental tool for achieving social change.

Moreover, the desire to change society and discomfort with the status quo are the main stimuli for SEVs to innovate (Prabhu, 1999). This makes them more sensitive to entrepreneurial opportunities that deal with social problems and unsatisfied social needs (Mair and Noboa, 2003a): they create value by building portfolios of resources to address unmet social needs.

Equally important is the aptitude for networking and cooperation. Because of its intersectorial nature, SE needs a strong ability to establish and manage multiple relationships. The ability to build external relations is also critical to establishing legitimacy with different constituencies (Prabhu, 1999). In conclusion, a strong bridging capacity has been demonstrated to be directly linked to the success of SE initiatives (Alvord, Brown and Letts, 2002).

Social entrepreneurs are also different from their nonprofit counterparts. As underlined by McLeod (1997), social innovators show a firm focus on outcomes and a market-based aptitude, reversing the traditional nonprofit accountability flow from the predominance of funding organizations to an accountability towards the overall stakeholder base. Furthermore social entrepreneurs demonstrate less fear of failure and often abandon 'cause-marketing tactics' to embrace a quality-oriented entrepreneurial process.

Summing up, social entrepreneurs are change promoters in society; they pioneer innovation within the social sector through the entrepreneurial quality of a breaking idea, their capacity building aptitude, and their ability to concretely demonstrate the quality of the idea and to measure social impacts.

Shifting from theory to practice

In order to obtain a preliminary corroboration of conclusions in the literature on SE and to paint a picture of critical areas in the functioning of SEVs, we now change perspective, directing our attention towards practitioners. This section of the chapter stands as an exploratory study, aimed at uncovering consistency in the aptitude of SEVs for social change and wealth creation through entrepreneurialism. This research relies on theoretical sampling, that is, cases were chosen for theoretical, not statistical, reasons, (Glaser and Strauss, 1967; Eisenhardt, 1989) to fill theoretical SE meanings and categories. Consistent with this view, the 35 analyzed case studies were preliminarily selected on the basis of both their wide recognition as examples of best practice in the field of nascent SE, and their own awareness of being SEVs. Sample organizations come from diverse regions, present different juridical forms (for-profit companies or nonprofit organizations), belong to different sectors – from the social services (employment training, homelessness, child services, hunger and poverty relief, rehabilitative services and community development) traditionally presided over by nonprofits – to the most innovative sectors such as information and communication technology, media and web services. Interesting SEVs have also been identified within traditional business sectors, such as financial services, pharmacology and energy. Data and information about the cases have been generated from published reports, as well as developed case studies and web resources.

Behavioral commonalities among the SEVs have then been grouped into four main areas of analysis:

- Mission, vision and organizational values
- Entrepreneurial opportunities and innovation
- Entrepreneurial model
- Social outcomes and social welfare impact

A first general commonality can be drawn from sectorial belonging:

Nonprofit SEVs are most likely to occur in traditional nonprofit sectors, even if only as innovative and pattern breaking actors. On the other hand, social change within business sectors is most likely to be pursued by for-profit SEVs.

This statement can be explained by beginning with the process of idea generation and the related, natural importance of previous experience in order to identify viable opportunities and collect resources (Dees, Emerson and Economy, 2001; Guclu, Dees and Battle Anderson, 2002; Mair and Noboa, 2003a). In this sense, nonprofit SEVs are predominantly devoted to the delivery of social services (for example, rehabilitative services or employment training for disadvantaged people) because of the past and progressive knowledge they have built up about problems, criticalities and sectorial points of reference (for example, critical relationships and sources of capital). For-profit SEVs deserve similar considerations.

Some exceptions, however, do exist. The Institute for OneWorld Health, the first nonprofit pharmaceutical company in the US, aims at serving 'as a positive agent for change by saving lives, improving health, and fulfilling the promise of medicine for those most in need' (http://oneworldhealth.org) and is a clear example of that hybrid organizational form so often stressed in theorization.

Mission, vision and organizational values

Mission, vision statement and company values are the most direct indicators of an organization's soul and beliefs. They should briefly describe the company service area, service recipients and the main outcome that organization is expecting to achieve. In so doing, they represent the first clear indicators as to whether an organization should be included in the SE field or not. In fact, the mission summarizes the three key elements – innovation, entrepreneurship and tension towards specific social change – that make organizations consistent with the SEV paradigm.

All of the SEVs analyzed present a mission statement and a value chart, both of which are distinctly displayed on a specific section of their websites, and SE principles are clearly visible from the verbal formulas they use.

An explanatory example of what we are talking about comes from Juma Ventures, a nonprofit organization mainly devoted to providing employment opportunities for San Francisco Bay Area youth in social enterprises it owns and operates. In its mission Juma Ventures declares that: 'all people deserve the opportunity and encouragement to reach their highest potential. Juma Ventures uses business enterprises as the vehicle to provide these opportunities to young people who have traditionally lacked access to them. We operate our businesses on a sound financial basis while seeking to create a new paradigm that simultaneously promotes both people and profits' (http://jumaventures.org). A second commonality can be identified with regards to mission and value statement:

SEVs tend to express their entrepreneurial orientation beginning with their mission: they present themselves as social actors with a strong orientation towards innovation, a self-sufficient and financially sound business strategy and specific expected outcomes.

Therefore, organizations seem to be aware of the importance of clarifying the company mission in order to identify goals and returns from the very beginning (Brinckerhoff, 2000). Mission represents the first step in the process of developing discovered entrepreneurial opportunities into concrete social outcomes and social change (Dees, Emerson and Economy, 2001).

A last consideration on social change: this element is viewed as crucial and founding in all the SEVs' declarations but it is never considered as a generic and abstract attempt to change the world in some way (poverty reduction or community development), rather, it is defined by specific social outcomes. Examples are: providing access to educational resources that increase the capacity of young people to become employable and self-reliant in today's global marketplace (Global Education Partnership, http://geponline.org/index.shtml), eradicating needless blindness by providing appropriate, compassionate and quality eye care for all (Aravind Eye Hospitals, http://aravind.org), or bridging economic, racial and social divisions by providing at-risk youth with the keys to self-sufficiency through paid employment in the arts (Artists for Humanity, http://afhboston.com/), and so on.

Entrepreneurial opportunities and innovation

The process of entrepreneurial opportunity identification goes hand in hand with mission statement definition: they influence each other. As stated above in the literature review, opportunities represent the core of entrepreneurship (Drucker, 1985) and provide one of the major commonalities between business and social entrepreneurialism. In fact in both cases, starting from a balanced mingling of past, personal experience, changes at every level, and available social assets (Guclu, Dees and Battle Anderson, 2002), opportunities can be recognized where unmet needs exist (Mair and Martí, 2004).

SEVs also stand out for focusing their attention on a different set of possibilities: innovative ways to create or sustain social change by bringing two different cultures – business and nonprofit – together under one innovative and hybrid organization.

In their own words, entrepreneurs are described as enlightened minds who, at a certain point of catharsis in their lives, understand how to change an unsustainable situation. In reality, it can be seen as a third commonality in the behavior of SEVs:

> Social entrepreneurial opportunities come into existence as a balanced result of both vision-oriented factors and crisis-oriented factors.

In fact, the analysis of organizational behavior shows the formation of a viable business idea, in turn resulting in a social entrepreneurial opportunity, as a combination of *internal factors* (or vision-oriented factors) and *external factors* (or crisis-oriented factors). The former are:

- *Personal experience*: this phrase refers to a kind of transformative event (Barendsen and Gardner, 2004), both at individual level (for example, living abroad and gaining perspective, directly experiencing a social breakdown, or dealing with a social issue), and at organizational level, that makes organizations aware of the possibility to contribute by changing an existing social situation
- *Previous experience*: this refers to past experience, both at individual level and at organizational level that makes organizations aware of the possibility of applying an acquired knowledge base to something different and socially significant (Dees, Emerson and Economy, 2001)

The latter – external factors – correspond to external, explicit and implicit requests for help or changes in the previous situation (for example, changes in the legal/normative situation, technological progress, a market niche left uncovered, unmet social needs, new sources of monetary and nonmonetary resources, or the possibility of establishing a partnership with unexpected actors).

Opportunity exploitation represents the starting base for organizations to innovate within the social sector. The innovations proposed by the SEVs analyzed here are very diverse. They range from microcredit services (Real Microcredito, CrediAmigo or Grameen Bank) to community venture capital (Aavishkaar); from new patterns in employment education (Artists for Humanity, Global Education Partnership or Golden Gate Community Inc.) to the delivery of goods and services to the poorest (Casas Bahia). Often innovation cannot be recognized in products and services per se, but with regards to market relations or to new methods of organization and production. In general:

> Innovation is not a one-dimensional construct. SEVs tend to innovate simultaneously or progressively on four different fronts: products and

services or new qualities of products and services, methods of organization and/or production, production factors and market relations.

SEVs can originate with a single innovation and progressively embrace other fields. A clear example of this process is once again Aravind Eye Hospitals. This SEV was first established as a more efficient way to bring eye care to the poorest people in rural and urban India (Prahalad, 2004). Therefore the initial innovation can be regarded not as service per se but above all as the organization of the workflow. Today the organization has grown and offers eye-camps, community-based rehabilitation projects, eye screening for school children and other innovative services to complement the initial, winning innovation.

Jumpstart, an organization devoted to addressing the social, economic and educational problems of school readiness, begins with a service innovation: delivering individualized tutoring to preschoolers in order to develop the literacy and social skills needed to succeed in school. From the beginning this kind of innovation grew out of an innovative business model consisting of creative production factors: a balanced combination of children (the 'clients'), their families (in order to support them during the learning process) and college students as tutors (the workforce).

It is possible to continue ad libitum with examples: however, it is important to clearly state the multidimensionality and the temporal dimension of innovation as crucial in the SE process.

A last consideration on social issues that are covered by social entrepreneurial innovation: practice shows innovation as widely spread within different action fields. It is not limited to traditional social sectors but can be found potentially everywhere.

Entrepreneurial model

Looking at the way SEVs manage social transformation, the most evident component of the business style of SEVs is their orientation towards the market. SEVs declare themselves to be explicitly market-driven, directing their efforts to customer and stakeholder satisfaction.

This statement confirms what has been said with regard to the change in the accountability flows of SEVs: 'In traditional nonprofits, it was the funding organizations that had to be satisfied first, then the executive director (usually the conduit to funding sources), then the employees and volunteers, and, only in the end, the people whose satisfaction was directly tied to the organization's mission in the first place' (McLeod, 1997: 4). SEVs, on the contrary, start from their community of reference, know their community of reference and choose businesses that match (in the first instance) their population's needs. Microcredits and community venture capital are two examples of what knowledge of the consumer base means for SEVs.

In looking for business where others (typically business actors) see nothing, SEVs start the entrepreneurial process from an explicit, combined evaluation of social and economic potential. In this sense, SEVs declare themselves to start business by evaluating their own aptitude to help the community and their ability to be self-sustaining. The key to sustainability is constantly pursued through combining low costs with efficiency, quality and profitability.

This tension also arises from a further characteristic element: the analyzed SEVs manifest rising trends and underline the adoption of a proper scalable business/social strategy.

In particular, the growth attitude is considered to be strictly linked to three factors:

- *Networking*: SEVs share a strong attitude to sustain growth with partnerships and collaborations with nonprofit partners, companies and public actors. The reasons that justify this behavior are diverse. SEVs can tend both to eliminate duplicative costs and excess capacity through shared facilities, services or activities, or can be pushed by critical input combinations. In fact, no single entity has all the inputs necessary to address effectively an identified social need. Other reasons that explain partnership-orientation are to be found in the necessity to increase impact by bringing together complementary capabilities or, on the other hand, to enlarge market or client bases and also to acquire new expertise or enhance contractual power towards funding institutions.
- *Flexibility*: most of the SEVs' organizational structures are extremely flexible, participatory and transparent. This characteristic can be explained by the newness that characterizes the phenomenon. In such a situation, where the scarcity of models of reference and acknowledged best practices makes the links among growth, innovation and the unpredictability of outcomes and impacts considerably strong, it becomes critical to share information and let it flow easily at each level of the organization in order to stimulate creativity.
- *Balancing the local dimension with the global dimension*: this last growth specificity has been noticed to be quite a constant of SEVs' behavior. To be sure of not losing out in quality, SEVs tend to maximize impact at each site through a sort of tied-up diversification. In

other words, they add new sites through a targeted new site development plan, often helping communities to independently replicate a community-built model. This can be read as an attempt to maintain a constant level of personality in the provision of social services and avoid the proved ineffectiveness of improving social conditions through standardized services (Borzaga and Defourny, 2004).

In generalizing we can say that:

SEVs aim at creating an overall vision that embraces both nonprofit and business culture. They constantly look for synergy, leveraging transferable skills and best practices, and business or social partners in order to enhance the general impact. They are based on a learning and participatory organizational structure, in order to promote innovative solutions. As a result, SEV emerges as an extremely adaptive culture.

Social outcomes and social welfare impact

The last critical research area concerns social outcomes and social change. This is a list of the fields in which social transformation is expected to be reached in the SEVs analyzed:

- Arts, culture and humanities
- Children and youth
- Community and economic development
- Disaster relief
- Education and research
- Employment training
- Environment and sustainable development
- Health enhancement
- Homelessness
- Hunger and poverty relief
- Rehabilitative services

Yet these are only fields of action: to be more specific, what kinds of social transformation can be identified in current practice?

A first area of SE contribution is *employment creation*: Juma Ventures, Pioneer Human Services and Rubicon Programs Inc. are all examples of how it is possible to create direct employment for at-risk people, otherwise excluded from access to the marketplace. But the contribution of SEVs, in this sense, is not limited to the employment training field, they may 'help in developing both demand and supply, as well as in reconfiguring public expenditure composition' (Borzaga and Defourny,

2004: 359). The fact that SEVs often employ low-income or at-risk workers does not imply quality reduction or less attention to attracting the best skills. On the contrary, these are major strengths of the SE approach:

> SEVs adapt traditional business practices to unexpected resources that are not characterized by low growth potential but that only need to be stimulated and balanced in accordance with innovative approaches.

Furthermore, SEVs' social outcomes extend to the field of *access to information*. Bay Area Video Coalition, International Network of Street Papers and Grameen Bank's telecommunications venture with Norwegian company Telenor are the most explicative examples of how it is possible to stimulate a nonexclusive flow of information. Especially encouraged by those SEVs that work at the bottom of the pyramid, gaining access to information through technological progress is the main driver to enhance democracy and reduce overall asymmetry (Prahalad, 2004).

Thirdly, SEVs can actually contribute to changing patterns of interaction in order to enhance *social cohesion* through personalization and participative approaches. 'By contributing to solving or to alleviating the problems of specific groups, and by favoring the integration of disadvantaged people into the labor market with higher wages than those paid by sheltered employment workshops and sometimes for-profit companies, social enterprises also contribute to improving life conditions, the well-being of communities and the level of social integration' (Borzaga and Defourny, 2004: 360). This objective is often supported by technology with a process of progressive dissemination and adaptation of technological progress to the different communities.

Finally, a general consideration: as innovation, social change is anything but a one-dimensional construct. SEVs tend to voluntarily and involuntarily pursue simultaneous, different social outcomes. In other words, it is hard to affirm that, for example, Rubicon Programs Inc. is an employment organization. Maybe this is what its mission states, but related outcomes, for example, community development, changes in patterns of interactions and the enhanced ability of workers to make independent choices, cannot be underestimated.

Discussion and conclusion

> Social entrepreneurs find what's not working, spread the solution, change the system from within, and persuade whole societies to change for the better. (http://www.aworldconnected.org).

SE represents now, the most innovative and challenging possibility in clearing the way for social change and social transformation.

Reframing the previous research, we propose a definition that complements all the components presented above. We define SE as a dynamic process created and managed by an individual or team (the innovative social entrepreneur), which strives to exploit social innovation with an entrepreneurial mindset and a strong need for achievement in order to create new social value in the market and community at large. SEVs are at the nexus of profit strengths and nonprofit culture, constantly looking for a precarious equilibrium between management profitability and the ability to pursue a social mission both superordinate to and sustained by the maximization of profits.

In light of the argument developed so far in the shift from theory to practice, we can now suggest a tentative framework for the SE process, as follows (Figure 5.1):

The process is composed of six main steps that refer to the research areas analyzed above. It begins with the definition of a clear, 'socially entrepreneurial' mission and the identification of a viable entrepreneurial opportunity stemming from vision-oriented and crisis-oriented factors. The mission and the opportunity to satisfy an unmet social

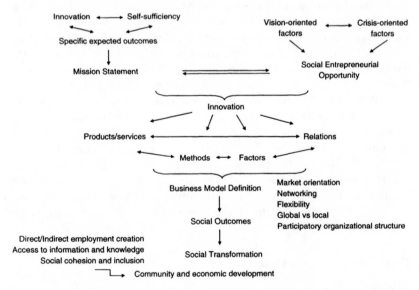

Figure 5.1 The point of view of the practitioner: a descriptive framework of the social entrepreneurial process

need turn into a concrete innovation that can embrace one to four main dimensions. As stated above, social innovation is not, in fact, a one-dimensional construct but can involve many company dimensions both contemporaneously and temporally.

To be effective a social innovation needs a fitting business model. Practitioners tend to address their business models towards market and stakeholder needs. All this is achieved through a strong networking orientation, organizational flexibility, a wise trade-off between local and global dimensions and a participatory management philosophy.

This business model is explicitly addressed towards a specific social outcome or outcomes and leads to general social transformation in the long run, in terms of direct and indirect employment creation, access to information and knowledge and social cohesion. As innovation, social transformation is a multidimensional construct consisting of concurrent or temporally subsequent employment creation, access to information, social cohesion and economic and community development.

Current research on SE still suffers from a lack of systematic empirical studies and, above all, the difficulty of comparing very diverse experiences without a common and shared starting base. To date, empirical contributions tend to focus themselves on a particular aspect of this original phenomenon, often leaving out the general framework.

As a consequence, the significance of this preliminary and ongoing research lies in the attempt to corroborate theory by looking for general commonalities among practitioners and well-established practices. In this way, it has also been possible to present a descriptive framework for social entrepreneurial process.

There are two major, natural next steps in the research process. The first includes studies on each single component of the proposed framework and relations among them. The second regards the analysis of correlations between elements and characteristics. For example: are there rule models regarding the relationship between types of innovation and organizational sizes or scale-up strategies? Given the importance of opportunity definition and exploitation, what is the reciprocal weight of different components within an entrepreneur's cognitive process? And so on.

In slightly different words, we suggest that we will not understand the phenomenon of SE if we do not consider each single element of the discourse; however we must also consider the links between these elements over time. SE scholars should focus their efforts on the nexus of entrepreneurial mindset, innovation and social issues, with reference to entrepreneurial opportunities, enterprising individuals or teams, and the mode of organization within the overall context of the dynamic environment.

Appendix 5A List of analyzed SEVs

	Social Entrepreneurial Venture	Country	Kick-off	Founder	Web Site	Sector
1	Aavishkaar	Singapore	2001	Vineet Rai	http://www.aavishkaar.org/	Financial Services
2	Aravind Eye Hospitals	India	1976	G. Venkataswamy	http://www.aravind.org	Health Care
3	Artists for Humanity	USA	1990	Susan Rodgerson	http://www.afhboston.com/	Education and Training
4	Bangladesh Rural Advancement Committee (BRAC)	Bangladesh	1972	Fazle Hasan Abed	http://www.brac.net	Development Services
5	Bay Area Video Coalition (BAVC)	USA	1976		http://www.bavc.org/	Media Services
6	Casas Bahia	Brazil	1952	Samuel Klein	http://www.casasbahia.com.br/	Retailing
7	CDI – Committee for the Democratization of Information Technology	Brazil	1995	Rodrigo Baggio	http://www.cdi.org.br	ICT
8	City Year	USA	1988	Michael Brown and Alan Khazei	http://www.cityyear.org	Voluntary Services
9	Coalition of Essential Schools	USA	1984	Ted Sizer	www.essentialschools.org	Education and Training
10	College Summit	USA	1993	J.B. Schramm	http://www.collegesummit.org/	Education and Training
11	Creative Capital	USA	1999	Peter Thomas Gow	http://www.creative-capital.org/	Arts and Culture Development Services
12	CrediAmigo	Brazil	1952	Banco do Nordeste		Financial Services
13	Freeplay Energy Group and Foundation	UK	1994	Rory Stear	http://www.freeplay.net	Energy
14	Global Education Partnership	USA	1994	Tony Silard	http://www.geponline.org/index.shtml	Education and Training
15	Golden Gate Community Inc.	USA	1981	Group of Citizens	http://www.ggci.org	Education, Training and Housing

Appendix 5A *List of analyzed SEVs – continued*

	Social Entrepreneurial Venture	Country	Kick-off	Founder	Web Site	Sector
16	Grameen Bank	Bangladesh	1983	Muhammad Yunus	http://www.grameen-info.org	Financial Services
17	International Network of Street Papers (INSP)	UK	1994	The Big Issue	http://www.street-papers.org/	Media Services
18	Juma Ventures	USA	1993	Rebecca Juhl, Malek Nativad	http://jumaventure.org	Education and Employment Services
19	Jumpstart	USA	1993	Yale University	http://www.jstart.org	Education and Training
20	KaBoom	USA	1995	Darell Hammond	http://www.kaboom.org/	Child Services
21	Koto	Vietnam	1966	Jimmy Pham	http://www.streetvoices.com.au	Education and Employment Training
22	Net4kids	Netherlands	1999	Loek van den Boog	http://www.net4kids.org/	Child Services
23	Institute for One World Health	USA	2000	Victoria Hale	www.OneWorldHealth.org	Pharmacology
24	Pioneer Human Services	USA	1962	Jack Dalton	http://www.pioneerhumanserv.com	Education and Employment Services
25	Real Microcredito	Brazil	2002	ABN-AMRO in partnership with ACCION	http://www.accion.org/about_where_we_work_program.asp_Q_T_E_24	Financial Services
26	Rubicon Programs Incorporated	USA	1973	Rick Aubry	http://www.rubiconprograms.org	Education and Employment Services
27	Sekem	Egypt	1968	Ibrahim Abouleish	www.sekem.com	Agriculture
28	Share Our Strength	USA	1984	Bill Shore	http://www.strength.org/	Hunger Relief
29	IDEAAS	Brazil	1992	Fabio Rosa		Renewable Energy
30	Teach for America	USA	1990	Wendy Kopp	http://www.teachforamerica.org/	Education and Training
31	TechnoServe	USA	1968	Ed Bullard	http://www.technoserve.org/home.html	Consulting Services

Appendix 5A List of analyzed SEVs – *continued*

Social Entrepreneurial Venture	Country	Kick-off	Founder	Web Site	Sector
32 The Big Issue	UK	1991	John Bird	http://www.bigissue.com	Education and Employment Services
33 The Delancey Street Foundation	USA	1971	John Maher	http://www.eisenhowerfoundation.org/grassroots/delancey/	Rehabilitative Services
34 Thibodeau's Centre for Hearing Health and Communication	Canada	1964	Ted Thibodeau	http://www.centreforhearing.com/	Health Care
35 Voxiva	Peru, India	2001	Paul Meyer, Pamela Johnson, Anand Narasimhan	http://www.voxiva.net	ICT

References

Alvord, S. H., Brown, L. D. and Letts, C. W. 2002. Social entrepreneurship and social transformation: An exploratory study. Working Paper 15, November 2002. The Hauser Center for Nonprofit Organizations and The Kennedy School of Government, Harvard University.

Bank of England 2003. *The financing of social enterprise*. London: Bank of England.

Barendsen, L. and Gardner, H. 2004. Is the social entrepreneur a new type of leader? *Leader to Leader*, Fall: 34.

Bornstein, D. 2004. *How to change the world. Social entrepreneurs and the power of new ideas*. Oxford: Oxford University Press.

Borzaga, C. and Defourny, J. (eds) 2004. *The emergence of social enterprise*. London: Routledge.

Borzaga, C. and Solari, L. 2004. Management challenges for social enterprises. In C. Borzaga, and J. Defourny (eds). *The emergence of social enterprise*: 333–49. London: Routledge.

Boschee, J. 1998. What does it take to be a social entrepreneur? National Centre for Social Entrepreneurs. Available: http://www.socialentrepreneurs.org/what-does.html. Accessed: 14 June 2005.

Boschee, J. and McClurg, J. 2003. Toward a better understanding of social entrepreneurship: Some important distinctions. Available: http://www.se-alliance.org/better_understanding.pdf. Accessed: 14 June 2005.

Brinckerhoff, P. C. 2000. *Social entrepreneurship. The art of mission-based venture development*. New York: John Wiley and Sons.

Bruyat, C. and Julien, P. A. 2000. Defining the field of research in entrepreneurship. *Journal of Business Venturing*, 16: 165–80.

Campbell, S. 1998. Social entrepreneurship: How to develop new social-purpose business ventures. *Health Care Strategic Management*, 16(5): 17–22.

Cannon, C. M. 2000. Charity for profit: How the new social entrepreneurs are creating good by sharing wealth. *National Journal*, 16 June: 1898–904.

Casson, M. 1982. *The entrepreneur – An economic theory*. Totowa, NJ: Barnes and Noble.

Cook, B., Dodds, C. and Mitchell, W. 2001. Social entrepreneurship: Whose responsibility is it anyway? The false premise of social entrepreneurship. Working Paper. Center of Full Employment and Equity and Department of Social Work, November 2001. University of Newcastle, Australia.

Dart, R. 2004. The legitimacy of social enterprise. *Nonprofit Management and Leadership*, 14(4): 411–24.

Dees, J. G. 1998a. The meaning of social entrepreneurship. Paper, Center for the Advancement of Social Entrepreneurship, Fuqua School of Business, Duke University, Durham. Available: http://www.fuqua.duke.edu/centers/case/documents/dees_SE.pdf

Dees, J. G. 1998b. Enterprising nonprofits: What do you do when traditional sources of funding fall short? *Harvard Business Review*. January/February: 55–67.

Dees, J. G. and Elias, J. 1998. The challenges of combining social and commercial enterprise. *Business Ethics Quarterly*, 8(1): 165–78.

Dees, J. G., Emerson, J. and Economy, P. 2001. *Enterprising nonprofits: A toolkit for social entrepreneurs*. New York: John Wiley and Sons.

Dees, J. G., Emerson, J. and Economy, P. 2002. *Strategic tools for social entrepreneurs. Enhancing the performance of your enterprising nonprofit*. New York: John Wiley and Sons.

Dorado, S. and Haettich, H. 2004. *Social entrepreneurial ventures: Worth a careful look?* Working Paper. UMASS – College of Management, Boston.

Drucker, P. 1985. *Innovation and entrepreneurship.* New York: Harper and Row.

Eisenhardt, K. M. 1989. Building theories from case study research. *Academy of Management Review*, 14(4): 532–50.

Foryt, S. 2002. Social entrepreneurship in developing nations. Working Paper. INSEAD, Fontainebleau.

Glaser, B. and Strauss, A. 1967. *The discovery of grounded theory. Strategies of qualitative research.* London: Wiedenfeld and Nicholson.

Grenier, P. 2002. The function of social entrepreneurship in the UK. Paper presented at the ISTR Conference, Cape Town, July.

Guclu, A., Dees, J. G. and Battle Anderson, B. 2002. The process of social entrepreneurship: Creating opportunities worthy of serious pursuit. Paper. Fuqua School of Business, Center for the Advancement of Social Entrepreneurship.

Henton, D., Melville, J. and Walesh, K. 1997. The age of the civic entrepreneur: Restoring civil society and building economic community. *National Civic Review*, 6(2): 149–56.

Hockerts, K. 2004. Bootstrapping social change: Towards an evolutionary theory of social entrepreneurship. Manuscript submitted to Academy of Management Review, June 2004.

Johnson, S. 2000. Literature review on social entrepreneurship. University of Alberta: Canadian Center for Social Entrepreneurship. Available: http://www.bus.ualberta.ca/ccse/Publications.

Kanter, R. 1999. From spare change to real change: the social sector as beta site for business innovation. *Harvard Business Review*, 77(3): 122–33.

Larson, A. L. 2000. Sustainable innovation through an entrepreneurship lens. *Business Strategy and the Environment*, 9: 304–17.

Laville, F. L. and Nyssens, M. 2004. The social enterprise: Towards a theoretical social-economic approach. In C. Borzaga, and J. Defourny (eds), *The emergence of social enterprise*: 312–32. London: Routledge.

Leadbeater, C. 1997. *The rise of the social entrepreneur.* London: Demos.

Letts, C. W., Ryan, W. P. and Grossman, A. 1999. *High performance nonprofit organizations. Managing upstream for greater impact.* New York: John Wiley and Sons.

Mair, J. and Martí, I. 2004. Social entrepreneurship: What are we talking about? A framework for future research. Working Paper 546, March. IESE Business School, University of Navarra, Barcelona.

Mair, J. and Noboa, E. 2003a. Social entrepreneurship: How intentions to create a social enterprise get formed. Working Paper 521, September. IESE Business School, University of Navarra, Barcelona.

Mair, J. and Noboa, E. 2003b. The emergence of social enterprises and their place in the new organizational landscape. Working Paper 523, October. IESE Business School, University of Navarra, Barcelona.

Margolis, J. D. and Walsh, J. P. 2003. Misery loves companies: Rethinking social initiative by business. *Administrative Science Quarterly*, 48: 268–305.

McLeod, H. R. 1997. Cross over, *Inc.* 19: 100–5.

Mort, G. S., Weerawardena, J. and Carnegie, K. 2002. Social entrepreneurship: Towards conceptualization. *International Journal of Nonprofit and Voluntary Sector Marketing*, 8(1): 76–88.

Paton, R. 2003. *Managing and measuring social enterprises*. London: Sage Publications.

Prabhu, G. N. 1999. Social entrepreneurial leadership, *Career Development International*, 4(3): 140–5.

Prahalad, C. K. 2004. *The fortune at the bottom of the pyramid. Eradicating poverty through profits*. Upper Saddle River, NJ: Wharton School Publishing.

Prahalad, C. K. and Hammond, A. 2002. Serving the world's poor, profitably, *Harvard Business Review*, 80(9): 48–57.

Prahalad, C. K. and Hart, S. L. 1999. Strategies for the bottom of the pyramid: creating sustainable development. Unpublished Draft Paper, August 1999.

Reis, T. 1999. Unleashing the new resources and entrepreneurship for the common good: A scan, synthesis and scenario for action. W. K. Kellogg Foundation, Michigan.

Schaltegger, S. 2002. A framework for entrepreneurship: Leading bioneers and environmental managers to entrepreneurship. *Greener Management International*, 38: 45–58.

Shane, S. 2000. Prior knowledge and the discovery of entrepreneurial opportunity. *Organization Science*, 11: 448–69.

Thompson, J., Alvy, G. and Lees, A. 2000. Social entrepreneurship – A new look at the people and the potential. *Management Decision*, 35(5): 328–38.

Volery, T. 2002. An entrepreneur commercialises conservation: The case of Earth Sanctuaries, Ltd. *Greener Management International*, 38: 109–16.

Waddock, S. and Post, J. 1991. Social entrepreneurs and catalytic change. *Public Administration Review*, 51(5): 393–401.

Walsh, J. P., Weber, K. and Margolis, J. D. 2003. Social issues and management: Our lost cause found. *Journal of Management*, 29(6): 859–81.

Part II

Opportunities and Intentions

6
Introduction to Part II – Exploring the Intentions and Opportunities Behind Social Entrepreneurship

Johanna Mair

The process by which scholars are struggling to establish social entrepreneurship (SE) as a legitimate field of study closely resembles the development of the field of business entrepreneurship. Similar to business entrepreneurship, which even today lacks a unifying paradigm (Shane and Venkataraman, 2000), SE has taken on a variety of meanings (Dees, 1998), and we still lack answers to the following questions: How do we define SE? Why and how should we study it? What differentiates SE from other 'social' initiatives? And finally, what is the relation between SE and traditional business entrepreneurship?

The world of ideas, innovation, and opportunity has traditionally been associated with economic value creation, a link that has attracted the attention of management scholars over the last decades. Although today it is increasingly recognized that ideas, innovation, and opportunity are not the exclusive domain of business entrepreneurs, we lack conceptual and empirical research to ascertain whether SE is a subset of 'traditional' entrepreneurship, or whether it is an independent field of study.

It could be argued that SE merely provides a different ('social') setting in which to examine entrepreneurial phenomena. On the other hand, we know that all entrepreneurial activity creates a certain amount of social value – it creates employment, stimulates innovation, and generates tax revenue. Is business entrepreneurship, which focuses predominately on economic value creation, therefore a subset of SE, which embraces both economic and social value creation?

In sum, the concept of SE is still poorly defined and its boundaries to traditional business entrepreneurship are still fuzzy. Approaches and constructs from existing entrepreneurship research have clearly shaped the first attempts to conceptualize SE. Now it is time to go one step further. The rise of SE, both as a practice and as a theoretical endeavor, provides a unique opportunity for the field of entrepreneurship to challenge, question, and rethink important concepts and assumptions in its effort towards discovering a unifying paradigm (Mair and Martí, 2005).

The two papers of this chapter provide a first step in this direction and advance our understanding of the social entrepreneurial process. Mair and Noboa offer a refreshing conceptualization of how entrepreneurs form intentions to create a social venture; and Robinson presents an insightful empirical study on how social entrepreneurs identify and evaluate opportunities. The authors of both papers explicitly build on existing research and literature in entrepreneurship. Mair and Noboa draw from the entrepreneurship literature on intention formation, as well as from foundational work in social psychology. Robinson, instead, builds on earlier work in economics: more specifically, he applies an Austrian approach and findings from research on market entry to the phenomenon of SE.

Both papers suggest that differences exist between business entrepreneurship and SE in terms of outcome and opportunities. Social entrepreneurship clearly aims at a double (if not triple) bottom line, combining social and economic value creation. Social entrepreneurial opportunities are also different. Robinson argues that, while the decision of business entrepreneurs to pursue a venture depends to a large extent on the economic barriers to entry, social entrepreneurs face social and institutional structures as barriers. Mair and Noboa further argue that social entrepreneurial opportunities, as well as the ways to pursue these (social) opportunities, are distinct.

While previous research on SE has mainly focused on the (social) entrepreneur or the outcome (social enterprise or venture), the papers in this chapter address the social entrepreneurial process. Here the major contribution lies in their emphasis on the cognitive aspects of the entrepreneurial process. For Robinson social entrepreneurs are special as they perceive and enact social opportunities that others do not see. Mair and Noboa suggest that social entrepreneurs perceive social ventures as desirable because of specific emotional and cognitive attitudes. Furthermore, the authors perceive them as feasible because they develop a high level of social entrepreneurial self-efficacy, that is, an enhanced perception of their ability to create a social venture.

The papers in this chapter add to the debate on whether SE constitutes a distinct field of research or whether it represents a subfield. The findings clearly indicate that examining cognitive processes is important in order to detect fundamental differences and similarities between business and SE processes. Both studies also shed new light on the antecedents of social ventures: the specific personal background and the situational context matter as to whether and how social entrepreneurs enact their venture ideas. Mair and Noboa, as well as Robinson, stress the importance of personal and work experience for forming social entrepreneurial intentions and detecting social entrepreneurial opportunities. Both chapters, Robinson in particular, point towards the importance of perceived context, namely the social and institutional structure to facilitate opportunity recognition.

The next paragraphs provide a short summary of the main arguments.

Robinson – How social entrepreneurs identify and evaluate opportunities

The prevailing theoretical perspective in entrepreneurship focuses on the nexus between enterprising individuals and valuable opportunities (Shane and Venkataraman, 2000; Venkataraman, 1997). Yet we still know very little about the nature of opportunities. Are opportunities made or found? Some authors talk about opportunity development (Ardichvili, Cardozo and Ray, 2003) or opportunity creation (McGrath and MacMillan, 2000), while others take the existence of opportunities for granted and talk about opportunity identification and recognition (DeTienne and Chandler, 2004; Gaglio and Katz, 2001). Robinson adds an interesting nuance to this debate. According to him social entrepreneurial opportunities exist, but they cannot be seen by everyone. Social entrepreneurial opportunities are special because they are embedded in a social sector market. The social market however, is highly influenced by (formal and informal) social and institutional factors which are perceived as entry barriers by some and not by others.

Robinson addresses some of the most prominent questions that we need to address at this early stage of research on SE: What makes social entrepreneurial opportunities different from other types of opportunities? What is unique about SE? And finally, how do social entrepreneurs discover opportunities?

In short, the findings of Robinson's paper suggest that social entrepreneurial opportunities are highly influenced by the social and institutional structures in a market and/or community, which can create entry barriers. As a consequence, SE has to be viewed as a process by which entrepreneurial strategies are used to address a social problem, and equally important, as a process of navigating social and institutional barriers to a market/community. Finally, whether social entrepreneurs discover an opportunity or not, depends on their personal and work experience and on the characteristics of the market/community they want to enter.

Robinson adds the necessary rigor and creativity to establish SE as a recognized field of study. His longitudinal analysis of six early stage social ventures combines the breadth and depth to generate insights and frameworks for further research. Robinson applies a mix of methods, ranging from business plan analysis to in-depth case studies, and is therefore able to capture the richness of the phenomenon.

Besides a refreshing view of entrepreneurial opportunities the paper provides a new perspective on how entrepreneurs navigate social and institutional barriers to markets. Adopting a sociological view of markets, Robinson introduces cognitive and strategic dimensions to consider entry barriers. His paper, therefore, is inspiring for future research in the area of SE as well as in strategy and entrepreneurship.

Mair and Noboa – How intentions to create a social venture are formed

How do social entrepreneurs form intentions to create a social venture? Mair and Noboa address this important question by building on well-established entrepreneurship literature on the intention formation process. Previous work has depicted intentions as a reliable predictor of entrepreneurial activity that culminates in the formation of new ventures. This research stream within the field of entrepreneurship has drawn from social psychology, which views intentions as powerful predictors of behavior, especially in the case of purposive, planned, and goal-oriented behavior (Bagozzi, Baumgartner and Yi, 1989). In the case of entrepreneurial behavior – aiming at social value creation – the degree of purpose might even be more pronounced.

Investigating the sources and antecedents of behavioral intentions to set up a social venture, Mair and Noboa contribute to a more comprehensive picture of SE. At the same time, they shed light on the fuzzy boundaries between entrepreneurship and SE. Bird (1988), one of the first authors to emphasize the importance of intentions for studying entrepreneurial phenomena, claimed that studying intentions allows us to distinguish between entrepreneurial activity and strategic management. Thus, studying the intention formation process of social entrepreneurs might indeed provide a more nuanced understanding of whether SE constitutes a separate field of study.

While the majority of existing intention formation models consider both individual and situational variables as important determinants of entrepreneurial intentions, Mair and Noboa focus on individual-based differences. Opting for a parsimonious approach they restrict their analysis to a specific set of dynamic and malleable variables. They build on and extend existing research in several ways. First, in line with existing models, Mair and Noboa draw from Ajzen's work on the origins of planned behavior (Ajzen, 1991) and Shapero and Sokol's seminal work on entrepreneurial event formation (Shapero and Sokol, 1982). They also include perceived desirability and feasibility as important antecedents of intentions. However, they go one step further, or better, one step backwards, and specifically look at the set of variables that affect perceived desirability and feasibility. In short, their model suggests that intentions to set up a social venture develop from perceptions of desirability, which are affected by emotional and cognitive attitudes (empathy and moral judgment), and from perceptions of feasibility, which are instigated by 'enabling' factors such as self-efficacy and social support. The second main contribution lies in the fact that the authors are the first to investigate intention formation in the context of ventures where social value creation is the primary objective.

Finally, the paper invites future empirical and conceptual research. To date, very little is known about the relationship between opportunity recognition and intentions development. Does one precede the other? By the same token, little is known about the way social entrepreneurs discover and exploit social opportunities. Do social entrepreneurs search for opportunities or suddenly discover them? Do they show an above-normal level of entrepreneurial alertness? What prior information is relevant for the discovery/exploitation of social opportunities? To what extent do social entrepreneurs rely on gut feeling to evaluate social opportunities?

To conclude, the contribution of the two papers in this chapter lies in the insightful description and conceptualization of the social entrepreneurial process. Mair and Noboa as well as Robinson succeed in advancing our understanding of SE without neglecting existing knowledge in entrepreneurship theory. They therefore make the first steps towards a comprehensive picture of the SE process and, at the same time, challenge and advance existing frameworks and concepts in the field of entrepreneurship. Both chapters provide an inspiring source for further empirical and theoretical research.

References

Ajzen, I. 1991. The theory of planned behavior. *Organizational Behavior and Human Decision Process,* 50: 179–211.

Ardichvili, A., Cardozo, R. and Ray, S. 2003. A theory of entrepreneurial opportunity identification and development. *Journal of Business Venturing,* 18(1): 105–33.

Bagozzi, R., Baumgartner, H. and Yi, Y. 1989. An investigation into the role of intentions as mediators of the attitude-behavior relationship. *Journal of Economic Psychology,* 10: 3–62.

Bird, B. J. 1988. Implementing entrepreneurial ideas: The case for intention. *Academy of Management Review,* 13(3): 442–61.

Dees, J. G. 1998. The meaning of social entrepreneurship. Paper. Centre for the Advancement of Social Entrepreneurship, Fuqua School of Business, Duke University, Durham. Available: http://www.fuqua.duke.edu/centers/case/documents/dees_SE.pdf.

DeTienne, D. R. and Chandler, G. N. 2004. Opportunity identification and its role in the entrepreneurial classroom: A pedagogical approach and empirical test. *Academy of Management Learning and Education,* 3(3): 242–57.

Gaglio, C. M. and Katz, J. A. 2001. The psychological basis of opportunity identification: Entrepreneurial alertness. *Journal of Small Business Economics,* 16: 95–111.

Mair, J. and Martí, I. 2005. Social entrepreneurship research: A source of explanation, prediction, and delight. *Journal of World Business:* forthcoming.

McGrath, R. G. and MacMillan, I. 2000. *The entrepreneurial mindset: Strategies for continuously creating opportunity in an age of uncertainty.* Boston, MA: Harvard Business School Press.

Shane, S., and Venkataraman, S. 2000. The promise of entrepreneurship as a field of research. *Academy of Management Review,* 25(1): 217–26.

Shapero, A. and Sokol, L. 1982. The social dimensions of entrepreneurship. In S. V. Kent (ed.), *Encyclopedia of Entrepreneurship.* Engelwood Cliffs, NJ: Prentice Hall.

Venkataraman, S. 1997. The distinctive domain of entrepreneurship research: An editor's perspective. In J. Katz, and R. Brockhaus (eds), *Advances in Entrepreneurship, Firm Emergence, and Growth,* **Vol. 3**: 119–38. Greenwich, CT: JAI Press.

7
Navigating Social and Institutional Barriers to Markets: How Social Entrepreneurs Identify and Evaluate Opportunities

Jeffrey Robinson

Introduction

Entrepreneurship research can be broadly placed into three categories: that which examines the people (entrepreneurs); that which examines the process and that which examines the entrepreneurial or business opportunities. This chapter specifically looks at social entrepreneurial opportunities and the process of identifying and evaluating these types of opportunities. I address three important questions:

- What makes social entrepreneurial opportunities different from other types of opportunities?
- What makes social entrepreneurship special?
- How do social entrepreneurs find social entrepreneurial opportunities?

The phenomenon of social entrepreneurship

For the purposes of this chapter, I define social entrepreneurship (SE) as a *process* (Shane and Venkataraman, 2000) that includes: the identification of a specific social problem and a specific solution (or set of solutions) to address it; the evaluation of the social impact, the business model and the sustainability of the venture; and the creation of a social mission-oriented *for-profit* or a business-oriented *nonprofit* entity that pursues the double (or triple) bottom line. This approach to defining SE allows for future research directions and for clearer distinctions from 'traditional' entrepreneurship.

Recently, there has been an explosion of interest in the phenomenon of *SE*. It is an attractive area for practitioners, policy makers, the media and business schools because it addresses several issues in society (Dees, 1998; Thompson, 2002; Alvord, Brown and Letts, 2004; Brainard and Siplon, 2004). SE is a uniting concept that demonstrates the usefulness of business principles in achieving social goals. The term SE is an umbrella term that includes social enterprises, social venture capital, and social purpose organizations. It is a term that is being used all around the world to describe the people, the ventures and the activities that innovate for social good. Social entrepreneurs who span these sectorial boundaries are particularly adept at innovation.

Social entrepreneurship has the potential to bring an interdisciplinary array of actors together leading to various boundary-spanning research and practical activities. The result of such boundary-spanning is the rearrangement and recombination of the existing organizational forms and roles. This hybridization of organizational forms and roles follows the law of requisite variety: difficult problems require innovative solutions. Social entrepreneurs are engaged in creating these innovative solutions.

Although SE is a global phenomenon, it has not happened in all of these places for the same reason. In developed nations, SE is on the rise because of the decline of the welfare state. Vital gaps in the social safety net and changes in the institutional environment have led to social entrepreneurial opportunities. As I report in this chapter, the ability to fill these gaps with innovative solutions is a phenomenon worthy of study. In less-developed, developing and emerging economies, SE arises out of a combination of distrust of the NGO community, apathy within the private sector, and the impotence of the government to provide services to the people. For example, in Soweto, South Africa, social entrepreneur Mdala Mentoor created *Soweto Mountain of Hope* in response to the dire conditions of poverty that existed in his community. His organization generated funds from the products and artwork developed onsite and from the businesses they are incubating. In both of these examples, those that pursue social entrepreneurial opportunities are using the same process to achieve their goals. I will discuss this process later in the chapter.

Initiating a research agenda in SE

Much of the media attention related to SE focuses on the exceptionalism of individual social entrepreneurs. While I agree that these actors are important, I believe that the process of SE is underexplored. It also concerns me that a focus on the actors alone will lead some to believe that the achievements of social entrepreneurs can only be made by an elite. Academic research must go further and demystify how SE takes place. To date, however, there has been little academic research conducted in this area. My own literature review of academic journals and working papers posted at universities revealed only 15 papers that directly addressed SE research issues.

The point here is that we need more than journalistic accounts of the phenomenon of SE. I propose that academic research exploring the phenomenon of SE can take two paths. One path is to analyze SE in the light of current explanations of organizational life. Alternatively, scholars may take a grounded theory approach and see what new theories might come out of an in-depth understanding of the phenomenon.

This chapter begins with a discussion of two relevant theoretical approaches to the phenomenon of SE: the Austrian approach and entry barriers. I then present a framework for understanding entry into *social sector markets* and demonstrate its relevance to SE. I discuss how this framework explains the first two steps in the SE process (identification and evaluation) and the navigation process that takes place. In the second half of this chapter, I apply the framework to an analysis of six social venture case studies and demonstrate its usefulness for future research on social entrepreneurs. Finally, I present three themes that arise out of a second analysis of the data, and the implications of these themes for research and practice.

Theoretical background

The Austrian approach to the economics of entrepreneurship is particularly useful for defining two important aspects of SE: 1) social sector markets; and 2) social entrepreneurial opportunities.

The Austrian approach emerges from a strong critique of neoclassical economics (Kirzner, 1997). In this critique, proponents of the Austrian school argue that the neoclassical approach cannot accommodate entrepreneurship into its theories of equilibrium. Following the Austrian theorists, Kirzner (1997) and Hayek (1945), I believe that markets are more often in disequilibrium than in equilibrium. Disequilibria in the economic, social and institutional environment lead to entrepreneurial opportunity. Alert entrepreneurs will discover these opportunities more readily than those who are not alert. Shane (2000: 450) summarizes the Austrian approach in three points:

1. People cannot recognize all opportunities,
2. Information about opportunities determines who becomes an entrepreneur,
3. The process depends on factors other than a person's ability and willingness to take action.

This tradition of entrepreneurship is relevant to the analysis of SE and social sector markets where it is clear that equilibrium conditions do not exist. In fact, SE may exist because of a desire by some highly motivated individuals to address the issues of disequilibria in the areas of wealth, income, employment, human capital, and social capital. Often, social entrepreneurs are working in parts of society that are impacted by transitions and inequalities in the economy. For this reason, the Austrian approach is relevant to defining both the social entrepreneurial opportunity and the social sector market.

Social entrepreneurial opportunities and markets

Entrepreneurship theorists have placed much emphasis on the existence of definable opportunities that entrepreneurs pursue (Shane and Venkataraman, 2000). The pursuit of business opportunity presupposes the identification and discovery of an opportunity and a subsequent evaluation that may (or may not) lead to the pursuit or exploitation of that opportunity. These are critical links for any research program related to foundings, new venture creation, new products and strategy.

Only recently have scholars struggled to define opportunity in a technical fashion. Singh (2001: 11) generically defines it as:

> ...a feasible, profit-seeking, potential venture that provides an innovative new product or service to the market, improves on an existing product/service, or imitates a profitable product/service in a less-than-saturated market.

Under this definition, opportunities exist in markets whether an entrepreneur or manager recognizes them or not. This is consistent with Kirzner (1997) and his fellow Austrian economists. They consider everyone a potential entrepreneur because there are potential opportunities everywhere. If we accept this definition of who can be an entrepreneur then it follows that we should also accept the premise that opportunities are everywhere. Is there something special about social entrepreneurial opportunities that makes them different from other opportunities? I argue here that social entrepreneurial opportunities are a special case of opportunities. They are a special case because they are embedded in a social sector market. The social sector is known by various names – the third sector, the independent sector and the citizen sector (Bornstein, 2004). It is the part of the economy that provides all of the social services and products in any community and has direct benefit to society. Those benefits can be strictly social or strictly environmental or both. Governmental agencies, nongovernmental organizations, private companies, and private citizens all participate in this sector of our global economy.

Social sector markets have two defining characteristics. First, they are social in nature: in other words, the context of these markets has a significant impact on greater society. Second, they are highly influenced by both formal – and informal – social and institutional factors. Often, social sector markets are geographical areas (neighborhoods, communities, regions, or states) where a particular social problem or issue is prominent. As a result, social sector markets are challenging because they typically arise from situations where the formal and the informal economy are tightly coupled.

The markets and communities where social entrepreneurs operate are certainly representative of this type of market. Portes (1994) and others have explored the intricacies of the informal market. The formal economy is supposed to be regulated, predictable and able to smoothly transact in a near-pure market. The informal economy is not regulated, irregular and more prone to the idiosyncrasies of personal relationships. Because of this tight coupling and the ebb and flow of economic and social conditions, social sector markets pose an enormous challenge to the potential entrepreneur or business manager. Social entrepreneurs may predict that their services have a high impact on the lives of residents in a poverty stricken area, but soon become disillusioned when their venture is isolated within the community and customers/clients do not come to receive their services. This type of situation speaks to the need for both creativity in identifying opportunities, and innovative business practices in executing a social venture plan. Fully understanding social sector markets is a critical step toward understanding SE. The characteristics of these types of markets are the source of the entry barriers to social sector markets and are important for this discussion.

Social and institutional entry barriers to social sector markets

Entry barriers are the other side of the opportunity coin. Entry barriers represent some of the criteria entrepreneurs use to evaluate business opportunities once they are discovered. The perception of these entry barriers will influence the entry decision. After several years of researching business entry and nonentry into inner city markets I have concluded that SE opportunities are best analyzed in the context of the social and institutional factors that help to create them. I call these factors social and institutional entry barriers. I argue in this section that social entrepreneurs understand how to navigate these barriers in the SE process.

The concept of barriers to entry is well-documented in the literature of economics and business. As early as 1907, economist John Bates Clark wrote about keeping 'potential competition' at bay. Bain (1956) coined the term 'barriers to new competition' in the seminal work on the subject. Scherer (1980), Porter (1980) and others have clearly stated the importance of five barriers to entry in business strategy: capital requirements, cost advantages, switching costs, distribution access and proprietary assets. These barriers are tangible and generally address the issues of economies of scale and scope. Overcoming these barriers is the key to survival.

The implication of this work instructs firms to create and deploy mechanisms of deterrence that would prevent competitors from entering their markets. Researchers from various perspectives have considered the efficacy of such entry barriers in small business economics and entrepreneurship (Casson, 1982; Acs and Audretsch, 1988; Acs, 1999), strategic management and industrial economics (Porter, 1980; Harrigan, 1981; Schmalensee, 1981; Wagner, 1994; Klepper and Simons, 2000) and organizational theory (Tucker, Singh and Meinhard, 1990; Hannan, Carroll, Dundon and Torres, 1995; Carroll, Bigelow, Siedel and Tsai, 1996). Porter (1980) presented a typology of entry barriers that has become the backbone of strategic management theory. Today, when we teach business strategy and entrepreneurship in business schools, we explain that entry barriers serve two functions. First, an entry barrier deters the entrepreneur from entering new markets. Put simply, if the barriers are 'too high', a firm cannot (or will not) enter the market. Second, we describe entry barriers as something that should be erected behind the entrepreneur to protect her from competitors seeking to enter the same market. These have been explained as the major investments, learnings and innovations that are made, found and implemented within the firm and that are difficult to imitate outside of the firm. These types of barriers to entry, however, do not explain the breadth of challenges and opportunities afforded to firms seeking to enter social network markets.

To advance this argument I propose that entry barriers fall into three categories. I refer to the traditional entry barriers described by Bain (1956) and Porter (1980) as *economic barriers*. Economic barriers are related to market structure (that is, the concept of structure-conduct-performance in Scherer, 1980). I refer to the second type of entry barriers as *social entry barriers*. Social entry barriers such as the lack of networks of resources and access to an appropriate workforce are related to the social structure of the market. The third type of entry barriers I refer to as *institutional entry barriers* (that is, norms, values and order) and these are related to the institutional structure of the market.

Before I further describe these types of barriers, it is important to note that this framework for entry barriers shares Granovetter's (1985; 1992; 1999) conclusion that all economic action takes place within a social and institutional structure. SE, in particular, lends itself to this approach because of the goal to solve complex social problems.

Types of Entry Barriers

Economic entry barriers

Economic entry barriers are those defined by Harrigan (1981) as investments in a business that build up its technology, resources, and competitive advantage to a level where it is difficult for others to compete. In this case, the deterrent is financial (economic) in nature. Examples of economic entry barriers include cost advantages, product differentiation, capital requirements, customer switching costs, technology investment and research and development investment.

Social entry barriers

Social entry barriers prevent an entrepreneur from using the social network of relationships that exist within a market to her advantage. These interfirm, employee-employer, formal economy-informal economy and other firm-to-resource relationships are embedded in the social structure of the market. There are at least five categories of social networks that may present barriers to firm entry: business owners, business organizations, civic organizations, political infrastructure and attractive labor markets.

Information is communicated and resources are delivered through these networks. The lack of access to these social networks can be a significant deterrent to market entry, especially for new ventures. It is well-documented that access to trust networks (Uzzi, 1997), information, market knowledge, and other resources can enhance the survival of new ventures (Burt, 1992; Ingram and Simons, 2000). The lack of such access may prove to be fatal for the firm steered into an unfamiliar market. When an entrepreneur is making the entry decision, and she does not have access to the network of actors in the target market, this poses a significant entry barrier.

Table 7.1   Examples of social entry barriers in social sector markets

Social entry barriers	Examples
Lack of access to local networks of business owners and other social ventures	• Memberships in local business owners organization • Access to informal trust networks
Lack of access to local networks of business organizations and resources	• Relationships with local business development organizations • Relationships with local banking institutions
Lack of access to local networks of community-based and social organizations	• Relationships with faith-based or community development organizations
Lack of access to political infrastructure	• Relationships with local political figures
Lack of access to pool of labor and talent	• Relationships with workforce development organizations

Institutional entry barriers

Institutional entry barriers prevent an entrepreneur from knowing or accommodating the rules, norms and values that contribute to the culture, order and practices of a market. They occur at multiple levels in a market and dictate the relationship between a firm and the consumer, and the firm and the community. These are related to the institutional structure of a market.

In describing the new institutionalism in economics, Ingram and Clay (2000) argue that institutions form the basis of order and help to smooth interactions among actors. These institutions can be public or private in their source and centralized or decentralized in their making. For the social sector market, the interdependence of the public (centralized and decentralized) and private-decentralized forms is of importance to strategy and entrepreneurship. My framework focuses upon these three forms of institutional entry barriers.

Formal (or public) institutional barriers

Governmental systems, laws, financial markets and lending institutions are codified and formalized institutional structures that smooth the transactions between actors. Formal institutional barriers may deter entry to a market if the market does not have the appropriate institutions to encourage entrepreneurial activity. For example, if the market opportunity is in a place where there is significant disorder and disregard for property rights, it may not be the most inviting market to enter. Some markets do not have active financial markets. For entrepreneurs engaged in commercial ventures, this could be disadvantageous for their firm. Some entrepreneurs will not consider these markets because they do not believe they can overcome the existing institutional barriers to create their social ventures.

Table 7.2   Examples of institutional entry barriers in social sector markets

Institutional entry barriers	Examples
Lack of knowledge of local norms, values and culture	• Knowledge of cultural holidays and celebrations
Lack of social order	• Significant criminal activity • Abandoned housing ('broken windows')
Lack of government/quasi-government 'attention' that creates an 'environment for business'	• Lack of significant business presence and low self-employment
Lack of active financial markets	• Redlining of neighborhoods • Inactive banking community

Cultural barriers

Cultural entry barriers are informal institutions. Language, slang, dress and etiquette are often critical to a firm's success in securing stakeholders' goodwill and trust. Cultural norms are the attitudes, beliefs, and expectations about behavior in a market. These forms of cultural capital (Bourdieu, 1984; Coleman, 1990) can take many forms: language, slang, dress, etiquette, legends, and even superstitions.

Cultural barriers have been addressed in the literature of international business (Karakaya and Stahl, 1989). The interactions between businesses and residents of a social sector market are full of unspoken norms and rules. These institutions are clearer to those who are embedded within the institutional structure (the culture) than to those outside of it. Understanding these institutions is critical for business success. The lack of mutual understanding may pose a serious entry barrier to the entrepreneur.

Social and institutional entry barriers and the identification and evaluation of SE opportunities

Previous research on opportunity recognition has argued for the importance of prior knowledge in recognizing opportunities (Shane, 2000). While I agree that prior knowledge is important I have also found in my own work that an additional factor influences the recognition of opportunities: perception of entry barriers (Robinson, 2004). Personal experiences and intentional searches form the basis of the entrepreneur's *perception* of any opportunity. I have found that opportunity identification is influenced by the entrepreneur's *perception* of what is required to pursue the opportunity. The entrepreneur asks herself strategic questions: what are the benefits of going after this opportunity for me and for others? Do I have the resources to take advantage of this opportunity? What are the risks? Are there any barriers to my pursuing this opportunity? As they ask these questions, entrepreneurs are influenced by their perceptions about the opportunity and then perform their own risk calculus to choose between the alternatives (Kahneman and Tversky, 1979).

Casson (1982) argues that experience will greatly influence how an opportunity is perceived. It follows that the entrepreneur's experience will also influence how an entry barrier is perceived. For any entrepreneur, experience has two dimensions: business and social. Business experience relates to experience in managing, owning or being employed in business. Social experience is life experience gained through family groups, educational systems or other social units. Relevant experience in either category can be valuable for entrepreneurs. Either category can enhance an entrepreneur's ability to identify and overcome social, economic, and institutional entry barriers. Nonrelevant experience may limit one's ability to see and understand barriers to entry or business opportunities. In other words, entrepreneurs with limited inner city experience may have a blind spot for the social and institutional barriers to entry. Social and institutional barriers to markets obscure entrepreneurial opportunities to those in unfamiliar markets: where most people would see barriers, some people see opportunity.

In the SE context, the social and institutional barriers are of highest importance because they are usually the factors that are driving the social problem the entrepreneur is attempting to solve. To this point I have argued that entry barriers influence all parts of entrepreneurship (as depicted in Figure 7.1).

Using this framework, we can better understand three things about SE. First, SE opportunities are different from other types of opportunities because they are highly influenced by the social and institutional structures in a market/community. Second, SE is not only a process by which social problems are solved using entrepreneurial strategies but it is also a process of navigating social and institutional barriers to the markets/communities they want to impact. Social entrepreneurs are successful because they are able to *execute* and *navigate*. The ability to do both well is part of what makes social entrepreneurs and SE so special.

Third, social entrepreneurs find opportunities in areas and under circumstances that they understand. I argue that an interaction takes place between the personal experiences and/or work experiences of the social entrepreneur and the characteristics of the market/community she is attempting to enter. This navigation process is one that is not understood by entrepreneurship scholars but is clearly an essential step toward the establishment of the venture.

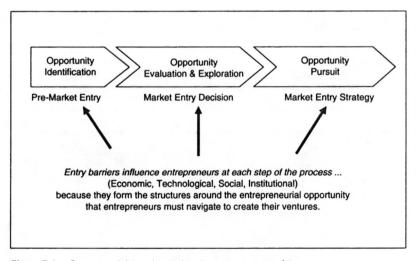

Figure 7.1   Opportunities orientation in entrepreneurship

Figure 7.2 attempts to summarize these arguments. The navigation of social and institutional barriers takes place in both the cognitive and the strategic dimensions. In the cognitive dimension, social and institutional barriers, as described above, may obscure opportunities from entrepreneurs who do not have the relevant experience and prior knowledge for a particular opportunity. They may also obscure the opportunity from entrepreneurs because the perception of the barriers leads to the conclusion that there is no opportunity.

Both types of navigation are important aspects of the SE process. Cognitive navigation of entry barriers is the key to identifying and evaluating social entrepreneurial opportunities. Strategic navigation of social and institutional barriers is important when pursuing an opportunity.[1] An entrepreneur must be able to navigate among the social and institutional factors present in a market/community to be successful in her venture. As with any navigational process, it is not perfect. There is often a need for mid-course corrections. Social entrepreneurs may start and sputter throughout the navigation process but this is part of the social entrepreneurial process where social entrepreneurs can add enormous value. They are adept at navigating the complexities of social sector markets to achieve their objectives and goals.

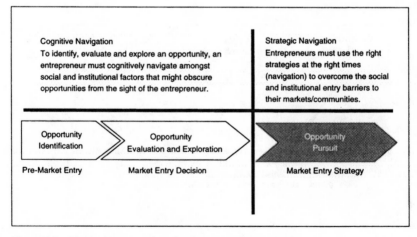

Figure 7.2 Navigating social and institutional entry barriers

Data and methods

It is important for any new research to do qualitative work that begins to make sense of the complexities that are inherent in underexplored phenomena (Eisenhardt, 1989; Yin, 2003). SE, as an area of study, is underexplored. To this end, I have used a case study approach to explore the social entrepreneurial process.

Data were collected from six early stage social ventures that were affiliated with the Berkley Center for Entrepreneurial Studies of New York University's Stern School of Business. These six ventures were part of a larger study of early stage social entrepreneurial ventures being conducted with a grant from the Satter Social Venture Fund of the Berkley Center for Entrepreneurial Studies.

Before settling on these six ventures, I first reviewed the business plans of 20 social ventures and 40 two-to-three page social venture concepts for simple comparison. There was some overlap between the set of 40 venture concepts and the 20 venture plans. From these ventures and venture concepts I chose six ventures to conduct in-depth case studies using a semi-structured interview protocol. Founders or cofounders of these six ventures were interviewed and the interview covered the founding of the venture, the background and experience of the founder/cofounder, the organization of the venture and financial aspects. I made several observations of these ventures during a six-month period from October 2004 to April 2005. During these six months, three of the ventures were in a business plan competition for social ventures of which I am a faculty advisor. The other three are ventures I had known prior to the six-month observation period and I used this opportunity to gather data directly from the cofounders.

Following recommendations from Yin (2003), these six ventures are representative of various social and institutional contexts, stages of development, industry sectors and types of founders. In reporting the observations and themes, I have used pseudonyms to disguise the names of each of the ventures.

I followed the circular qualitative data analysis process recommended by Miles and Huberman (1994): data collection, data reduction, and data display. After reducing and/or displaying the data, I drew inferences or conclusions about the data that was collected with respect to the theoretical framework presented earlier in this chapter. I noted where the data was consistent with the framework and where it was not. My final step in the analysis process resulted in three themes that were consistent across all six case studies. I report here a summary of the findings from the data analysis process from the six case studies.

Findings

Tables 7.3 and 7.4 summarize the details about the six social ventures that I studied in-depth.

Table 7.3   Case details of social entrepreneurs in an inner city context

	Foster care	Community arts	Education and training
Stage	Seed	Startup – 1 year	Startup – 2 years
Context of opportunity	Inner City	Inner City	Inner City
Background of social entrepreneurs	Family history of foster care	Activist and artist, educator	Former school teacher and social worker
Problem to solve	Inefficiencies and ineffective foster care system	Community arts education	Urban education programs and consulting
Examples of barriers	Social – connections to support organizations	Social – access to laundry suppliers and services	Social – connections to community-based organizations
	Institutional – political will to change system	Institutional – cultural differences	Institutional – inertia in the educational system
Organizational form	For-profit	Nonprofit	For-profit

Table 7.4   Case details of social entrepreneurs <u>not</u> in an inner city context

	Medical translation	Eco-design	Eco-tour
Stage	Startup – 1 year (with funding)	Seed	Seed
Context of opportunity	A major US metropolitan area	A major US metropolitan area	East Asia and Pacific islands
Background of social entrepreneurs	Medical professionals and public health	Ecofriendly, interior designers	International affairs, adventure tour participant

Table 7.4   Case details of social entrepreneurs <u>not</u> in an inner city context
– *continued*

	Medical translation	Eco-design	Eco-tour
Problem to solve	English translation for doctors' offices (HIPPA)	Environmentally friendly interior design	Ecotours and ecopreservation
Examples of barriers	Social – network of doctors' offices	Social – access to distributors/ suppliers and deal flow	Social – community/family networks in country
	Institutional – regulatory issues, cultural differences	Institutional – development of a local market for environmentally friendly interior design and furniture	Institutional – international business environment, cultural differences
Organiza- tional form	For-profit	For-profit	For-profit

A brief description of the social venture case studies

Six social ventures were studied in-depth to explore the issues of identification and evaluation of the social entrepreneurial opportunities. The pseudonyms chosen for these six ventures are as follows: *Foster Care, Community Arts, Urban Education and Training, Medical Translation, Eco-design,* and *Eco-tour*. These pseudonyms will be used throughout the rest of this chapter.

Foster Care is a venture that provides a new model of foster care services for urban youths aged 12–18 years. This population has been the most difficult to service and is often the most problematic. The underlying premise of *Foster Care* is that the current system is broken and there is a need for an alternative system that equips the children to be active and productive citizens. At the time of my last observation, *Foster Care* was in the seed stage and attempting to revise its business plan to present to potential funders and partners.

Community Arts is a venture whose mission is to bring visual arts to the people of inner city neighborhoods through arts education, art shows, and artist-in-residence programs. The cofounders believe that it is important to have a place where art can be accessible to the people and have developed an exciting, innovative and sustainable way to accomplish their goal. Their choice of a revenue-generating business model for their community arts venture has gained support from a national SE seed fund. As of my last observation, the founders were preparing their operational plan and seeking startup funds for the venture.

Urban Education and Training is a venture that is more than two years old. The cofounders started the venture to provide consulting services to urban school districts, youth agencies and community organizations in the area of youth development. Their specialty is teacher training and the development and implementation of youth development programs. At the time of my last observation, they had five employees and had recently moved into new office space in the inner city area of one of the largest urban areas on the east coast of the US.

Medical Translation was the recipient of social venture seed money and venture funding. It provides real time translation services for doctors' offices and medical facilities which have patients with limited English language proficiency. At the time of my last observation, the founders were pursuing their first contracts with the largest hospitals in a major US city.

Eco-design is an environmentally conscious interior decorating and design company that stresses the principles of the triple bottom line. They provide a unique service for clients who want a true green building environment and consult with developers and individuals interested in lifestyles of health and sustainability. At the time of my last observation, *Eco-design* had received seed funding from a local social venture fund.

Eco-tour is an ecotourism company that aims to provide small scale ecotour services to its customers while providing responsible ecostewardship to fragile environmental areas in Southeast Asia. As a part of their philosophy, the cofounders insist upon hiring local tour guides, assistants and services and have implemented a local youth program to impact the next generation of local citizens. At the time of my last observation, these social entrepreneurs were competing in a social venture competition and were seeking startup capital to begin operations.

The background of the social entrepreneurs

The social entrepreneurs studied were connected to their ventures through their professional and/or personal experiences. It was evident from both the interviews, and the business plans and venture descriptions, that each of the entrepreneurs had experiences which served as an important resource in the development of their venture. For example, the cofounders of the *Community Arts* venture were involved in community organizations for many years before starting their venture. One of the cofounders describes herself as coming from 'a long family history of social change'; she has worked on projects related to HIV/AIDS, arts, and education. The second founder was in corporate marketing before cofounding the venture but her real 'love' was art. Prior to working on this social venture, she had been volunteering with many different types of community-oriented organizations and was seeking a way to combine her love of art with a desire to serve as a 'community change agent'.

These responses are similar across all six case ventures as evident in Tables 7.3 and 7.4. It is easy to see the relationship between the social entrepreneurs and the ventures they created. This does not mean that the social entrepreneurs were trained specifically to do their social ventures, however the interviews revealed experiences that were related to the problem or issue they wanted to solve with their social venture.

The context of opportunity

I reviewed 40 social ventures prior to selecting six for in-depth exploration. I purposely selected three ventures that focused on inner city markets/communities and three that did not. I believed that this categorization would be an important source of variation for the study and was important to expanding the previous inner city business research to another context. This was the only criteria that I used in the selection of the cases.

Inner city markets are unique because they usually contain communities and neighborhoods where poverty rates are high, educational attainment is low, and unemployment is high. In many instances they also have higher concentrations of immigrants and racial/ethnic minorities. This context is vastly different from contexts that are not focused on disadvantaged geographical areas in the US.

The ventures that were coded as inner city (*Foster Care*, *Community Arts*, and *Urban Education and Training*) are ventures that focus their efforts and their energies on inner city areas where the problems they are trying to address are the most severe. The other three ventures (*Eco-design*, *Eco-tour*, and *Medical Translation*) did not focus solely on inner city areas. In two of the cases, the venture addressed environmental issues. The environmental issues they chose to address were not in inner city areas. In the third case, the services were being provided in various communities and neighborhoods. These communities and neighborhoods varied in income, education and employment levels. By coding for inner city or noninner city context, I was able to account for the influence (if any) of the context on the development of the social venture.

The existence of barriers to entry

In response to the question about the founding of the social venture, each of the subjects described the social and institutional factors that were unique to their social sector market opportunity. I frame these challenges using language I presented earlier in the paper. Each of the founders described social and institutional factors that challenged them as they entered the market. Tables 7.3 and 7.4 present examples of the barriers they described.

For example, the *Eco-tour* venture faced both formal and informal institutional barriers from legal constraints and cultural norms. These factors were considered early and certainly influenced the decision to pursue SE. In the case of *Urban Education and Training*, the founders described severe challenges in dealing with the bureaucracy of the educational system in the urban school districts they were working in. Additionally, they found it challenging to collaborate with the various community-based organizations in these areas.

Organizational form

In the US, social ventures can elect to be legally organized as a 'for-profit' company or a 'nonprofit' organization. The implications of either of these choices may place another type of variation into this study. There are two differences between the for-profit and nonprofit entities. Nonprofit companies cannot pay any dividends to board members because they are not 'shareholders' of the company. There is no mechanism for building personal wealth through a nonprofit organization and all profits from year to year must be reinvested in the organization. As a result of this legal structure, nonprofit organizations have tax-exempt status under federal and state law. They do not have to pay any income or sales tax and can accept donations and contributions from individuals, corporations, foundations and other nonprofit organizations. The contributing organizations are given incentives to donate funds and resources to these organizations because the contributors are given significant tax alleviation for doing so. In the age of SE, the decision to be a for-profit or a nonprofit company is an important one because of the message it sends to potential stakeholders and funders. As these six social ventures developed, the 'for-profit or nonprofit?' question was one that they took under careful consideration. Some were concerned that their possible funding sources only wanted to fund nonprofit organizations. Other founders saw the for-profit choice as central to their SE believing that the choice to be a for-profit social venture signaled to the environment that they were 'serious' about organizing their venture with efficient business processes.

In this study, five of the six social ventures were for-profit companies with social missions. While I don't believe that these six ventures are representative of the proportion of new social ventures who choose for-profit organizational forms over nonprofit forms of organization, I do believe they are illustrative of the changing trend in the US. It is not unusual to see social ventures that are for-profit companies.

An additional observation should be noted at this point. All of the ventures made it clear that their organizations had a mission but there was a difference in how the for-profit and nonprofit companies described themselves. When I reviewed the business plans and the literature of the for-profit social ventures, they were specific about how their *services* were the mechanism of change. As clients purchased their services, these social ventures were adding value or solving problems. However, *Community Arts,* the only nonprofit social venture in this study, was focusing on entrepreneurship as a means towards greater sustainability of its venture.

Themes

After reviewing the interviews, business plans, and any other information available on these ventures (websites, brochures, and so on) for common patterns, three themes emerged from the analysis of this qualitative data:

Theme #1: Successful social entrepreneurs will identify opportunities in social and institutional contexts they believe they understand.
Theme #2: Successful social entrepreneurs will consider social and institutional factors when evaluating opportunities to create social ventures.
Theme #3: During the process of exploring new social venture opportunities, successful social entrepreneurs will directly address social and institutional barriers to markets/communities.

In the discussion section of this chapter, I present each of these themes in detail and describe how these themes can be interpreted.

Discussion

The process of developing a social venture follows the process of every entrepreneurial venture. The purpose of this chapter is to explore the early stages of social ventures and to understand what might influence the identification, discovery, and evaluation of social entrepreneurial opportunities. The data collected and explored in this chapter points toward three themes that require further research.

Identification and discovery

Theme #1: Successful social entrepreneurs will identify opportunities in social and institutional contexts they believe they understand

In each of the six ventures I observed, it was clear that the social entrepreneurs: 1) had relevant experience or a deep and long standing interest in the areas they eventually created a venture in, and; 2) used this knowledge to navigate the social and institutional contexts of their ventures. This is an interesting finding because it is a slight departure from previous studies of traditional entrepreneurship.

In studies of entrepreneurship we find evidence that entrepreneurs pursue opportunities that are related to their experience and also those unrelated to their experience. Shane (2000) has made a good case for the prior knowledge perspective but there is also evidence from serial entrepreneurship that successful entrepreneurs do not always have experience in the industry or business they go into (Ronstadt, 1988; McGrath and MacMillian, 2000). From this set of case studies, the prior knowledge logic seems to be at work. Social entrepreneurs create ventures where they see a need that they can clearly identify.

This theme fits the theoretical framework that I presented in Figure 7.1. Social sector markets are complex and only entrepreneurs who have prior experience and knowledge about these types of markets will see, and subsequently act upon, these opportunities. Without the specific knowledge about the problem area and issue context, a potential social entrepreneur may not identify or discover the social entrepreneurial opportunity seen before her. She may only see the problem and this becomes just as real an entry barrier to this market as any access to capital storyline. Social and institutional barriers are certainly at play in social sector markets and influence the all important first step in the social entrepreneurial process: identification.

There is one caveat to this discussion. I cannot be certain that the social entrepreneurs were not engaging in some post hoc analysis. I was careful to ask general and open ended questions about the founding of the venture and the background of the founders so as to elicit narratives instead of direct answers to my questions. This allowed the subjects ample leeway to make connections between themselves and their venture. When asked about the founding of their ventures, most of the subjects were forthcoming about how they became interested or engaged with the issues or social problems they were trying to solve. I believe that the research approach and line of questioning reasonably ruled out any tendency to cater to the interviewer in these six cases.

Evaluation

Theme #2: Successful social entrepreneurs will consider social and institutional factors when evaluating opportunities to create social ventures

When considering the possibility of creating a social venture, the social entrepreneurs who were interviewed for this study described a process of evaluating various social and institutional factors in the markets in addition to the economic and financial aspects of their ideas. In the course of their narratives, many of the entrepreneurs described how the problem they were trying to solve was connected to social and institutional factors. These factors were similar to the social and institutional barriers I presented in the first half of this chapter. By simply taking into consideration these social and institutional aspects of the opportunity, the subjects have diverged from traditional entrepreneurship. Most discussions of evaluating market opportunities do not address the social and institutional factors that give rise to the opportunity. Yet, the subjects in this study specifically addressed them during their evaluation of the business idea (that is, before the business plan).

Medical Translation came into being when a US federal law for medical privacy was enacted in 2002. One aspect of this new law was a provision that required medical offices and hospitals to have qualified medical translation for their patients who are not proficient English speakers. The founders of *Medical Translation* recounted that their idea became a reality when they finally took a patented technology and applied it to the social problem of language translation in medical offices as they saw the laws changing. The opportunity was evaluated as a good one because they saw the convergence of the social (large immigrant population) and institutional (changes in the law) factors as the source of a unique social sector market opportunity they could address. The cofounders of *Urban Education and Training* were already addressing the complex issues around urban youth in their respective jobs as a high school teacher and social worker before they created their venture. They turned their frustration into a social venture. From their perspective the social and institutional issues that make youth development and empowerment so difficult provided the perfect opportunity for them to make a difference and to make a living.

As a final example, I return to the cofounders of *Community Arts*. In this excerpt of my interview with them, it is clear that they thought through the complex social and institutional factors related to their specific social entrepreneurial opportunity.

> I: How did the idea begin? How did the organization come into form?
> #1: So, the idea for ...[*Community Arts*] was about trying to make art more accessible on every level... so trying to make art accessible, in particular, to black communities and communities within under-served communities... trying to think of why people weren't going to museums, why weren't people interested in what already was there. We realized it was that there were a number of issues of access and a number of barriers: one of them being financial, another being physical and geographic, and another being conceptual in the terms of what the actual experience was like to go look at art. And so... even if we came up with a solution for how to change the way art is experienced it would matter where, right?
>
> So it was about thinking about where people are already... that is a familiar space, an accessible space in and of itself, and feels like a space that we owned; that whatever is in that space is something we owned by extension... limiting the amount of financial burden that has been added by having that experience.

Social entrepreneurs are able to see through the complexity of social problems to the entrepreneurial opportunity. This is consistent with the framework presented in Figure 7.2 in this chapter because it demonstrates that social entrepreneurs practice a form of cognitive navigation of the social and institutional factors while developing and evaluating their ideas.

Addressing the barriers

Theme #3: During the process of exploring new social venture opportunities, successful social entrepreneurs will directly address social and institutional barriers to markets/communities

This was also apparent in the business plans of these social ventures. A draft of *Foster Care's* business plan specifically identified the social and institutional factors leading to the problems in the current foster care system and what they would do differently. The *Eco-design* business plan tells readers that their mission and goals are:

1. To create beautiful interiors that support better health and productivity for users while increasing client profitability,
2. To shift attitudes towards environmentally preferred materials usage, and
3. To set industry standards for environmentally-conscious and profitable interior design methods.

When the founders of *Eco-design* identify the social and institutional factors that make their solution possible, they write:

There are multiple trends and factors that make healthful, cost-efficient commercial interiors an attractive and growing market:

Consumer Preference for Green Home Products

Many mainstream retailers are offering products that are gentler on the environment. These include ethically sourced woods such as in xxx furniture, nonpetroleum ingredients such as in xxx detergents, and recyclable carpets such as that found at xxx Hardware stores ...

Government Emphasis for Green Buildings and Interiors

There is a growing emphasis for healthful buildings from the government. Tax credits and other incentives are part of broader green building assistance programs offered by a growing number of state and local governments across the country.

Certain green buildings are eligible to receive tax breaks under the Green Building Tax Credit program. Also, a growing number of states provide green tax credits for Leadership in Energy and Environmental Design (LEED) certified buildings and are encouraging all new construction to be green.

Building Industry Preference for Green Buildings and Interiors

Industry executives experienced or familiar with green buildings are becoming aware of the financial advantages, aside from tax benefits. Roughly 66% of executives at organizations involved with green buildings have reported that their projects have generated a higher return on investment (ROI) than other buildings.

This theme was consistent across all six ventures. As discussed in the theoretical framework in Figure 7.2, these factors are important to framing the social entrepreneurial opportunity. The cognitive navigation of social and institutional barriers is an essential aspect of SE. Where most people see difficult problems and complex issues, social entrepreneurs seem to be able to see solutions and opportunities.

Conclusion

A central question I attempt to answer through my research is how a sociological view of markets (that is, organization theory) can enhance the business strategy of entrepreneurs and managers. Because of the focus in business schools on industrial markets and large firms in the strategy literature, we have overlooked some key elements of the market entry story. If we are to believe that markets are social structures then it follows that social and institutional barriers to these markets will be just as salient as economic barriers to markets. I have previously argued that social and institutional forces play a significant role in the entry and nonentry of firms to new and unfamiliar markets. I call these barriers to market entry, social and institutional barriers to entry and have argued here that these barriers are important right from the beginning of the entrepreneurial process. I used this theoretical perspective as a starting point for my exploration of SE in this chapter. My purpose in exploring SE using this framework was to consider how these social and institutional factors have relevance for the understanding of SE. Interestingly, the framework seems to fit for SE as well as it fitted the inner city entrepreneurship context it was originally theorized for. The reason for this convergence was not clear to me until I reviewed the qualitative data in preparation for writing this chapter. Now I realize how closely inner city entrepreneurship is related to SE and vice versa. The types of markets that each engage have the same features. Both social sector markets and inner city markets are highly influenced by social and institutional factors. In fact, these factors are the structures that form the barriers to entry to these markets while simultaneously giving rise to the market opportunities that those with experience in these specific markets can pursue. Social entrepreneurship and the research that should follow it, should force us to look at markets in a completely different light. This is important work for those who are willing to engage in it.

Note

1. Since this is not the subject of this chapter, I will not use space here to expand on it further.

References

Acs, Z. 1999. *Are small firms important? Their role and impact*. Norwell, MA: Kluwer.

Acs, Z. and Audretsch, D. 1988. Innovation in small and large firms: An empirical analysis. *American Economic Review*, 78(4): 678–90.

Alvord, S. H., Brown, D. L. and Letts, C. W. 2004. Social entrepreneurship and societal transformation: An exploratory study. *The Journal of Applied Behavioral Science*, 40(3): 260–83.

Bain, J. S. 1956. *Barriers to new competition*. Boston: Harvard University Press.

Bornstein, D. 2004. *How to change the world: Social entrepreneurs and the power of new ideas*. New York: Oxford University Press.

Bourdieu, P. 1984. *Distinction: A social critique of the judgement of taste*. Cambridge, MA: Harvard University Press.

Brainard, L. A. and Siplon, P. D. 2004. Toward nonprofit organization reform in the voluntary spirit: Lessons from the internet. *Nonprofit and Voluntary Sector Quarterly*, 33(3): 435–57.

Burt, R. S. 1992. *Structural holes: The social structure of competition*. Cambridge, MA: Harvard University Press.

Carroll, G. R., Bigelow, L. S., Siedel, M. L. and Tsai, L. B. 1996. The fates of De Novo and De Alio producers in the American automobile industry, 1885–1981. *Strategic Management Journal*, 17: 117–37.

Casson, M. 1982. *The entrepreneur*. Totowa, NJ: Barnes and Noble Books.

Clark, J. B. 1907. *The Essentials of Economic Theory*. New York: Macmillan.

Coleman, J. S. 1990. *Foundations of social theory*. Cambridge, MA: Harvard University Press.

Dees, J. G. 1998. The meaning of social entrepreneurship. Paper. Centre for the Advancement of Social Entrepreneurship, Fuqua School of Business, Duke University, Durham. Available: http://www.fuqua.duke.edu/centers/case/documents/dees_SE.pdf.

Eisenhardt, K. 1989. Building theories from case study research. *Academy of Management Review*, 14(4): 532–50.

Granovetter, M. 1985. Economic action and social structure: The problem of embeddedness. *American Journal of Sociology*, 91(3): 481–510.

Granovetter, M. 1992. Problems of explanation in economic sociology. In N. Nohria and R. G. Eccles (eds), *Networks and organizations, structure, form and action*: 25–56. Boston: Harvard Business School Press.

Granovetter, M. 1999. The economic sociology of firms and entrepreneurs. In A. Portes (ed.), *The Economic Sociology of Immigration: Essays in Networks, Ethnicity and Entrepreneurship*: 128–65. New York: Russell Sage Foundation.

Hannan, M. T., Carroll, G. R., Dundon, E. A. and Torres, J. C. 1995. Organizational evolution in a multinational context: Entries of automobile manufacturers in Belgium, Britain, France, Germany and Italy. *American Sociological Review*, 60: 509–28.

Harrigan, K. R. 1981. Barriers to entry and competitive strategies. *Strategic Management Journal*, 2: 395–412.

Hayek, F. 1945. The use of knowledge in society. *American Economic Review*, 35(4): 519–30.

Ingram, P. and Clay, K. 2000. The choice-within-constraints New Institutionalism and implications for Sociology. *Annual Review of Sociology*, 26: 525–46.

Ingram, P. and Simons, T. 2000. State formation, ideological competition, and the ecology of Israeli workers cooperatives, 1920–1992. *Administrative Science Quarterly*, 45(1): 25.

Kahneman, D. and Tversky, A. 1979. Prospect theory: An analysis of decisions under risk. *Econometrica*, 47: 313–27.

Karakaya, F. and Stahl, M. J. 1989. Barriers to entry and market entry decisions in consumer and industrial goods markets. *Journal of Marketing*, 53(2): 80.

Kirzner, I. 1997. Entrepreneurial discovery and the competitive market process: An Austrian approach. *Journal of Economic Literature*, 35: 60–85.

Klepper, S. and Simons, K. L. 2000. Dominance by birthright: Entry of prior radio producers and competitive ramifications in the US television receiver industry. *Strategic Management Journal*, 21: 997–1016.

McGrath, R. and MacMillian, I. 2000. *The entrepreneurial mindset*. Boston: Harvard Business School Publishing.

Miles, M. B. and Huberman, A. M. 1994. *Qualitative data analysis*. (2nd edn) Thousand Oaks, CA: Sage Publications.

Porter, M. 1980. *Competitive Strategy*. New York: Free Press.

Portes, A. 1994. The informal economy. In N. J. Smelser and R. Swedberg (eds) *The handbook of economic sociology*: 426–49. Princeton: Sage Foundation.

Robinson, J. A. 2004. An economic sociology of entry barriers: Social and institutional entry barriers to inner city markets. Unpublished Doctoral Dissertation, Columbia University, Graduate School of Business – Management, New York.

Ronstadt, R. 1988. The corridor principle. *Journal of Business Venturing*, 3: 31–40.

Scherer, F. M. 1980. *Industrial market structure and economic performance*. Chicago: Rand McNally.

Schmalensee, R. 1981. Economies of scale and barriers to entry. *Journal of Political Economy*, 89: 1228–38.

Shane, S. 2000. Prior knowledge and the discovery of entrepreneurial opportunities. *Organization Science*, 11(4): 448.

Shane, S. and Venkataraman, S. 2000. The promise of entrepreneurship as a field of research. *Academy of Management Review*, 25(1): 217.

Singh, R. P. 2001. A comment on developing the field of entrepreneurship through the study of opportunity recognition and exploitation. *Academy of Management Review*, 26(1): 10–12.

Thompson, J. L. 2002. The world of the social entrepreneur. *The International Journal of Public Sector Management*, 15(4/5): 412–32.

Tucker, D. J., Singh, J. V. and Meinhard, A. 1990. Organizational form, population dynamics, and institutional change: The founding patterns of voluntary organizations. *Academy of Management Journal*, 33: 151–78.

Uzzi, B. 1997. Social structure and competition in interfirm networks: The paradox of embeddedness. *Administrative Science Quarterly*, 42: 35–67.

Wagner, J. 1994. The post-entry performance of new small firms in German manufacturing industries. *The Journal of Industrial Economics*, 52: 141–54.

Yin, R. K. 2003. *Case study research: Design and methods* (3rd edn) Thousand Oaks, CA: Sage Publications.

8

Social Entrepreneurship: How Intentions to Create a Social Venture are Formed

Johanna Mair and Ernesto Noboa

Introduction

Entrepreneurship aiming at social benefits has become ubiquitous. Social entrepreneurship (SE) involves innovative approaches to address issues in the domains of education, environment, fair trade, health and human rights and is widely regarded as an important building block of the sustainable development of countries.

Although entrepreneurial initiatives aimed at social and economic wealth creation are not new, they have only recently raised increasing interest among scholars (Wallace, 1999). Therefore, we still know relatively little about the particular dynamics and processes involved in SE. The few existing papers are mainly descriptive and rely on anecdotal evidence: studies based on rigorous empirical and theoretical research approaches are rare. This paper aims at clarifying important concepts and illuminating the process of SE.

We believe that the core of entrepreneurship – in Schumpeter's words, 'the carrying out of new combinations' – is context free, that is, it is the same regardless of where it takes place (Schumpeter, 1934). Yet SE differs from traditional 'business' entrepreneurship in several aspects. First, social entrepreneurs are moved by different motivations to discover and exploit a distinct category of opportunities; second, the way they pursue opportunities might diverge from typical business approaches; and third, the outcome social entrepreneurs aim for involves both social and economic aspects. In sum, the distinct characteristics of social entrepreneurs, the particular category of opportunities they pursue, and the outcomes of their initiatives, invite us to discuss whether SE stands as a distinct field of investigation (Prabhu, 1999).

SE has been previously defined as the 'creation of viable socioeconomic structures, relations, institutions, organizations and practices that yield and sustain social benefits' (Fowler, 2000: 649). While this definition provides an answer to what SE aims at, it lacks a description of how to achieve the intended results. We view SE as a set of interlocking opportunity-based activities by competent and purposeful individuals who – through their actions – can make a difference in society and are bounded by context. We conceptualize SE as a process that involves individuals (social entrepreneurs) engaging in a specific behavior (social entrepreneurial behavior) with tangible outcomes (social ventures or enterprises). For the purpose of this chapter we define SE as the innovative use of resource combinations to pursue opportunities aiming at the creation of organizations and/or practices that yield and sustain social benefits. We deliberately do not delimit the definition to initiatives in the nonprofit sector and imply a notion of helping behavior.

In the first part of this chapter we review the existing literature to clarify key constructs. We elaborate on the distinguishing features of social entrepreneurs and identify key antecedents of the SE intention formation process. Subsequently, we address how behavioral intentions to create a social venture are formed, and present a model of socially entrepreneurial intentions. We conclude by discussing implications for future research and contributions.

Mapping social entrepreneurship

Numerous definitions have been offered, each stressing different aspects and dimensions of SE. One group of researchers refers to SE as nonprofit initiatives in search of alternative funding strategies and management schemes to create social value (Boschee, 1998; Austin, Stevenson and Wei-Skillern, 2003). A second group of researchers understands it as the socially responsible practice of commercial businesses engaged in cross-sector partnerships (Waddock, 1988; Sagawa and Segal, 2000). And a third group views SE as a means to alleviate social problems and catalyze social transformation (Alvord, Brown and Letts, 2004). For the purpose of this chapter, we view SE as the innovative use of resource combinations to pursue opportunities aiming at the creation of organizations and/or practices that yield and sustain social benefits.

What is special about the social entrepreneur?

In very practical terms, social entrepreneurs – also known as social entrepreneurial leaders and civic entrepreneurs – are 'ordinary people doing extraordinary things' yet we still do not know much about them.

Traits and skills

Although research on social entrepreneurs is still scarce, anecdotal evidence suggests a few distinguishing traits and skills. Thompson, Alvy and Lees (2000) suggest that vision and fortitude are necessary traits to implement a social venture. Drayton (2002: 123) describes social entrepreneurs as creative individuals with a 'powerful new, system-change idea'. Finally, Boschee (1998) considers candor, passion, clarity of purpose, commitment, courage, values and customer focus to be required by social entrepreneurs, along with strategy, flexibility, a willingness to plan and the ability to think like a business as critical factors to successfully embark on social entrepreneurial activities.

However, many of these characteristics may not be exclusive to social entrepreneurs; they may very well be shared by nonentrepreneurs. In addition, social entrepreneurs who share the same traits may very well differ in the social impact of their initiatives. Hence, Drayton (2002: 124) claims that the factor which distinguishes the average from the successful entrepreneur is 'entrepreneurial quality'. Entrepreneurial quality is a very special and scarce trait. It is much more than altruistic motivation, and much more than the traits previously mentioned. It is the relentless motivation to change a whole society, shared by only a very small percentage of the population.

Behavior

We still know very little about the content and behavior of entrepreneurial initiatives aimed at social objectives. The main sources so far for enhancing our knowledge are foundations such as Ashoka or the Schwab Foundation, which provide support to SE initiatives. Having worked with hundreds of social entrepreneurs, these organizations provide descriptive accounts of their characteristics, motivations, and experiences. Nevertheless, a more rigorous approach is needed to map the SE process.

Thus far, several behavioral attributes have been associated with SE: the courage to accept social criticism, less failure-anxiety, a receptivity to the feelings of others, perseverance, communication skills, an ability to appear trustworthy, the ability to satisfy customer needs, goal orientation, creativity, and working capacity (McLeod, 1997; Prabhu, 1999). However, as in the traditional debate on the use of trait-based approaches (Gartner, 1988), many of these attributes may equally apply to business entrepreneurial behavior, with one exception, receptivity to the feelings of others, or put differently, empathy. According to the Webster's dictionary, empathy is defined as the ability to share in another's emotions or feelings. Although it is not yet clear whether empathy is a trait (dispositional empathy) or a behavior (situational empathy), we consider empathy as a cognitive and emotional antecedent in our model of social entrepreneurial intentions discussed in the next section.

Context and background

In addition to traits and behaviors, context and background are important aspects to understand entrepreneurs and their initiatives (Bird, 1988). The background of the social entrepreneur is critical for triggering the desirability of launching a social enterprise (Prabhu, 1999). 'I was raised in the spirit of charity and giving', 'I grew sensitive to other people's feelings', and 'I felt uneasy about the problems of the poor' are typical responses of social entrepreneurs; they indicate that social, moral and educational background play a vital role in forming entrepreneurial intentions aimed at fulfilling a social objective. Another aspect of background, that of previous entrepreneurial experience (Prabhu, 1999), is also central to understanding SE as a process. Such experience facilitates self-beliefs – social entrepreneurs' perceived capability to act socially entrepreneurial – and the creation of supporting networks. Both self-efficacy and social support 'enable' the entrepreneur to view the social venture as something feasible and, therefore, are important elements in the process of formation of SE intentions.

The context of social entrepreneurs, that is, their involvement with the social sector or their exposure to social issues, not only allows them to recognize social opportunities, but also seems to turn them into altruistic citizens: they are unsatisfied with the status quo, loyal to their values and philosophy, motivated to act socially responsibly, and they value the respect, success and lifestyles of other social entrepreneurs (Prabhu, 1999).

Overall, we argue that background and context explain a large part of social entrepreneurs' enhanced level of loyalty to their values and philosophy, which is typically associated with an elevated level of moral judgment (discussed in detail in the following section). Given the established empirical relationship between moral judgment and prosocial behavior (cf. Comunian and Gielen, 1995), we assume that moral judgment is a relevant parameter in distinguishing social from traditional entrepreneurs.

A model of socially entrepreneurial intentions

In order to further explore the specific features of the SE process, we focus on one particular aspect: intention formation. In particular, we propose a model for how behavioral intentions to create a social venture are formed, and introduce the previously identified variables – namely empathy and moral judgment – as well as self-efficacy and social support as salient antecedents of intention formation.

The intention formation process is a well-established subfield within social psychology and entrepreneurship literature. Intentions reflect the motivational factors that influence behavior and are a reliable indicator of how hard a person is willing to try and how much effort he/she makes to perform a behavior (Ajzen, 1991: 181). As a result, intentions are widely seen as a powerful predictor of behavior, especially in the case of purposive, planned, and goal-oriented behavior (Bagozzi, Baumgartner and Yi, 1989).

Entrepreneurial behavior is typically seen as purposive behavior directed towards a specific entrepreneurial event, such as the creation of a new company or new products. It can be argued that, in the context of SE, the degree of purpose is even more pronounced. Investigating the sources and antecedents of the behavioral intentions to set up a social venture therefore seems an important first step towards a comprehensive theory of SE.

The model presented here draws from existing work on intention formation in the entrepreneurship literature. A number of authors have developed intention-based models to explain entrepreneurial processes. Bird (1988) claims that intentions are key for distinguishing entrepreneurial activity from strategic management. Krueger (1993) emphasizes perceived feasibility and desirability, social norms and precipitating events as important antecedents of intentions (Krueger, 1993; Krueger and Reilly, 2000).

In sum, traditional models in the entrepreneurship literature argue that both individual and situational variables are important to determine intentions to behave entrepreneurially. Situational variables include the social, economic and political factors present (Bird, 1988), and are often discussed in the context of precipitating or triggering events (Shapero and Sokol, 1982; Krueger and Brazeal, 1994). The most prominent individual-based factors discussed as antecedents of entrepreneurial intentions are personality, background, dispositions, and proactiveness, which represent rather stable traits or characteristics (Bird, 1988; Krueger, 1993).

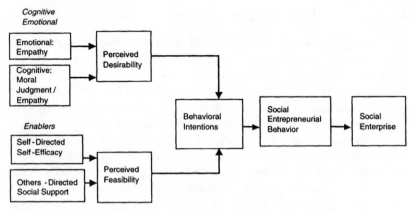

Figure 8.1   A model of social entrepreneurial intention formation

While we acknowledge the importance of situational factors and inter-action effects in predicting behavioral intentions, in this chapter we focus on individual-based differences and confine our analysis to a specific set of dynamic and malleable variables. In a nutshell, our model suggests that intentions to set up a social venture develop from percep-tions of desirability, which are affected by emotional and cognitive attitudes (empathy and moral judgment), and from perceptions of feasi-bility, which are instigated by 'enabling' factors such as self-efficacy and social support. Figure 8.1 summarizes our model.

Aiming at a parsimonious model of intention formation, we build on Ajzen's (1991) work on the origins of planned behavior and Shapero and Sokol's (1982) seminal work on entrepreneurial event formation. Com-plementing previous studies that have integrated these streams of research (Krueger, 1993; Krueger and Reilly, 2000), this chapter identifies and examines a specific set of variables that affect perceived desirability and feasibility in the context of SE.

In the next paragraphs we elaborate on the different elements in our model. The selection of variables is by no means exhaustive. A number of variables are necessary, but no single one is sufficient (Shapero and Sokol, 1982). Also, they work in combination rather than as single predictors.

Perceived social venture desirability and feasibility

In their seminal work on the formation on entrepreneurial events Shapero and Sokol identified perceived desirability and feasibility as important elements in the company formation process (Shapero and

Sokol, 1982). Perceived desirability refers to the attractiveness of generating the entrepreneurial event, that is, forming a company, while perceived feasibility refers to the degree to which one believes that he or she is personally capable of forming a company.

Their model suggests that individuals vary in their perceptions of what they find feasible and what they find desirable. These perceptions, which are shaped by the individuals' cultural and social environment, largely determine which actions are taken in order to set up a company (Shapero and Sokol, 1982).

Krueger incorporated the term 'intention' into Shapero's model by establishing a link with Ajzen's theory of planned behavior (TPB) (Krueger, 1993). TPB suggests that behavioral intentions are affected by attitudes towards the behavior, subjective (social) norms and perceived behavioral control (Ajzen, 1991). Krueger aligned the terminology in a simplifying way and proposed that perceived desirability corresponds to social norms and attitudes, while perceived feasibility relates to self-efficacy beliefs, a concept associated with behavioral control (Krueger and Brazeal, 1994). In short, his model proposes that stable individual traits and situational factors do not exert a direct effect on intentions and behavior but do so indirectly through perceptions of desirability and feasibility (Krueger and Reilly, 2000).

We build on this and specify the antecedents of perceived desirability and feasibility in the context of SE. Although we are conscious of the complexity of the phenomenon and the reciprocal nature of relationships, we confine our analysis to a restricted number of variables and links. We believe that the links chosen are illustrative of the particularities of SE. Thus, in the following paragraphs we first discuss two attitudinal antecedents of perceived social venture desirability (empathy and moral judgment), which embrace both an emotional and cognitive dimension. Second, we elaborate on two factors, one 'self-directed' (self-efficacy) and one 'other-directed' (social support), which affect perceptions of social venture feasibility and therefore 'enable' the formation of corresponding behavioral intentions. Our model highlights the particularities of the SE process and, at the same time, aligns itself with TPB in that the primary antecedents of behavioral intentions – attitudes, social norms and behavioral control – are reflected in the model's antecedent variables.

Antecedents of perceived desirability

A meta-analysis empirically shows that intentions predict behavior but also that attitudes predict intentions (Kim and Hunter, 1993). TPB emphasizes attitudes towards behavior as powerful antecedents of intentions. In the context of entrepreneurship Krueger and Brazeal have related these attitudes directly with perceived desirability (Krueger and Brazeal, 1994). In this paper we stress an additional set of attitudes, namely empathy and moral judgment.

Empathy. While it is widely agreed upon that empathy represents a multifaceted concept, no consensus seems to exist on a single definition. Traditionally the literature has distinguished between affective (emotional) and cognitive empathy (Mehrabian and Epstein, 1972). Authors following the former approach refer to empathy as an affective response; as something to be aroused. Authors who agree with the latter approach refer to empathy as the ability to adopt the perspective, or point of view, of other people and regard it as a basic requirement of all social behavior (Hass, 1984). For the purpose of this paper we define empathy as the ability to intellectually recognize and emotionally share the emotions or feelings of others.

Empathy has been studied extensively in the context of 'helping behavior', a concept that is related to the spirit of SE. Several studies do support the positive link between empathy and helping responses. Barnett, Thompson and Pfeifer (1984), for example, found that perceived helping skills increased the likelihood that empathy triggers a helping response. Building on this evidence that empathy is positively associated with helping responses, we suggest that a person who is capable of intellectually recognizing and emotionally sharing another person's emotions and feelings will develop a desire to help and do whatever is necessary to avoid another's suffering.

Specific research in SE indicates that sensitivity to others' feelings motivates social entrepreneurs to create social enterprises (Prabhu, 1999). However, not everybody with the ability to experience empathy is a social entrepreneur. Thus, we consider empathy as a necessary but not sufficient condition in the SE process. Furthermore, we expect a minimum threshold in this attitudinal antecedent. In other words, a certain level of empathy is needed in order to trigger perceived social venture desirability, which in turn will lead to intentions to create a social venture.

In sum, we claim that empathy represents an important attitudinal element in the SE process affecting perceived social venture desirability. Accordingly, we propose,

Proposition 1: Empathy is positively associated with perceived social venture desirability.

Moral judgment. Moral judgment represents an additional concept that is frequently employed to explain helping responses (Kohlberg and Hersh, 1977; Comunian and Gielen, 1995). Under the assumption that moral norms regulate the actions of individuals, for the purpose of this chapter we define moral judgment as the cognitive process that motivates an individual to help others in search of a common good.

Kohlberg and Hersh (1977) claim that moral judgment develops in human cognition through a sequential series of six stages which increasingly demonstrate a higher capacity for empathy and justice. The most basic form of moral judgment (stage 1) is when individuals consider the goodness or badness of actions depending on their physical consequences regardless of their human meaning or value (punishment-and-obedience orientation). As an individual educates his/her moral judgment, he/she passes through more sophisticated stages of moral reasoning until reaching the sixth stage (the universal-ethical-principle orientation), the most developed form of moral judgment.

Among others, the following important factors have been found to affect the level of an individual's moral judgment. First, the exposure to social experiences that make an individual deal with the needs, values, and viewpoints of others (Comunian and Gielen, 1995); and second, the perceived magnitude of the consequences (that is, the perceived harm or good done to an individual) and the social consensus (the level of agreement on the goodness or evil of a proposed act) (Morris and McDonald, 1995).

Furthermore, higher levels of moral judgment typically correlate positively with anti-authoritarian attitudes, a high tolerance towards minority groups, and moderate political beliefs. Comunian and Gielen (1995) found support for the hypothesis that involvement in prosocial volunteer activities is associated with higher levels of moral judgment.

It should not be surprising to find that social entrepreneurs are individuals who display a high level of moral judgment. Prabhu (1999) found that social entrepreneurs are motivated by a need to be loyal to their own principles, and to be socially responsible. By the same token, Johnson (2000) claimed that social entrepreneurs crave social justice.

Not everybody with moral judgment is a social entrepreneur. Thus, we consider moral judgment as a necessary but not sufficient condition in the SE process. We expect that a minimum threshold is necessary in order to trigger perceptions of social venture desirability and propose,

Proposition 2: Moral judgment is positively associated with perceived social venture desirability.

Antecedents of perceived feasibility

In the context of this paper, perceived feasibility refers to whether an individual believes that he/she is able to create a social venture. Based on anecdotal evidence in the field of SE and existing literature in relevant fields, we suggest two important antecedents. First, we propose that perceived feasibility is affected by the person's perceived ability to perform the specific behavior required for setting up the social venture (self-efficacy beliefs); and second, that it is influenced by the person's social capital, that is, by the social support he/she generates from the social network. We conceive the former antecedent as a 'self-directed' enabling factor and the second antecedent as an 'other-directed' enabling factor in the SE process.

Self-efficacy. In a broad sense self-efficacy refers to 'people's belief in their capabilities to mobilize the motivation, cognitive resources, and courses of action needed to exercise control over events in their lives' (Wood and Bandura, 1989: 364). It is considered highly relevant to entrepreneurial phenomena (Stevenson and Jarillo, 1990), and various authors provide empirical evidence for the positive relationship between entrepreneurial self-efficacy beliefs and performance. Moreover, self-efficacy beliefs have been considered an anchor of formal theory-driven models of entrepreneurial intentions (Krueger and Brazeal, 1994), and have been shown to be powerful predictors of actual entrepreneurial behavior (Mair, 2005).

Self-efficacy has been conceived as a central construct in examining behavioral self-regulation (Gist and Mitchell, 1992). In a more narrow and behavioral sense, self-efficacy therefore refers to the perceived ability to perform a specific task. In the context of SE a high level of self-efficacy allows a person to perceive the creation of a social venture as feasible, which positively affects the formation of the corresponding behavioral intention. Thus, we propose:

Proposition 3: Self-efficacy beliefs are positively associated with perceived social venture feasibility.

However, not all individuals who believe that they are able to set up a social venture are social entrepreneurs. As in the case of all the variables in our model, self-efficacy beliefs trigger perceptions of social venture feasibility only in combination with the other antecedent variables.

Social support. Entrepreneurs do not and cannot succeed alone, they need support. It has been demonstrated that – depending on the particular context – successful entrepreneurs rely on efficient networks. Networks include all the persons connected by any kind of relationship (Aldrich and Zimmer, 1986) and can refer to venture capital, suppliers, facilities, clients and so on. (Reynolds, 1991). The social support entrepreneurs need is typically based on their social capital, a term commonly associated with trust, civic spirit, and solidarity. Thus, we conceive social support as trust and cooperation derived from social networks (Backman and Smith, 2000).

Social support relates to tangible outcomes such as the 'actual and potential resources individuals obtain from knowing others, being part of a social network with them, or merely from being known to them and having a good reputation' (Baron and Markman, 2000: 107). We view social support – trust and cooperation through a social network – as an enabling factor in the SE process. It facilitates the provision of resources needed to engage in SE and create a social venture.

The link between social support and entrepreneurship is well-established in the traditional literature on entrepreneurship. Aldrich and Zimmer (1986) for example, consider entrepreneurship as rooted in networks of recurrent social relations, which can act as a facilitator but also as a constraint. And it is widely agreed upon that entrepreneurial networks and networking activities affect the entrepreneurial process.

In the SE context, Shore, an experienced social entrepreneur himself, claimed that 'ambitious civic projects can't be achieved by government, business, or religious institutions alone. They require all of civic society' (Shore, 1999: 20). As a result, the presence of different stakeholders in the process not only increases the perception of feasibility, but also facilitates the birth of a social venture.

Also in this case we suggest that a minimum amount of social support is needed to affect perceptions of feasibility which trigger the formation of behavioral intentions to set up a social venture. We propose:

Proposition 4: Social support is positively associated with perceived social venture feasibility.

We don't perceive social support as a discriminating element among social entrepreneurs, entrepreneurs and/or managers. Yet we consider it as a vital element in the SE process, a necessary but not sufficient condition for the development of perceptions regarding the feasibility of a social venture. Social support represents a second enabling force in this process. While self-efficacy implies a self-directed enabling process, social support refers to an others-directed process.

Future research

This paper represents a first, modest step towards a theory of the SE process and points to a number of promising topics for future research. We have argued that empathy and moral judgment are antecedents of perceived venture desirability and that they positively affect the intention to behave entrepreneurially. But a gap still exists between behavioral intentions and actual behavior, which could be explored by introducing recent developments in the field of behavioral self-regulation. Kuhl's theory of action control might provide a fruitful conceptual and empirical base (Kuhl, 1994).

Trigger events might also play an important role in the social sector, interacting with the emotional and cognitive variables proposed in this paper. It is reasonable to assume that a person with a minimum level of empathy and/or moral judgment will choose to become a social entrepreneur after being exposed to a particular social problem (the trigger event). Why, then, do some individuals become social entrepreneurs after being exposed to a trigger event while others do not?

To date, very little is known about the relationship between opportunity recognition and intentions development. Does one precede the other? By the same token, little is known about the way social entrepreneurs discover and exploit social opportunities, and we suspect that the understanding of this process in the social sector will also give us new and richer insights into entrepreneurship per se. From the entrepreneurship literature we know that 'opportunity' is a multifaceted word. Do social entrepreneurs search for opportunities or suddenly discover them? Do they show an above-normal level of entrepreneurial alertness? What prior information is relevant for the discovery and exploitation of social opportunities? To what extent do social entrepreneurs rely on gut feeling to evaluate social opportunities?

Conclusion

Combining insights from traditional entrepreneurship literature and anecdotal evidence in the field of SE, we proposed that behavioral intentions to create a social venture are influenced, first, by perceived social venture desirability, which is affected by attitudes such as empathy and moral judgment; and second, by perceived social venture feasibility, which is facilitated by social support and self-efficacy beliefs.

Given the early stage of the field, we have aimed at providing a parsimonious rather than a comprehensive model on intention formation. We are well aware that the approach chosen is not free of controversy. First, we adopted the key assumption of TPB that intentions almost automatically lead to behavior and that behavior is purposive and planned. We recognize that entrepreneurship embraces unconscious and unintended behavior: however, in this paper, we focus on behavior which is directed towards the formation of a social venture and assume that creating a social venture indicates purposive and planned behavior.

Second, we focused on a particular – individual-based – set of variables to explain behavioral intentions. In contrast to previous studies, we did not rely on situational variables or stable traits in predicting intentions but introduced a set of dynamic variables, malleable in space and time, which act as facilitators and catalysts of behavioral intentions. Thus, instead of following the rather deterministic research tradition prevailing in previous studies, we chose a more proactive, almost volitional, approach. It is important to note that the variables chosen are by no means exhaustive in explaining intentions. However, we speculate that they are important in illuminating differences in the entrepreneurship process that may exist in the for-profit and the nonprofit contexts.

Third, the paper integrates knowledge from existing intention-based models with insights of SE and presents a conceptual account of only one particular part – the intention formation part – of the SE process. Additional conceptual and empirical work is needed to enhance our understanding of the whole process.

References

Ajzen, I. 1991. The theory of planned behavior. *Organizational Behavior and Human Decision Processes*, 50: 179–211.

Aldrich, H. and Zimmer, C. 1986. Entrepreneurship through social networks. In D. Sexton and R. Smilor (eds), *The Art and Science of Entrepreneurship*: 3–23. Cambridge, MA: Ballinger Publishing Company.

Alvord, S. H., Brown, L. D. and Letts, C. W. 2004. Social entrepreneurship and societal transformation. *Journal of Applied Behavioral Science*, 40(3): 260–82.

Austin, J., Stevenson, H. and Wei-Skillern, J. 2003. Social entrepreneurship and commercial entrepreneurship: Same, different or both? Working Paper, Harvard Business School.

Backman, E. V. and Smith, S. R. 2000. Healthy organizations, unhealthy communities? *Nonprofit Management and Leadership*, 10(4): 355–73.

Bagozzi, R., Baumgartner, H. and Yi, Y. 1989. An investigation into the role of intentions as mediators of the attitude-behavior relationship. *Journal of Economic Psychology*, 10: 35–62.

Barnett, M. A., Thompson, M. A. and Pfeifer, J. R. 1984. Perceived competence to help and the arousal of empathy. *The Journal of Social Psychology*, 125: 679–80.

Baron, R. A. and Markman, G. D. 2000. Beyond social capital: How social skills can enhance entrepreneurs' success. *Academy of Management Executive*, 14(1): 106–16.

Bird, B. J. 1988. Implementing entrepreneurial ideas: The case for intention. *Academy of Management Review*, 13(3): 442–61.

Boschee, J. 1998. Merging mission and money: A board member's guide to social entrepreneurship. National Center for Nonprofit Boards, Washington, DC. Available: http//www.ncnb.org.

Comunian, A. L. and Gielen, U. P. 1995. Moral reasoning and pro-social action in Italian culture. *The Journal of Social Psychology*, 135(6): 699–706.

Drayton, W. 2002. The citizen sector: Becoming as entrepreneurial and competitive as business. *California Management Review*, 44(3): 120–32.

Fowler, A. 2000. NGDOs as a moment in history: Beyond aid to social entrepreneurship or civic innovation? *Third World Quarterly*, 21(4): 637–54.

Gartner, W. B. 1988. 'Who is the entrepreneur?' is the wrong question. *American Journal of Small Business*, 12: 11–32.

Gist, M. E. and Mitchell, T. R. 1992. Self-efficacy: A theoretical analysis of its determinants and malleability. *Academy of Management Review*, 17: 183–211.

Hass, R. G. 1984. Perspective taking and self-awareness: Drawing an E on your forehead. *Journal of Personality and Social Psychology*, 46(4): 788–98.

Johnson, S. 2000. Literature review on social entrepreneurship. Canadian Centre for Social Entrepreneurship, University of Alberta School of Business, Canada. Available: http://www.bus.ualberta.ca/ccse/Publications.

Kim, M. S. and Hunter, J. E. 1993. Relationships among attitudes, behavioral intentions, and behavior. *Communication Research*, 20: 331–64.

Kohlberg, L. and Hersh, R. H. 1977. Moral development: A review of the theory. *Theory into Practice*, 16(2): 53–9.

Krueger, N. F. 1993. The impact of prior entrepreneurial exposure on perceptions of new venture feasibility and desirability. *Entrepreneurship Theory and Practice*, 18(1): 5–21.

Krueger, N. F. and Brazeal, D. V. 1994. Entrepreneurial potential and potential entrepreneurs. *Entrepreneurship Theory and Practice*, Spring: 91–104.

Krueger, N. F. and Reilly, M. D. 2000. Competing models of entrepreneurial intentions. *Journal of Business Venturing*, 15(5–6): 411–32.

Kuhl, J. 1994. *A theory of action and state orientation*. Seattle: Higrefe and Huber.

Mair, J. 2005. Entrepreneurial behavior in a large traditional firm: Exploring key drivers. In T. Elfring (ed.) *Series on International Studies in Entrepreneurship Research: Corporate Entrepreneurship and Venturing*, Vol. 10: 49–72. New York: Springer.

McLeod, H. 1997. Cross Over, *Inc.* 19: 100–5.

Mehrabian, A. and Epstein, N. 1972. A measure of emotional empathy. *Journal of Personality*, **40**: 525–43.

Morris, S. A. and McDonald, R. A. 1995. The role of moral intensity in moral judgments: An empirical investigation. *Journal of Business Ethics*, **14**: 715–26.

Prabhu, G. N. 1999. Social entrepreneurship leadership. *Career Development International*, **4**(3): 140–5.

Reynolds, P. D. 1991. Sociology and entrepreneurship: Concepts and contributions. *Entrepreneurship Theory and Practice*, **16**(2): 47–70.

Sagawa, S. and Segal, E. 2000. Common interest, common good: Creating value through business and social sector partnerships. *California Management Review*, **42**(2): 105–22.

Schumpeter, J. 1934. *Capitalism, socialism and democracy*. New York: Harper and Row.

Shapero, A. and Sokol, L. 1982. The social dimensions of entrepreneurship. In S. V. Kent (ed.), *Encyclopedia of Entrepreneurship*: 72–90, Englewood Cliffs, NJ: Prentice Hall.

Shore, B. 1999. *The cathedral within*. New York: Random House.

Stevenson, H. H. and Jarillo, J. C. 1990. A paradigm of entrepreneurship: Entrepreneurial management. *Strategic Management Journal*, **11**: 17–27.

Thompson, J., Alvy, G. and Lees, A. 2000. Social entrepreneurship – A new look at the people and the potential. *Management Decision*, **38**(5): 328–38.

Waddock, S. A. 1988. Building successful social partnerships. *Sloan Management Review*, **4**: 17–22.

Wallace, S. L. 1999. Social entrepreneurship: The role of social purpose enterprises in facilitating community economic development. *Journal of Development Entrepreneurship*, **4**(2): 153–74.

Wood, R. and Bandura, A. 1989. Social cognitive theory of organizational management. *Academy of Management Review*, **14**(3): 361–84.

Part III
Strategy, Structure and Outcome

9

Introduction to Part III – Understanding the Strategy, Structure and Outcomes in Social Ventures

Jeffrey Robinson

In early 2005, one of my doctoral students and I completed an initial scan of the published academic papers and working papers on the topic of 'social entrepreneurship' (SE) between 1990 and 2004. We found nine papers that had been published in peer-reviewed journals and five working papers. This might not be a problem for a fledging research area if the nine papers were influential. Unfortunately, it was painfully clear to us once we reviewed the papers that there was a lack of theory building being done in the area of SE during this time period. Furthermore, we believed that too much was being made of definitions and not enough effort was devoted to exploring the phenomenon as a means toward becoming more definitive.

One of the reasons that this volume exists is to get beyond the 'quagmire of definitions' (Hockerts, Chapter 10 this volume) and begin to explore how strategy and structure interact in social ventures. We have chosen to accommodate the broadest definition of SE in this book in order to address the broadest possible audience of researchers. There are two reasons for this approach. First, when charting the landscape of an emerging phenomenon this is the best way to understand what is happening in the field. Second, the collection of theoretical approaches, methods and contexts provides fertile ground for future research debates and directions.

Research in SE can take two routes from this juncture. We can use existing theory to explain the phenomenon of creating and sustaining social ventures. Alternatively, we can consider how the phenomenon brings to light practices, themes and concepts where existing theories do not explain what we see on the ground. As you will see in this section, these two approaches are not mutually exclusive. Each of the authors of these chapters draws upon theories and concepts from organization studies, strategic management and entrepreneurship but is clearly not constrained by them. In this section we explore the boundaries of social entrepreneurial organizations and the strategies they use to achieve their noteworthy goals.

Strategy, structure and outcomes

Recent scholarship in organization theory has stressed the importance of exploring social issues management (Perrow, 2000; Hinnings and Greenwood, 2002; Walsh, Weber and Margolis, 2003). While these calls for research may open up the academic journals to publishing works in SE there is at least one distinction that should be made between the previous work in social issues management and the types of organizations we are exploring in this volume. The calls for research in social issues management typically consider how established firms interface with their societal environment or manage challenging social issues in and around their firms (see Wood, 1991 for a review).

Haugh's grounded research of ventures in north-east Scotland could be viewed as an answer to this call. In her reporting of a longitudinal qualitative study of six social enterprises we get a glimpse of the complex interactions between these ventures and the community development of a region. By seeing beyond the economic and financial outcomes of these ventures, she is able to deeply explore the social and environmental impacts they have at the community, group and individual levels. This framework certainly points to future directions for those scholars who are interested in making the links between the organizations and their communities.

Organization scholars interested in social issues should also take note of Hockerts' chapter on 'social purpose business ventures'. There has been some scholarship in organization studies and strategic management describing established companies that do good works in communities (commonly referred to as corporate social responsibility). Hockerts proposes a framework for understanding the creation of 'hybrid enterprises straddling the boundary between the for-profit business world and social mission-driven public and nonprofit organizations'. He argues that the sources of the social entrepreneurial opportunity (activism, self-help, and philanthropy) are important for understanding the structure of a social venture. By making this argument he effectively moves the conversation from organizations that do good works to organizations that were created with a purpose to do good works. This is an important step forward in the building of conceptual frameworks for SE.

Desa and Kotha's chapter explores another aspect of the hybridization of organizational forms: technology social ventures. By exploring the organizational structure and strategy of an incubator, they have uncovered an incredibly interesting framework for relating the activist, philanthropic and volunteer environments to the strategic management of technologies for social innovation. What is particularly exciting about this research project is the potential for this exploration to yield new directions for those who study technology ventures and for those that study entrepreneurship.

These papers represent a cross-section of theory and evidence about the organization, strategy and outcomes of social entrepreneurial actors. In each of these chapters, the concepts and frameworks developed are but the first steps in creating a comprehensive set of theories that inform our understanding of organizations and strategic management. I am convinced that these chapters form the first wave of scholarship that goes beyond battles over definitions and begins to develop theory that has relevance and impact. At this juncture in the development of theories explaining the advent and the evolution of SE, it is to our field's advantage to follow the examples and the direction set out by these scholars.

References

Hinnings, C. R. and Greenwood, R. 2002. Disconnects and consequences in organization theory? *Administrative Science Quarterly*, 47(3): 411–21.

Perrow, C. 2000. An organizational analysis of organization theory. *Contemporary Sociology*, 29(3): 469–77.

Walsh, J. P., Weber, K. and Margolis, J. D. 2003. Social issues and management: Our lost cause found. *Journal of Management*, 29(6): 859–81.

Wood, D. J. 1991. Corporate social performance revisited. *Academy of Management Review*, 16(4): 691–718.

10
Entrepreneurial Opportunity in Social Purpose Business Ventures

Kai Hockerts

Literature on social entrepreneurship (SE) embraces an exceedingly broad range of topics. It covers individual, organizational, as well as interorganizational level phenomena (Boschee, 1995; Bornstein, 1996; Leadbeater, 1997; Brinckerhoff, 2000; Dees, Emerson and Economy, 2001a; Drayton, 2002; Johnson, 2002; Emerson, 2003; Mair and Martí, 2004). This paper focuses on the organizational level phenomenon of social enterprises. However, even this term leaves ample room for ambiguity.

Scholars have used the expression to describe:

- A specific ownership structure – cooperatives and other mutually owned organizations (such as producer or consumer cooperatives) are often referred to as social enterprises,
- Fundraising ventures – subsidiaries of nonprofit organizations, whose only purpose is to raise funds for the principal charitable objective (such as in the case of the WWF merchandising arm), can also be considered social enterprises (Dees, 1998a; Fowler, 2000),
- Social purpose business ventures – a final variety of social enterprise refers to for-profit businesses (such as in the case of many fair trade companies) whose main purpose of existence is to create (external) social benefits (Campbell, 1998; Larson, 2000; Foryt, 2002; Schaltegger, 2002; Volery, 2002; Hockerts, 2003; Mair and Noboa, 2003a).

Scholars may find the sources of entrepreneurial opportunity that I suggest below to be of relevance to cooperatives and fundraising ventures as well. However, in this paper I am principally interested in the third type of social enterprise – the social purpose business venture (SPBV). The existence of SPBVs is puzzling from a purely economic point of view. SPBVs purport to exist primarily to create a public good. However, while the benefits they create are public they are nonetheless incurring private costs. How can they manage to do so? Putting social welfare first and still being a profitable business is counterintuitive. Management research has no theoretical explanation for these phenomena, nor does it offer guidance for social entrepreneurs who need to navigate the fault line delineating for-profit strategies from the domain of public and nonprofit management.

In this paper I will outline a conceptual framework for the sources of entrepreneurial opportunity for social purpose business ventures. First, I review briefly the extant literature on SE. Then, I develop a conceptual framework for SE identifying three types of social entrepreneurial opportunity.

SE as a new organizational construct

The term SE has emerged from practice rather than academic debate. Accordingly, even today, the definition of SE remains quite fuzzy, as remarked upon by Foryt:

> 'Social Entrepreneurship' is a broad term that does not have a widely accepted precise definition. In practice, it is used to describe everything from revolutionary leaders in third world countries who are not at all involved in business to first world businessmen and women who start a socially responsible business in their home country. Thus Mahatma Gandhi and Ben Cohen of Ben and Jerry's could be thrown into the same category. (Foryt, 2002: 1)

Although the motivation to build a viable business can be part of SE, many authors do not think this to be a necessary condition. Social entrepreneurs can thus be community leaders, activists in nonprofit groups, or government employees who identify and implement any kind of innovation that furthers social well-being. The term 'social entrepreneurship' emerged in the late 1990s in the US (Boschee, 1995; Henton, Melville and Walesh, 1997; Bornstein, 1998; Dees, 1998a; 1998b; Brinckerhoff, 2000; Dees, Emerson and Economy, 2001a; Drayton, 2002); and in the UK (Leadbeater, 1997; Warwick, 1997; Zadek and Thake, 1997; SSE, 2002). However, as Mair and Martí (2004) emphasize, examples of SE can be found around the globe.

The definitions for SE emerging from the literature are very disparate. At the individual level SE focuses on persons driving social change and innovation. These *social or civic entrepreneurs* can be individual citizens, community activists (Henton et al., 1997; Leadbeater, 1997; Swamy, 1990; Thompson, Alvy and Lees, 2000); or civil servants (Leadbeater, 2000; James, 2001) who use entrepreneurial spirit in order to reach social objectives. Bornstein defines a social entrepreneur as 'a path-breaker with a powerful new idea, who combines visionary and real-world problem solving creativity, who has a strong ethical fiber and who is "totally possessed" by his or her vision for change' (Bornstein, 1998: 36). Mair and Noboa (2003b) identify empathy, moral judgment, self-efficacy, and social support as the key aspects that distinguish social entrepreneurs.

At the organizational level SE is conceptualized in three different ways. A first perspective could by described as *commercializing a nonprofit organization*. In essence this view of SE brings a 'for-profit' philosophy to the many nonprofits that experienced a financial crunch in the 1980s as they found it more and more difficult to finance their work through donations and grants. Boschee (1995: 21) reports that, while nonprofits had 27 per cent of their annual operating funds in reserve in 1977, this proportion had fallen to just 1.4 per cent by the mid-1990s. By going at least partly 'for-profit' some organizations have started to sell what they used to give away for free in order to raise alternative income. Many nonprofits remain fearful of commercial operations undercutting their social mission (Dees, 1998a; Fowler, 2000). However, a viable business can often be the best option to generate a dependable income to pay for charitable actions (Grimm, 2000).

A more upbeat interpretation of SE in nonprofit organizations is the notion that a good dose of market-orientation will help social organizations to deliver more social value for the money they spend. By applying successful business practices (that is, by focusing on the most effective programs and using strategic planning and control mechanisms) nonprofit organizations can increase their efficiency and thus have a higher impact with a given budget (Drucker, 1989; Boschee, 1995; Warwick, 1997; Dees, 1998a; Dees et al., 2001a; 2001b; Sagawa and Segal, 2000; Zietlow, 2001; SSE, 2002). This approach of 'bringing business expertise and market-based skills to the nonprofit sector' (Johnson, 2000: 6) can be best summarized as *efficient nonprofit management*.

There is also a research tradition to link a specific ownership structure to social enterprises. Cooperatives and other mutually-owned organizations are often referred to as social enterprises by certain scholars.

A fourth view at the organizational level found in literature is that of SE as *social purpose business ventures* (Campbell, 1998; Larson, 2000; Foryt, 2002; Schaltegger, 2002; Volery, 2002; Hockerts, 2003; Mair and Noboa, 2003a) In this case an emerging social innovation is seen as a business opportunity and turned into a commercial for-profit business creating, in the process, new market space while also attaining a social objective. Typical examples would be The Body Shop or Whole Foods Market.

At the societal level SE is often understood as *networks for social entrepreneurs* and *venture philanthropy*. In this case information and practical support, as well as charitable donations or equity capital, are made available to entrepreneurial individuals and organizations that have a clear social mission and require a targeted amount of funds to realize it (Christopher, 2000; EMFK, 2002; Joshua Venture, 2002; Orloff, 2002). A typical example is the Ashoka Fellow program that has networked over 1200 recipients worldwide who are working on radical social innovation and provided grants to allow them to realize their objectives (Bornstein, 1998; Ashoka, 2002; Drayton, 2002). Bill Drayton, a former McKinsey consultant and assistant administrator at the US Environmental Protection Agency (EPA), founded Ashoka in the early 1980s, and is probably one of the most vocal promoters of SE. Other examples include The Schwab Foundation for Social Entrepreneurship in Geneva and London-based UnLTD – the Foundation for Social Entrepreneurs.

So far practitioners have been the main driving force for SE. Research contributions have tended to 'spread the word' through anecdotal evidence and descriptive case studies. A literature review conducted by the Canadian Centre for Social Entrepreneurship yielded only seven journal articles against a host of 16 contributions from news magazines and websites. Not surprisingly the author concludes that 'research on social entrepreneurship lags far behind the practice' (Johnson, 2000: 2); a finding shared by other scholars (Prabhu, 1999; Thompson et al., 2000).

In analyzing social enterprises I focus this paper on the sources of entrepreneurial opportunities for social purpose business ventures.

Sources of social entrepreneurial opportunity

Social purpose business ventures are hybrid enterprises straddling the boundary between the for-profit business world and social mission-driven public and nonprofit organizations. Thus they do not fit completely in either sphere. In order to keep their balance these social enterprises need to discover and exploit opportunities to create both social and economic value. Emerson calls this 'blended value' creation (Emerson, 2003). In this paper I introduce three sources of social entrepreneurial opportunity that can explain the existence of social purpose business ventures: activism, self-help, and philanthropy. I propose the main actors that contribute to the generation of opportunities as well as their social and economic value propositions.

Table 10.1   A conceptual framework for social entrepreneurial opportunities

Opportunity	Main actors	Economic value proposition	Social value proposition
Activism	Activists	Provides moral legitimization to the social enterprise Communication and distribution through activist networks	Social concerns championed by the activist group
Self-help	Beneficiaries	Cheap labor and marketing Cheap and patient capital Loyal and patient clients	Social needs or concerns of main beneficiaries of the social enterprise
Philanthropy	Donors	Charitable grants and donations Business development advice Networking with other social entrepreneurs	Social issues defined by the donor

Activism

One source of social entrepreneurial opportunity is activist interference in the market place. Activists aim to influence politicians and managers through mostly confrontational and sometimes cooperative campaigns (Rondinelli and London, 2003; Spar and La Mure, 2003; Yaziji, 2003). Yet, upon realizing that they may best meet their goals through the support of social purpose enterprises, some activist groups have begun to explore that route more systematically.

A typical example is the fair trade movement. Traditionally development activists lobby politicians to provide more development aid to poor countries and blast multinationals they perceive to exploit smallholder producers in underdeveloped countries. However, in recent years they have also initiated and supported fair trade enterprises such as Cafédirect (today the sixth largest coffee brand in the UK) or Agrofair (a fast growing fair trade fresh fruit wholesaler in the Netherlands). These organizations are not only successful businesses in their own right, but they are also governed by the principle of social welfare maximization for the producers of cash crops in developing countries (Robins and Roberts, 1997; Tallontire, 2000). The reason these enterprises have succeeded in a competitive market place lies in two kinds of support they have received from activists.

Firstly, development activists provide legitimization in the market place. Implicit or explicit endorsement from organizations such as Oxfam and CAFOD in the UK or Steun Onderontwikkelde Streken (SOS) and Solidaridad in the Netherlands, has helped to make fair trade a product distinction that customers trust. At the same time campaigns put industry incumbents like Kraft, Nestlé, Procter and Gamble, and Sara Lee on the spot, a good example being Oxfam's campaign report: 'Mugged – Poverty in your coffee cup' (Economist, 2002; Oxfam, 2002).

Secondly, activists organized in church groups, development initiatives, or local citizen committees provide free marketing and distribution to fair trade enterprises. Knocking on doors, staging boycotts outside local retailers until they list fair trade products, and spreading news by word of mouth, all provide invaluable free marketing to these budding businesses.

As the market share of fair trade has grown, traditional players have started to crowd in on this opportunity. In the UK, Sainsbury's and the Coop, for example, have launched their own brand fair trade labels that are registered with the activist groups and bear the official fair trade mark. Even Kraft Foods Inc. has begun to sell fair trade coffee certified by the Rainforest Alliance. Increasing economic pressure has been driving some fair trade pioneers out of the market. Oxfam, for example, stopped its own importing of fair trade products focusing instead on development (Stevens, 2001). Other fair trade enterprises such as Cafédirect have since revamped their communications toward stressing product quality and thus moving more into the direction of traditional business.

Activism provides social enterprises with a set of social entrepreneurial opportunities primarily by making the key assets of activist groups

available to the social enterprise. Yaziji (2003) suggests legitimacy, awareness of social forces, distinct networks, and specialized technical expertise as the most relevant resources that activist groups possess. For
budding social venture startups these resources can make the difference
between survival and failure. However, activism-driven social enterprises
are also at risk since public pressure groups usually have a short attention
span. They operate in a world of campaigns and thus, ultimately, media
attention. As soon as social enterprises become established, activist
groups begin to lose interest as they are not in the institution-building
business.

In the long run activist-based social enterprises face two options.
Either they tone down their social welfare mission and mutate into traditional businesses competing primarily on price and quality, or they
leave the business side to the incumbents and slide back into the
activist world. The latter is not necessarily a failure. Oxfam's decision
to stop importing fair trade products was, at the same time, testimony
to the fact that the activist organization had succeeded in kickstarting
the fair trade movement. Now that more and more professional fair
trade enterprises have emerged, Oxfam can move back to its original
mission of alleviating poverty and lobbying policy makers.

Self-help

The beneficiaries of the social enterprise are a second source of social
entrepreneurial opportunity. Usually beneficiaries of social initiatives
would be expected to be powerless. Why else would they need support
and protection from social enterprises? However, often the needy can
pull themselves up given the opportunity. Thus, roping the beneficiaries into the business can be another source of opportunity for social
enterprises; they can provide the enterprise with valuable resources.

Take the example of microfinance (Bornstein, 1996). Traditionally
aid organizations have focused on providing donations. Yet charity is
not the most effective way to help the poor. From this realization a
host of microfinance enterprises have emerged that provide the poor
with microloans, which in turn help them escape from poverty. How
can social enterprises succeed at this task when traditional banks have
failed at providing such services to the poor profitably? A primary asset
of microfinance is the fact that it encourages the poor to save. These
funds are, in turn, used to finance the microloans. Secondly, social
enterprises such as Grameen Bank use their beneficiaries as employees
thus reducing labor costs. Finally, knowing that they are the beneficiaries, clients of microfinance banks are highly loyal clients and this

results in lower default rates than pure for-profit banks encounter. Attracted by a growing market for financial services among the poor, banks and insurance providers have recently begun to duplicate the ideas of microfinance in a for-profit context. This, in turn, is putting the pioneering social enterprises under pressure and forcing them to choose between a return to the fold of charity or a move forward into commercial competition with the market incumbents.

Self-help can be a strong asset for social enterprises in all kinds of areas. GrameenPhone, for example, is emulating the village bank concept in bringing mobile telephony to the poor in rural Bangladesh (Quadir, 2003; Malaviya, Singhal, Svenkerud and Srivastava, 2004). Car sharing is another phenomenon taking on market incumbents by leveraging on its clients. This type of social enterprise has grown out of the desire of a small number of people to share their vehicles. These people were critical about car ownership from an ecological point of view, but still had an occasional need to use a car. Starting as an informal self-help network founded by a handful of people, car sharing cooperatives have mushroomed all over Europe. The market leader, Mobility Car Sharing (MCS) in Switzerland, serves over 50,000 clients and owes its strong position largely to its cooperative members (Hockerts, 2004). Apart from putting up capital, cooperative members also donate time and effort to operating the car sharing system while spreading news about the business by word-of-mouth.

Social enterprises, drawing on self-help as a source of entrepreneurial opportunity, find this reflected in three primary categories. Firstly, beneficiaries are a source of cheap and patient capital. While the individual contribution of each participant is small, the aggregate result can be considerable. Secondly, recipients can provide cheap access to labor. They can also knock on doors and get the word out. In contrast to activist-driven enterprises, beneficiaries bring the additional advantage of being the social enterprise's clients. Thus their message will be perceived as more objective than that of a political activist. Thirdly, self-help enterprises can be sure of their clientele. Where commercial operators might lose frustrated clients, the customers of social enterprises have a higher level of patience. This is essential as they are often figuring out their business models on the fly. At least initially, this may result in lower quality products.

A drawback for self-help inspired social enterprises lies in their inertia. Here they are the exact opposite of activist enterprises. Having grown out of a very specific need of their beneficiaries, self-help enterprises will tend to stick to the interests of these recipients, even when it would make sense to employ the resources of the social enterprise in new regions or to address new target groups.

Philanthropy

A third source of opportunity can be philanthropic venture capitalists (Roberts, Emerson and Tuan, 1999). Whereas commercial businesses are expected to generate competitive rates of return this is not true for philanthropy-driven enterprises. Here the altruistic mission can be sufficient payback for philanthropic investors. As a consequence of subsidized capital, social enterprises can compete with market incumbents.

Good examples of philanthropy-driven enterprises are Rubicon Bakery and Rubicon Landscape Services, based in the Bay Area, California (Moore, 1999). Both businesses compete with traditional firms while providing jobs and training for disabled or homeless people. In order to deliver its products and services at a competitive price Rubicon relies on charitable support from philanthropic venture funds. The Roberts Enterprise Development Fund (REDF) is one of the contributors to Rubicon. REDF assists its portfolio organizations in a variety of ways, most notably by providing financing for organizational infrastructure, access to additional funds for capital expenses and strategic business development assistance. It also provides access to business networking opportunities, social outcome measurement and technological tools and training.

Over the past years venture philanthropists focusing particularly on social enterprises have sprung up in many countries. They include organizations such as Ashoka in the US, the Schwab Foundation for Social Entrepreneurship in Geneva, and London-based UnLTD – the Foundation for Social Entrepreneurs.

Philanthropy-driven social enterprises benefit from three advantages. Firstly, venture philanthropists are a source of subsidized capital. Secondly, rather than just providing charitable grants venture philanthropy comes with valuable advice on launching and growing social enterprises. Finally, social enterprise funds link their portfolio investments, in the process creating unique networks of social enterprises in which to learn and cooperate.

At the same time venture philanthropists demand, more than any other partner, accountability for an enterprise's social performance. This requires the social enterprise to keep its eye very closely on its social mission and thus avoid a drift away from the underlying social welfare objectives. At the same time philanthropy-driven enterprises may also be restricted by the altruistic focus of their investors. More importantly, most philanthropic funds have investment cycles; once they come to an end, social enterprises are expected to be able to succeed in the market place on their own. Those which cannot achieve this will tend to drift into a nonprofit state of mind.

Conclusions

Scholars working on developing a theory of SE face two challenges. Firstly, their contributions risk being lost in a quagmire of definitions. Grand social entrepreneurial theory needs to cover so broad an area that the result is often unconvincing. More focused mid-range theory seems to offer a more promising venue to move SE research from its infancy stage to a more rigorous theoretical level. I have, therefore, focused this paper on just one element in the mosaic that is SE. By studying the sources of entrepreneurial opportunity for social purpose business ventures I intend to provide scholars in our field with an initial framework that I hope will be further developed and extended by future research.

A second challenge of SE research lies in the lack of rigorous empirical studies grounding or testing theories about SE. A particular problem is the lack of systematic data on social enterprises. To date, there is no Compustat equivalent for social enterprises. A notable research endeavor in this context is the Stanford Project on Emerging Nonprofits (SPEN), studying 200 randomly selected operating charities in the US and in the process, generating a valuable body of data. It would be highly desirable to see a similar effort for social purpose business ventures. Future research could also profitably use matched pair designs to study social enterprises. It might, for example, be illuminating to study three otherwise similar social purpose business ventures, one of which is primarily activist-driven, one of which is self-help-based, and one of which is drawing on philanthropic capital as its primary source of success.

Researchers may find the conceptual framework proposed in this paper useful in two ways. Current literature often intimates that there exists some generally applicable management rules for social enterprises. The framework introduced here suggests that practitioners need to think systematically about the type of entrepreneurial opportunity underlying their social enterprise. Depending on the primary source of opportunity they may have to adopt significantly different strategies. A second avenue of research could be the study of organizations that draw simultaneously on several sources of opportunity. Here it would

be interesting to study tensions between activism, self-help, and philanthropy. The result would be a more fine-grained understanding of
how the different sources of opportunity interact with each other.

References

Ashoka. 2002. What is a social entrepreneur? Available: http://www.ashoka.org/
fellows/social_entrepreneur.cfm. Accessed 3 October 2002.

Bornstein, D. 1996. *The price of a dream: The story of the Grameen Bank.* Chicago:
University of Chicago.

Bornstein, D. 1998. Changing the world on a shoestring. *The Atlantic Monthly,*
281(1): 34–9.

Boschee, J. 1995. Social entrepreneurship. *Across the Board,* 32(3): 20–4.

Brinckerhoff, P. C. 2000. *Social entrepreneurship: The art of mission-based venture
development.* New York: John Wiley and Sons.

Campbell, S. 1998. Social entrepreneurship: How to develop new social-purpose
business ventures. *Health Care Strategic Management,* 16(5): 17–18.

Christopher, A. 2000. Flatiron launches fund, foundation. *Venture Capital
Journal,* 40(5): 22–3.

Dees, J. G. 1998a. Enterprising nonprofits. *Harvard Business Review,* 76(1):
54–66.

Dees, J. G. 1998b. The meaning of social entrepreneurship. Paper. Center for the
Advancement of Social Entrepreneurship, Fuqua School of Business, Duke
University, Durham. Available: http://www.fuqua.duke.edu/centers/case/
documents/dees_SE.pdf.

Dees, J. G., Emerson, J. and Economy, P. 2001a. *Enterprising nonprofits: A Toolkit
for Social Entrepreneurs.* New York: John Wiley and Sons.

Dees, J. G., Emerson, J. and Economy, P. 2001b. *Strategic tools for social entrepreneurs: Enhancing the performance of your enterprising nonprofit.* New York: John
Wiley and Sons.

Drayton, W. 2002. The citizen sector: Becoming as entrepreneurial and competitive as business. *California Management Review,* 44(3): 120–32.

Drucker, P. F. 1989. What business can learn from nonprofits. *Harvard Business
Review,* 67(4): 88–93.

Economist. 2002. Coffee: Mug shot, coffee companies prepare for a roasting.
Economist, 21 Sept: 67.

Emerson, J. 2003. Blended value map. Available: http://www.blendedvalue.org/.

EMKF. 2002. Ewing Marion Kauffman Foundation – Social entrepreneurship.
Available: http://www.kauffman.org/. Accessed 16 October 2002.

Foryt, S. 2002. Social entrepreneurship in developing nations. Research Paper,
INSEAD, Fontainebleau.

Fowler, A. 2000. NGDOs as a moment in history: Beyond aid to social entrepreneurship? *Third World Quarterly,* 21(4): 637–54.

Grimm, R. T. J. 2000. Profits to charity. *Foundation News and Commentary,* 41(2):
64.

Henton, D., Melville, J. and Walesh, K. 1997. Grassroots leaders for a new
economy: How civic entrepreneurs are building prosperous communities.
National Civic Review, 86(2): 149–56.

Hockerts, K. N. 2003. Sustainability innovations, ecological and social entrepreneurship and the management of antagonistic assets. Unpublished PhD Thesis, University St. Gallen.

Hockerts, K. N. 2004. Mobility car sharing, from ecopreneurial start-up to commercial venture. Case study. INSEAD, Fontainebleau.

James, C. 2001. Social entrepreneurs. *New Zealand Management*, 48(9): 58.

Johnson, S. 2000. Literature review on social entrepreneurship. Canadian Centre for Social Entrepreneurship, University of Alberta School of Business, Canada. Available: http://www.bus.ualberta.ca/ccse/Publications.

Johnson, S. 2002. Social entrepreneurship literature review. *New Academy Review*, 2(2): 42–56.

Joshua Venture. 2002. Social entrepreneurs. Available: http://www.joshuaventure.org/entre-path.html. Accessed 16 October 2002.

Larson, A. L. 2000. Sustainable innovation through an entrepreneurship lens. *Business Strategy and the Environment*, 9: 304–17.

Leadbeater, C. 1997. *The Rise of the Social Entrepreneur*. London: Demos.

Leadbeater, C. 2000. Sir Humphrey needs venture capital. *New Statesman*, 27 Nov: 29–30.

Mair, J. and Martí, I. 2004. Social entrepreneurship: What are we talking about? A framework for future research. Working Paper 546. IESE Business School, University of Navarra, Barcelona.

Mair, J. and Noboa, E. 2003a. The emergence of social enterprises and their place in the new organizational landscape. Working Paper 523. IESE Business School, University of Navarra, Barcelona.

Mair, J. and Noboa, E. 2003b. Social entrepreneurship: How intentions to create a social enterprise get formed. Working Paper 521. IESE Business School, University of Navarra, Barcelona.

Malaviya, P., Singhal, A., Svenkerud, P. J. and Srivastava, S. 2004. Telenor in Bangladesh: the prospect of doing good and doing well? Case study. INSEAD, Fontainebleau.

Moore, T. 1999. *Rubicon Programs, social purpose enterprises and venture philanthropy in the new millennium*, Vol. 3: Practitioner profiles. San Francisco: Roberts Enterprise Development Found (REDF).

Orloff, A. 2002. Social Venture Partners Calgary: emergence and early stages. Edmonton, Alberta: Canadian Centre for Social Entrepreneurship.

Oxfam. 2002. *Mugged: Poverty in your Coffee Cup*. Oxford: Oxfam International.

Prabhu, G. N. 1999. Social entrepreneurial leadership. *Career Development International*, 4(3): 140–5.

Quadir, I. 2003. Bottom-up economics. *Harvard Business Review*, 81(8): 18–20.

Roberts, G., Emerson, J. and Tuan, M. T. 1999. *Social purpose enterprises and venture philanthropy in the new millennium*. San Francisco: Roberts Enterprise Development Found (REDF).

Robins, N. and Roberts, S. 1997. Reaping the benefits: Trade opportunities for developing producers from sustainable consumption and production. *Greener Management International*, Autumn (19): 53–67.

Rondinelli, D. A. and London, T. 2003. How corporations and environmental groups cooperate: Assessing cross-sector alliances and collaborations. *Academy of Management Executive*, 17(1).

Sagawa, S. and Segal, E. 2000. Common interest, common good: creating value through business and social sector partnerships. *California Management Review*, 42(2): 105–22.

Schaltegger, S. 2002. A Framework for ecopreneurship: Leading bioneers and environmental managers to ecopreneurship. *Greener Management International*, 38: 45–58.

Spar, D. L. and La Mure, L. T. 2003. The power of activism: Assessing the impact of NGOs on global business. *California Management Review*, 45(3): 78–102.

SSE. 2002. Background. Available: http://www.sse.org.uk/network/index.shtml. Accessed 16 October 2002.

Stevens, A. 2001. Communication to Oxfam's fair trade producer groups. Oxford: Oxfam Fair Trade.

Swamy, R. 1990. The making of a social entrepreneur: The case of Baba Ampte. Vikalpa. *The Journal for Decision Makers, Indian Institute of Management*, 15(4): 29–38.

Tallontire, A. M. 2000. Partnerships in fair trade, reflections from a case study of CaféDirect. *Development in Practice*, 10(2).

Thompson, J., Alvy, G. and Lees, A. 2000. Social entrepreneurship – A new look at the people and the potential. *Management Decision*, 38(5): 328–38.

Volery, T. 2002. An entrepreneur commercializes conservation: The case of Earth Sanctuaries Ltd. *Greener Management International*, 38: 109–16.

Warwick, D. 1997. Will social entrepreneurs blossom or hit bottom? *People Management*, 3(20): 56.

Yaziji, M. 2003. From gadflies to allies. *Harvard Business Review*, 82.

Zadek, S. and Thake, S. 1997. Send in the social entrepreneurs. *New Statesman*, 26(7339): 31.

Zietlow, J. T. 2001. Social entrepreneurship: Managerial, finance and marketing aspects. *Journal of Nonprofit and Public Sector Marketing*, 7(1/2): 19–44.

11
Ownership, Mission and Environment: An Exploratory Analysis into the Evolution of a Technology Social Venture

Geoffrey Desa and Suresh Kotha

Introduction

Despite the recognition that technology is not a panacea for social ills (UNDP, 2001), some of the largest and most active philanthropic organizations in the US (for example, The Bill and Melinda Gates Foundation, The Open Society Institute, and The MacArthur Foundation) are committed to technology-based solutions to social problems. Similarly, like-minded entrepreneurs are beginning to address social problems through technology.

The literature on technology and innovation however, is yet to discuss this growing phenomenon. In general, one of the main thrusts of the technology and innovation literature deals with how established companies: (a) use technology to gain a competitive advantage (Bettis and Hitt, 1995); (b) have difficulty adapting to technological change (Henderson and Clark, 1990; Utterback, 1994; Christensen and Bower, 1996; Rindova and Kotha, 2001); and (c) seek ways to stay technologically innovative (Nelson and Winter, 1982; Dosi, 1988; Cohen and Levinthal, 1990; Leonard-Barton, 1992; Ahuja and Katila, 2001). Similarly, the literature on entrepreneurship deals almost exclusively with commercial ventures (Moore, 1991; Ahuja and Lampert, 2001; Shane and Stuart, 2002; Agarawal, Echambadi, Franco and Sarkar, 2004) and, only occasionally, addresses how technology-based startups satisfy social welfare needs. Finally, the literature on social entrepreneurship (SE) addresses issues pertaining to how social ventures differ from 'traditional' entrepreneurship and is yet to address issues specific to technology-based ventures (Mair and Martí, 2004).

The purpose of this study is to better understand technology social ventures (TSVs), an area that falls at the nexus of two fields: SE, and technology innovation. We base our study on the following premises: (a) social enterprises increasingly develop and use technology to solve critical social problems; (b) technological-innovation frameworks developed for 'for-profit' ventures may not be readily applicable to the SE context; and (c) management research can benefit from studying innovation in the SE area (Drucker, 1989; Kanter, 1999).

We explore the following research question: *How do technology social ventures originate, develop and grow in a resource-limited context?* We address this question by studying Benetech, a Silicon Valley-based, TSV incorporated in 2000. The goal is to understand this firm's evolution and discuss how it uses technology to benefit social innovation, and how it continues to expand through technology-based projects into multiple arenas. Benetech has multiple projects in various stages of venture formation from idea/opportunity generation to venture growth. The firm's founder, Jim Fruchterman, is a strong advocate for technology in social ventures and has addressed leaders and policy makers at venues such as the World Economic Forum, which meets annually in Davos, Switzerland. The firm is widely regarded as an exemplar, and thus is a 'revelatory' case (Yin, 1994) that warrants academic study.

Below we discuss the emerging literature on SE to provide a context for our detailed study of Benetech's approach to technology SE. We then discuss Benetech's evolution and growth, and highlight the propositions that emerge from our study of this firm. We conclude with a few observations for research on TSVs.

Background literature

One emerging research stream attempts to define SE as a field and help distinguish it from that of 'for-profit' ventures using individual and organizational characteristics (Hockerts, 2004; Mair and Martí, 2004). Although the definition of SE remains fuzzy (Boschee, 1995; Dees, 1998; Brinckerhoff, 2000), SE according to this stream is broadly defined as the innovative use of resources to explore and exploit opportunities that meet a social need in a sustainable manner (Mair and Martí, 2004). The mission statements of social ventures often address a social need (or problem) that is either ignored by the 'for-profit' sector or inadequately addressed by the government sector. In contrast, the mission statements of 'for-profit' ventures typically mention the market segment addressed or financial returns to be expected from the venture's pursuit to providers of capital. Thus, it is addressing a 'social' need that forms the defining characteristic of a social venture. Social ventures can take on a complex array of forms (for-profit, nonprofit and intermediate hybrids) (Mair and Martí, 2004) and since they operate at the nexus of public, economic, and social authorities they serve multiple masters (Leadbeater, 1997; Mair and Noboa, 2003a; Shaw and Carter, 2004).[1]

Drawing from opportunity recognition literature in entrepreneurship research (Shane and Venkataraman, 2000), a second stream focuses on highlighting how social entrepreneurs recognize opportunities worthy of pursuit (Hockerts, 2004). As they attempt to discover and exploit venture opportunities, social entrepreneurs invariably straddle the boundaries between the 'for-profit' business world and the social mission-driven 'nonprofit' organization. Hockerts (2004), for example, conceptualizes social entrepreneurial opportunity recognition as emerging from one of three sources: philanthropy, self-help, and activism. Activist groups use a distinct set of resources (for example, legitimacy, awareness of social forces, distinct networks, and technical expertise) to influence politicians and managers through confrontational or cooperative campaigns, and thus involve them in addressing social needs. Self-help sources or volunteers, often beneficiaries of the social enterprise themselves, provide the venture with valuable resources through volunteering time, effort, or cheap and patient capital. Finally, philanthropic venture capitalists form a third source of opportunities by providing subsidized capital and know-how on social ventures.

Since entrepreneurship research involves the study of two phenomena, the presence of enterprising individuals and the presence of lucrative opportunities (Shane and Venkataraman, 2000), it is not surprising that a third research stream focuses on one or both these phenomena. For example, Mair and Noboa (2003b) attempt to explain why entrepreneurs start social ventures using four factors: empathy, moral-judgment, self-efficacy, and social support. They propose that behavioral intentions to create a social venture are influenced by constructs of perceived social venture desirability, and social venture feasibility.[2] Their framework provides a useful starting point for studying how entrepreneurial intentions results in social venture formation.

The emerging literature, however, is yet to address the phenomenon of TSV (that is, ventures that develop and deploy technology-driven solutions to address social needs in a financially sustainable manner) dotting the SE landscape. Not unlike other social ventures, TSV's address the twin cornerstones of SE – ownership (financial return) and mission (social impact) using advanced technology.

From a technology venture perspective, Shane and Stuart (2002) focused on the situational and background characteristics of entrepreneurs to predict the probability of venture formation. They looked at the resource endowments (such as social relations, prior industry, startup experience and technological assets) of technology entrepreneurs and found that these resource endowments significantly predicted who secured external funding. This external funding then allowed founders to pursue the discovered opportunities.

In another study, Shane (2000) demonstrated that people can discover entrepreneurship opportunities without actively searching for them as portrayed in the traditional entrepreneurship literature. Using case studies of eight potential entrepreneurs seeking to exploit a single MIT innovation, he shows that, despite all potential entrepreneurs having access to the same information, each discovered and pursued only those market segments which were related to his or her prior background knowledge.

Recently, a few academics have highlighted the transformative and innovative power of TSVs. Prahalad (2005), for example, through case studies of social venture organizations, advocates for technologically empowered social ventures that treat the poor as consumers and sources of innovation rather than as a problem or as recipients of aid. One of the examples Prahalad and his coauthors chronicle is Voxiva (Casas, Lajoie and Prahalad, 2003), a startup social venture that provides practical technology solutions that let distributed organizations exchange information and communicate more effectively. However, beyond this and a few other cases (for example, Project Impact, OneWorld Health, and eChoupal), we know little about this emerging form of technology-based SE, and how it fits within the larger domain of entrepreneurship (Schumpeter, 1934; Venkataraman, 1997) and SE (Dees, 1998; Drayton, 2002; Skloot, 2002; Mair and Martí, 2004). Thus, the current study is an exploratory attempt to address this important nexus between technology and SE, an area that deserves academic attention.

Table 11.1 Technology social venture projects within Benetech (circa. mid-2004)

Project	Description
Bookshare.org	An Internet library where members of the blind, visually-impaired and reading-disabled community can legally store and share scanned publications.
Martus	Provides for the creation, encryption and secure storage of reports of human rights abuses. The system improves the accessibility of human rights information to help assure that violations will be recorded and those responsible held accountable.
Human Rights Data Analysis Group	Applies information technology solutions and statistical techniques to help human rights advocates build evidence-based arguments.
All-Link	Internet service providing best-practice reading and writing instruction to students with significant disabilities.
Bookaccess	An initiative delivering digital books to improve access to information for poor and illiterate populations in the developing world.
Landmine Detector Project	Adapts cutting-edge technologies to the needs of humanitarian landmine removal.
Project Libre	Seeks to bring truly affordable and usable open source software to users in the developing world and schools, nonprofits and government agencies in the industrialized world.
ReadingCam Project	Developing a prototype device for people with visual disabilities that can locate, recognize, and speak text found in the general environment.

Source: Adapted from http://www.benetech.org.

Approach and methods

Since our research questions are aimed at exploring the evolution of de novo TSVs, they demand the richness, holism and sustained period observations offered by a qualitative case study (Lee, 1998; Whetten, 1989; Pettigrew, 1990). We recognize that the processes which underlie the evolution of Benetech can be unique and difficult to identify or measure with great precision. Often, in such cases, many processes underlying the phenomenon can be generalized (Tsoukas, 1989; Kotha, 1998). Using the Benetech case, we incrementally refine definitions of the constructs proposed by moving between existing theory, the data, and the emerging propositions.

Choice of organization

We chose Benetech for its pioneering role as a social technology venture. The firm has been the recipient of numerous social venture industry awards including the Skoll Award for Social Entrepreneurship, the Schwab Foundation Award for 2003, and the Social Capitalist award from Fast Company, Inc. For these reasons, Benetech may be considered an exemplar, which represents a 'revelatory' case (Yin, 1994).

We look at Benetech, a technology incubator with multiple projects (see Table 11.1 for details). These projects are in diverse fields of SE, for example, human rights, education, literacy, disability access, civic participation and the environment; and as such are representative of the wide range of applications of SE. Studying multiple projects allows us to draw certain normative implications from a descriptive evaluation of the data (Eisenhardt, 1989; Yin, 1994).

Data sources

We used archival information and interviews about the different social venture projects being undertaken at Benetech. The data utilized (from Benetech's inception in year 2000 to 2004) include: newspaper articles; an independent nonprofit study; project summaries; business plans; press releases; nonretrospective quarterly data from the president; blog summaries of meetings (captured by independent participants); and archived public speeches and presentations. We supplemented these with interviews with the various project leaders of Benetech, including the company's CEO Jim Fruchterman. At quarterly intervals, we interviewed senior personnel to get 'lived meanings' (Miles and Huberman, 1994) and supplement the archival data collected. Then, following Eisenhardt (1989), we prepared case summaries for each project, utilizing multiple sources of data, which represent the qualitative equivalent of statistical degrees of freedom.

The evolution of a technology social venture

Genesis of Benetech

Jim Fruchterman's quest for a hybrid blend of business and altruism began at Caltech while studying 'smart' bomb technology in an applied physics course. Jim saw the potential for turning warfare technology to a new use:

> At Caltech ... I was learning about optical pattern recognition, and one of the applications for it is making a 'smart' bomb. I was thinking of what, other than military targets, you could recognize with optical pattern recognition [technology]. The one idea I came up with was that you could make a reading machine for the blind using the same technology (Hillberry, 2004).

After completing his undergraduate degree in engineering and graduate work in applied physics, Jim headed off to pursue a doctorate at Stanford. But he interrupted his studies to work on a rocket project which blew up during the launch. Following this, he started another rocket company, but failed to secure the necessary venture capital to grow the venture.

Undeterred, in 1982, using his expertise and background in pattern recognition technology, he cofounded Calera Recognition Systems, a manufacturer that developed optical character recognition machines. After serving in different executive positions at Calera, he left it in 1989 to found RAF Technology, a software company based on his background in pattern recognition. Businesses and the US Postal Service now use mail address-recognition systems (hardware and software) created by this venture. At RAF Technology, Jim served initially as the company's CEO and later as its CFO. However, he became increasingly frustrated that the projects he wanted to pursue, those offering the greatest benefit to help people, weren't profitable. Notes Jim:

> I felt strongly that I have a missionary role: to sell technologists on how much good technology can do in the world. We fail to give technologists a model between making scads of money on an idea or charity, and I think that technology can do so much for the people who can least afford it, as long as the cost is accessible (Hillberry, 2004).

In 1989, to address this challenge, he started Arkenstone, once again using his expertise in pattern recognition. This venture was a nonprofit supplier of reading machines and software tools for the visually impaired. Arkenstone delivered these tools in a dozen languages to thousands of individuals globally. In June 2000, Freedom Scientific, a for-profit company, bought Arkenstone's operations for $5 million (all currency units quoted in this chapter are US dollars). This infusion of cash paved the way for Jim's next venture – Benetech. According to Jim:

> Benetech is a nonprofit venture that combines the impact of tech-nological solutions with the SE business model to help disadvan-taged communities in our society and across the world. It grew out of my recognition that most big companies don't address *small markets*. We think of ourselves as a high-tech company but our cus-tomers are people who most high-tech companies won't go after. I like to spread the original, very successful Arkenstone model to more fields, all with the common thread of technology in the service of humanity (Fruchterman, 2005).

A technology incubator in a resource-constrained environment

Benetech addressed projects in which the social need was apparent, but the market size, as seen by venture capital investors, was too small to warrant adequate financial returns. These projects were unable to attract the financial capital from venture capitalists when compared to technology-based ventures that focused on larger market segments with greater market and financial potential. Jim notes:

> The goal of a technology social enterprise is to maximize social impact while breaking even financially. This is a much easier standard to meet than that of the typical for-profit high technology company that needs to aim for a $50 million market and deliver a 30–40 per cent annual return on investment. These double-bottom line enter-prises can fill the gap between what's possible and what's profitable in the social applications of technology (Fruchterman, 2004b).

Consequently, Jim conceived Benetech as a holding corporation incor-porating 'for-profit' and 'nonprofit' arms right from the start. Benetech served as a technology incubator where the management team and the board decided to fund the initial technology and business develop-ment plans for different ideas that faced difficulty attracting funding in the traditional venture community. Depending on the venture, the finances were either obtained from an internal unrestricted operating budget or from external corporate, public, or private funding sources. Jim goes on to elaborate:

> Technology social enterprises present exciting options. The development of technology grants advantages of leverage that are exploited by high technology business and should be further exploited by the social sector. The first is high margins. Creating the original unit incurs the majority of the cost of a technology-based product: every additional unit has relatively low manufacturing costs. The second advantage is ease of replication worldwide. If the unit of service is a piece of information or a technology product, as opposed to an hour of human time, the possibility of going to scale is greatly enhanced. (Fruchterman, 2004b).

Figure 11.1 documents the Benetech process of taking a venture idea from inception, through seed funding, business plan development, financing, and operations. Jim and his associates used this process to develop and manage the project.

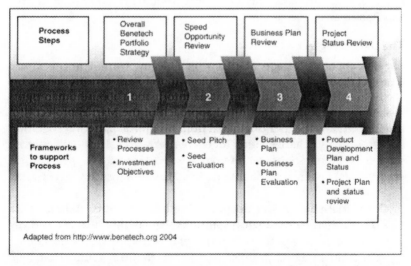

Figure 11.1 Project development process at Benetech (based on the venture capital model)

The process as, described in Figure 11.1, takes place in the context of specific investment objectives, which specify areas of nonprofit activity and investments, established by the Board to guide the Benetech venture process.

All initiatives are started with long term sustainability in mind and, as this initiative moved through the various developmental stages, the funding sources generally changed depending upon the stakeholders enticed or invited to participate, back or support the venture. Such changes often affected the project scope, its strategic mission, as well as the markets served by the new initiative. Such changes in turn enabled the venture to draw upon or seek new sources of funding, as well as technology contributions, from individual or private donors interested in supporting the evolving venture. Jim described this 'investment-driven dynamic' as follows:

> Benetech, in many ways acts as a venture capital partner, making investment decisions on behalf of society and our limited partners who have donated the seed capital. Additionally, it provides a corporate home, and often the management for a nonprofit technology venture, since there is no economic motive for independent ownership of the venture. Moreover, the process to set up a nonprofit is much more involved than for a high technology for-profit company (Fruchterman, 2004b).

Jim's first ventures after Benetech was founded in 2000 were Martus and Bookshare.org.

The Martus project

The idea/opportunity stage. Martus, which means, 'witness' in Greek, was a project designed to provide technology tools to assist the human rights sector in collecting and disseminating information about human rights violations. In recalling the initial approach of the Martus project, Jim mentioned how the idea originated from his optical pattern recognition background, but changed after an encounter with Patrick Ball, a senior adviser on human rights technology who had served as expert witness on genocidal hearings at the International Court of Justice in The Hague:

> Our initial thoughts of documenting human rights violations via sophisticated technological solutions like satellite imagery and spy drones were foregone for a more practical approach after talking with human rights groups. The Benetech team found that field workers did not want fancy technology; they had a hard time managing text and online access was slow and expensive (WAC, 2004).

The prototype/founding stage. Benetech provided the initial seed funding of $150,000 for prototype development. In early 2001, the

Benetech team visited with human rights activists in Sri Lanka, Cambodia, and Guatemala. The objective as Jim puts it was to 'gain real-world insight into the need for technology in the human rights field, and for specific input for our Martus prototype'.

Aimed at a 'grassroots activist' with the skills to use email and the internet, the prototype consisted of a simple and secure application with an email type of interface for gathering, organizing, and backing up the documentation of human rights abuse around the world. Additionally, any information earmarked as public was published to a human rights information search engine on the internet. Notes Jim:

> In addition to building this basic client solution [software] for just about any social justice group documenting and monitoring violations, Benetech has a high-end database solution designed for doing statistics on large-scale human rights issues. We serve truth commissions and international courts with the analysis of what happened in a country, helping that society answer the crucial questions for moving forward following a period of tremendous suffering: how many people died, was it genocide, and who was responsible! (Fruchterman, 2002)

The Martus prototype was presented by Marc Levine and Patrick Ball to several international human rights organizations in January 2001. It received extensive participation from small nongovernmental organizations (NGOs) on the ground to large international groups in the US, Sri Lanka, Guatemala, and Russia.

Funding the Growth Stage. The total development cost of Martus was estimated to be $1.5–2 million, a large amount for a nascent nonprofit organization. Benetech leveraged its initial $150,000 investment to gain support from other funders. Pledging an additional $100,000 to initial product development, Benetech received two-year grants of approximately $500,000 from the Open Society Institute and the MacArthur Foundation.

Martus, the human rights project, continued to expand and develop a large base of users. Receptivity from a wide range of social justice groups made it apparent to the Martus team that the product had a wide variety of applications. In July 2001, Jim wrote,

> In the last six months we have met with representatives of several dozen organizations in five countries, representing human rights, women's rights and gay and lesbian rights. Martus tools have a wide

variety of potential applications – from documenting international human rights abuses, to monitoring domestic violence offenders within the state of California, to tracking environmental 'hot spots' within a city or county. The reaction to Martus by these potential users has been very enthusiastic. (Fruchterman, 2001)

By January 2004, just after 11 months of operation, users from 47 countries downloaded the product. Martus was regularly used by NGOs in over 10 countries and the user interface had been translated into six languages.

With the Martus project operating in the background, and with the Arkenstone model in mind, Jim had started actively thinking about how to use technology to increase access to people with print disabilities when he stumbled on the idea of using this knowledge of pattern recognition technology to share books.[3]

The Bookshare.org project

The idea/opportunity stage. Early in January 2001, Jim, returning home, stopped by to say hello to his teenage son when he noticed a program called Napster running on his son's computer. A demonstration later, he was completely intrigued by the music and file sharing program which allowed users to access and share thousands of files. The acting CEO of Napster happened to live two doors down and so Jim talked to her about Napster. Recalls Jim: 'That's pretty cool, I thought. What if you can do something similar for digital books? Perhaps an online digital book distribution service for the blind?' Thus, out of this chance encounter emerged the Bookshare.org initiative. Jim conceived Bookshare.org as a subscription service providing an extensive online library of accessible digital books to US residents with print disabilities.

Currently, established providers such as the National Library Service of the Library of Congress (NLS) and Recording for the Blind and Dyslexic (RFBandD) made a small percentage of available books in accessible formats such as Braille and audiotape. Notes Jim:

> Today less than 5 per cent of books are produced in accessible forms such as Braille or audiotape. Bookshare.org's goal is to exponentially increase the breadth and depth of digital books available to our member community. Our service objective is to provide access to each member's desired book selection at least 50 per cent of the time. Because creating accessible books is expensive, the range of materials from existing providers is quite small (Fruchterman, 2005).

The prototype/founding stage. As Jim envisioned it, the Bookshare.org initiative complemented the services of NLS and RFBandD. It did so, by focusing on providing books not offered by these two services and by offering them in a superior, easily portable text-based digital format.[4] At the time, the most common method for accessing printed books was a labor intensive scanning process. A scanner combined with optical character recognition enabled an individual to scan a book directly, with the book text then either 'spoken' aloud, or presented in Braille format. It took between two and four hours to scan an average book, presenting a significant barrier to literacy and reading enjoyment. By enabling the tens of thousands of individuals who regularly scanned books to share those materials, Bookshare.org hoped to eliminate significant duplication of effort and to create a forum for leveraging the efforts of this community. The project prototype consisted of volunteer contributions of digital or hard-copy books to create a digital library. Books were scanned and digitized on-site at Benetech and made available online through an accessible user interface. Benetech provided the initial seed investment of about $1.5 million.

Many scanned books were received from volunteers and from a cross-list of accessible books from other nonprofit sources and participating publishers. Jim drew from his experience with Arkenstone and utilized numerous speaking engagements with the Silicon Valley technology community to spread awareness about the project and garner visibility and attention in the media.

With the prototype well under way, the Bookshare.org website was created in April 2001 with a trial-user interface. In June 2002, the website went live, and was described by Jim Fruchterman as 'acting as sort of an accessible Amazon.com.' Over 1000 people were signed up by November 2002, and the project was nominated as a finalist in the Yale/Goldman Sachs Nonprofit Business Plan Competition. By mid-March 2003, the Bookshare.org initiative had made more than 12,100 books available to people with disabilities.

Funding and changing scope. By July 2003 Bookshare.org sought additional funding for venture development and growth. While the initial plan called for revenue generated from individual print-disabled user subscriptions, the team realized the need for additional funds to grow the library. Initial contributions from publishers like O'Reilly were mainly technical books, and individual user subscriptions for technical books were insufficient to sustain the project financially on an ongoing basis. Benetech applied for and received a grant from the California Community Technology Foundation. But the funds came with the requirement that Bookshare.org expand its service to Spanish books in order to qualify for funding support. In other words, the scope of the project broadened to accommodate the interests of the funders.

The project also received a $195,000 grant from the Lavelle Fund for the Blind to support the New York metro area blindness-focused outreach, and a $25,000 grant from the NEC Foundation to support learning disability issues in K-12 school programs. Thus, project members began working with universities and schools to extend the reach of Bookshare.org to disabled students. This funding resulted in broadening the scope of the project again, to accommodate the interests of these new funders.

Broadening mission, establishing legitimacy. By July 2004, about 25 per cent of the Bookshare.org operating budget came from user-subscriptions, a funding level insufficient to maintain financial sustainability. Bookshare.org entered the educational institutional market, and announced Institutional Access, a program which provided teachers of students with learning and visual disabilities, or staff at disability student services with the option to download books for their students. However, for Bookshare.org to be accepted by educational institutions, technical compatibility with the hardware-electronic readers used by the institutions was important. Bookshare.org team members focused on building strategic partnerships with leading disability-hardware manufacturers and also focused on developing a strong presence in institutional disability-access standards committees.

Venture legitimacy was also important for assembling library content. Bookshare.org gained access to philanthropic support and publisher content based on a copyright honor system. When downloading a book from Bookshare.org customers are reminded of the copyright notice with the statement, 'If you post this book on the internet, you screw the blind community. Don't do it' (Zuckerman, 2004). Benetech also developed credibility with the publishing community by removing ebooks that violated copyright requirements from the site and generally assuring publishers that it was not trying to put them out of business, but instead was trying to help the blind. By early 2005, the Bookshare.org book collection had passed the 20,000 mark, and continued to grow.

New stakeholders: Expanding the Bookshare.org platform. The success of Bookshare.org provided a platform for Benetech to start working on

Bookaccess, an international project intended to use the same technology to benefit students in the developing world, a much larger market. Jim mentioned:

> Our vision of expanding literacy and book access doesn't stop with people with disabilities. We think that electronic books are critical for disadvantaged groups such as students around the world, and are actively proposing expansions of Bookshare.org. ...We look forward to building the critical support in the author and publishing communities required to bring affordable ebooks to villages that will never be able to have a library of physical books (Fruchterman, 2004a).

While the project initially looked at universities in Angola, in May 2004, Bookaccess sought and received funding from USAID. However, this new funding narrowed Jim's vision by requiring that his team work in Iraq. Benetech started working to deliver journals, textbooks, and reference books for the departments of medicine, nursing and public health/sanitation at the University of Mosul in northern Iraq.[5]

With the Martus and Bookshare.org projects underway, the Benetech team began to consider other social ideas from the technology and social entrepreneurial communities in Silicon Valley and around the US. Among the numerous projects examined, few passed into the idea/ opportunity stage. The first of those that did was the Landmine Detector Project followed by All-Link, Project Libre, and the ReadingCam Project (see Table 11.1). By early 2005, the Benetech organization continued a process of formalization and the projects were consolidated under two divisions, Literacy and Human Rights.

Discussion

This study addresses the following research question: *How do TSVs originate, develop and grow in a resource-limited context?* Our in-depth analysis of the Benetech case confirms some of the earlier observations made in the social venture literature and, at the same time, suggests some interesting nuances and differences to technology-based social venturing.

Opportunity recognition

Our first observation highlights how Jim recognized the opportunity for Benetech and its numerous projects. The extant literature provides evidence that entrepreneurial resource endowments (for example, social relations, prior industry and startup experience) predict the discovery of technological opportunities (Shane and Stuart, 2002); and that entrepreneurs discovered and pursued those technology-based opportunities which were related to his or her prior background knowledge. Our analysis of Benetech's origins suggests that in a resource-limited social venture context, the entrepreneur's prior technical expertise and social relations were particularly important during the early stages (that is, the idea/opportunity and prototype/founding stages) of the venture.

The initial project ideas for the Martus and Bookshare.org Projects (and other projects including the Landmine Detector Project, the ReadingCam Project, All-Link, and Project Libre) were each formed by the founding team after discussion or chance-encounters with members of their social network. These included members of human rights activist groups, and technologists in Silicon Valley. Initial technical specifications for each project were also based on the technical expertise of the founding team members. This suggests that TSVs originate in a similar way to for-profit technology ventures (Shane, 2000; Shane and Stuart, 2002).

Proposition 1a: The social entrepreneur's social networks and past experience will predict sources of opportunity recognition for technology social ventures (TSVs).

However, in examining Jim Fruchterman's background, we found that his foray into SE was a direct result of his dissatisfaction with for-profit ventures' inability to address social problems. Jim, as noted earlier, became increasingly frustrated that some of the projects he wanted to pursue, those offering the greatest benefit to help people, weren't turning out to be profitable. He felt that he had to assume a missionary role to 'sell technologists on how much good technology can do in the world'. Also, more importantly, we found that Jim is what one would consider as a 'serial' entrepreneur with 'for-profit' experience, who founded three companies Calera Recognition Systems, RAF Technology and Arkenstone, before delving into SE. While extant literature has little to say about prior entrepreneurship experience and social venture startups, the Benetech case suggests that people who start technology-based social ventures are likely to be experienced entrepreneurs with considerable 'for-profit' technology experience. In other words,

Proposition 1b: Entrepreneurs who start TSVs are more likely to have prior 'for-profit' technology experience.

Investment needs and rapid growth

Another observation focuses on the investment needs for a TSV and the potential speed with which the venture might evolve and grow. Our analysis of the two main projects implemented by Benetech, Bookshare.org and Martus, indicates that each required over $1 million worth of investments, from the idea/opportunity stage to product launch. This initial investment is higher than the typical operating budget of similar service-based nonprofit organizations. For example, 62 per cent of startup nonprofit organizations (founded after 1990) in the same disability-access category as Benetech (NTEE classification code G41) had assets of less than $100,000 (NCCS, 2005). This comparison suggests that TSVs, in general, require greater initial funding outlay than other typical nonprofits.

Our observations also indicate that the two initial projects (Martus and Bookshare.org) have grown rapidly and manage to serve large constituencies relatively quickly. The Bookshare.org project, for example, has evolved from an idea in the year 2000 to a full product launch in late-2002, with a collection exceeding 20,000 books in 2004. It has also spun-off other projects such as the focused Institutional Bookshare, International Bookshare, and Bookaccess all in a relatively short time period. The Martus product, launched in early 2003, received worldwide attention and has been downloaded by users from 47 countries and used by NGOs in over ten countries. The scope of these projects is especially remarkable considering that Benetech has only 30 employees.

In contrast, traditional nonprofit ventures (those using social workers who assist various constituents) generally grow at a much slower rate given the difficulty in hiring and training workers. Often the ability to scale the services offered by ventures is directly proportional to the amount of funding required to hire and train additional workers to support the growth. It appears that technology-based ventures offer greater ability to expand more rapidly. Often, it is creating the original unit that incurs the majority of the cost of a technology-based product: every additional unit has relatively low costs. This ability to replicate, often with high margin returns, conforms well to the goal of social enterprise, which is to maximize social impact whilst breaking even financially and reaching sustainability. In other words, TSVs may require greater initial funding, but can be replicated (across projects and regions) at a faster rate and with less expense than traditional social ventures. These observations suggest the following proposition:

Proposition 2: TSVs, in general, will grow at a faster rate with fewer resources than traditional social ventures and reach a greater number of people.

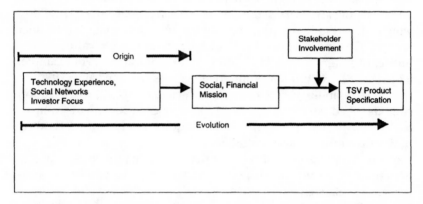

Figure 11.2   Emerging propositions from Benetech case: factors affecting TSV origin and evolution

TSV evolution: emphasis on legitimacy

Social enterprises operate in market transactions that rely on legitimacy gained through reputation and trust. Benetech's projects, especially after product launch, operate in environments that rely heavily on reputation and trust. Martus, for example, as a project designed to document sensitive human rights information, is only viable in a trust-based environment. Social workers will only use an encryption-based program if they trust that the information cannot be used indiscriminately by a third party. Martus designers were acutely aware of this and wrote the human rights program in nonproprietary open source software to allow users to verify the security and privacy of their human rights information.

The emphasis on product reputation is also seen on the Bookshare.org website which maintains a character recognition quality log for each digital book to allow customers to verify the quality, accessibility and interoperability of digital book formats. Product legitimacy was also important for assembling library content. Volunteer contributions of books were essential in getting the digital library started. Bookshare.org gained access to philanthropic support based on a copyright honor system. The copyright notice reminding people that irresponsibly posting Bookshare.org content would hurt the blind community, is a strong visual reminder of the importance of maintaining legitimacy in a TSV.

Proposition 3a: TSVs will emphasize trust and legitimacy during product launch.

Social enterprises take care to defer to social authority and to maintain their reputation in order to ensure that their financial interests do not alter their nonprofit social nature (Hansmann, 1980; O'Regan and Oster, 2000). As the TSV grows, resource constraints force the venture to search for additional sources of funding, which in turn requires that it demonstrate product legitimacy to the new funders. For example, the shift to providing institutional access meant that Bookshare.org would require large volumes of library content, only accessible from publishers. Gaining access to this content required a constant emphasis on legitimacy to demonstrate that Bookshare.org was not a threat to publishers. Bookshare.org developed credibility with the publishing community by removing ebooks that violated copyright requirements from the site. Bookshare.org also implemented a strong digital rights management system to assure publishers that the project was not trying to put them out of business but instead was trying to help only the print-disabled communities.

Proposition 3b: As the TSV grows, addition of new funders will increase the emphasis on product legitimacy.

TSV evolution: Social mission and stakeholder effects

As Benetech projects moved from the idea/opportunity stage through the postlaunch funding and growth stages, new stakeholders came on board. Stakeholders included additional investors, interested third party nonprofit and corporate organizations and customers. These stakeholders appeared to reshape the mission and identity of the Benetech projects. Bookshare.org was encouraged to expand the scope of its mission through funding received from the Lavelle Foundation (for New York), NEC (for schools) and the California Community Technology Foundation (for Spanish books).

   As Bookshare.org passed into the growth stage, the founding team decided to create Bookaccess, a more ambitious literacy project targeted at developing parts of the world. The initial aim of Bookaccess was to reach university students in Angola. However, restricted funding was received from USAID a government agency to develop a digital book project for Iraq and not Angola. The first field implementation of Bookaccess was conducted in Iraq, at the University of Mosul.

The effect of the environment and stakeholder involvement is also illustrated in the Martus project. During the prelaunch phase the mission of the Martus project was specifically defined in terms of the reporting and communication of human rights abuses. While the initial prototype was focused on the area of human rights, field tests and market feedback during the postlaunch phase expanded the project scope to a broader range of applications including election monitoring, human trafficking, and environmental abuse (WAC, 2004). Widespread acceptance and use of the developed product led to increased visibility in previously overlooked stakeholder environments – women's rights groups and gay and lesbian groups. The strategic orientation of the project broadened to encompass a wide range of social justice projects to meet many needs across the nonprofit sector. Philanthropic sources of support broadened to include The Open Society Institute, The MacArthur Foundation, The Asia Foundation and the US Department of State.

The resource-constrained environment in which a TSV operates, encourages the venture to continuously seek additional sources of funding. Limited grants for targeted activities require that the social venture continuously tailor its mission as new funders come on board. Increasing visibility within the community also brings in the support of other stakeholders including third party nonprofits (for example, Martus and the Asia Foundation) and corporate partners (such as NEC). As illustrated in Figure 11.3, the identity and mission of the social venture gets continuously reshaped as new funds are injected and new stakeholders come on board.

Proposition 4: As the TSV evolves from the idea/opportunity stage to the venture growth stage new stakeholders reshape the identity and mission of the social venture.

We summarize below the emerging propositions on the origin and evolution of TSVs. At origin, during the idea/opportunity and prototype/founding stage, technology experience, social networks and investor (grant-maker) focus are important factors in determining sources of opportunity. As the project evolves, secures additional funding and

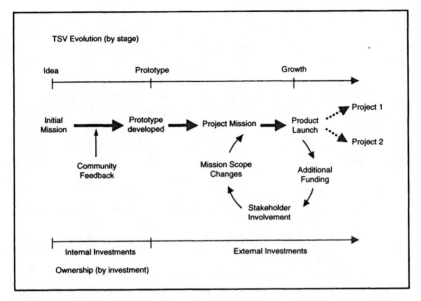

Figure 11.3 Emerging propositions: effects of TSV evolution and ownership on project mission and scope

starts to grow, venture legitimacy and the investment/grant duration play an important role as new stakeholders reshape the identity and mission of the social venture.

Conclusion

The purpose of this study was to gain a better understanding of TSVs, an area that falls at the intersection of two fields – SE and technology innovation. TSVs represent startup ventures that develop and deploy technologies to address social needs in a financially sustainable manner. While the TSV has received considerable practitioner interest there has been little research at the intersection of technology and SE. We used Benetech, an exemplar TSV, as a case to chart the evolution of a TSV.

This study leads toward some interesting implications for future research on the differences between the venture development process in TSVs and conventional for-profit ventures. Opportunity recognition is contingent on founder background and social networks. However for-profit technology experience appears to play an important role in developing a TSV. Compared to traditional social ventures, TSVs require higher initial investment, but appear to grow faster and reach more people. While operating aspects of a TSV are uncertain, these ventures typically differ from high-tech startups, in that they adopt developed technologies with the intent of minimizing technical uncertainty and maximizing social return. The uncertainty in the product development process for a social venture then lies in interaction with the sociopolitical dynamic – the activist, philanthropic and volunteer communities. The mission of the social venture evolves as new stakeholders play important roles in the resource-constrained social venture environment.

Notes

1. Social authority represents the communities, voluntary organizations and corporations, which operate in the same field as the focal venture. Public authority refers to regulatory government organizations that represent and aim to protect and promote public welfare, while financial markets represent the economic authority.
2. Mair and Noboa define perceived venture desirability as the attractiveness of generating the entrepreneurial event (such as forming a company), and posit that it is affected by empathy and moral judgment; factors that help characterize the entrepreneur. Perceived venture feasibility is the degree to which one believes that he or she is personally capable of forming such a company, and this they posit is facilitated by social support and self-efficacy beliefs, factors normally attributed to the environment.
3. Print disabilities may be defined as the inability to read print materials due to vision, physical or cognitive disabilities.
4. The digitization employed the open source Braille reading format (BRF) and DAISY formats, which allowed book marking and the conversion of text into the user's preferred format (for example large print, speech, Braille).
5. A pilot project in Iraq was designed as a test-bed to serve underserved communities, partner libraries, universities, and community centers around the world, in accordance with the potential for nonprofit licensing. However, by late 2004 the project was impacted significantly by the escalating violence in Iraq. In order to meet the goals proposed in the original proposal of Bookaccess, Benetech shipped 3000 pounds of books in a shipping container from various publishers around the US to Iraq. The project moved beyond developing software and into logistics, customs brokerage, shipping, and labeling – areas outside Benetech's expertise. The director of the Bookaccess program mentioned that the project would not continue, but from an international standpoint she believed that Benetech had learned a great deal about the different laws in each country (Carter, 2005).

References

Agarawal, R., Echambadi, R., Franco, A. M. and Sarkar, M. B. 2004. Knowledge transfer through inheritance: Spin-out generation, development, and survival. *Academy of Management Journal*, **47**(4): 501–22.

Ahuja, G. and Katila, R. 2001. Technological acquisitions and the innovation performance of acquiring firms: A longitudinal study. *Strategic Management Journal*, 22(3): 197–220.

Ahuja, G. and Lampert, C. M. 2001. Entrepreneurship in the large corporation: A longitudinal study of how established firms create breakthrough innovations. *Strategic Management Journal*, 22(3): 521–43.

Benetech. 2004. http://www.benetech.org.

Bettis, R. A. and Hitt, M. A. 1995. The new competitive landscape. *Strategic Management Journal*, 16(Special Summer Issue): 7–19.

Boschee, J. 1995. Social entrepreneurship. *Across the Board*, 32(3): 20–4.

Brinckerhoff, P. C. 2000. *Social entrepreneurship: The art of mission-based venture development*. New York: John Wiley and Sons.

Carter, J. 2005. Interview with Janice Carter, Director of Benetech's Literacy Program. 14 May 2005.

Casas, C., Lajoie, W. and Prahalad, C. K. 2003. Voxiva. University of Michigan Business School. Available: http://www.bus.umich.edu/BottomOfThePyramid/xMAP2003.htm.

Christensen, C. and Bower, J. 1996. Customer power, strategic investment, and the failure of leading firms. *Strategic Management Journal*, 17(3): 197–218.

Cohen, W. M. and Levinthal, D. A. 1990. Absorptive capacity: A new perspective on learning and innovation. *Administrative Science Quarterly*, 35: 569–96.

Dees, J. G. 1998. Enterprising nonprofits. *Harvard Business Review*, 76(1): 54–66.

Dosi, G. 1988. Sources, procedures, and microeconomic effects of innovation. *Journal of Economic Literature*, 6(3): 1120–71.

Drayton, W. 2002. The citizen sector: Becoming as entrepreneurial and competitive as business. *California Management Review*, 44(3): 120–32.

Drucker, P. F. 1989. What business can learn from nonprofits. *Harvard Business Review*, 67(4): 88–93.

Eisenhardt, K. M. 1989. Building theories from case study research. *Academy of Management Review*, 14: 532–50.

Fruchterman, J. 2001. President's update. Available http://www.benetech.org/about/presup_jul2001.shtml. Accessed 13 June 2005.

Fruchterman, J. 2002. President's update. Available: http://www.benetech.org/about/presup_jan2002.shtml. Accessed 13 June 2005.

Fruchterman, J. 2004a. President's update. Available: http://www.benetech.org/about/presup_may2004.shtml. Accessed 13 June 2005.

Fruchterman, J. 2004b. Technology benefiting humanity. Ubiquity, association for computing machinery 5(5). Available: http://www.acm.org/ubiquity/views/v5i5_fruchterman.html. Accessed 13 June 2005.

Fruchterman, J. 2005. Interview with authors, April.

Hansmann, H. 1980. The role of nonprofit enterprise. *Yale Law Journal*, 89: 835–901.

Henderson, R. and Clark, K. 1990. Architectural innovation: The reconfiguration of existing product technologies and the failure of established firms. *Administrative Science Quarterly*, 35: 9–30.

Hillberry, R. 2004. From Smart Bombs to Reading Machines. *Caltech News*, 36(3). Available: http://pr.caltech.edu/periodicals/CaltechNews/archive.html.

Hockerts, K. 2004. Bootstrapping social change – towards an evolutionary theory of social entrepreneurship. Working Paper, INSEAD, Fontainebleau.

Kanter, R. M. 1999. From spare change to real change: The social sector as a beta site for business innovation. *Harvard Business Review*, 77(3): 123–32.

Kotha, S. 1998. Competing on the internet: How Amazon.com is rewriting the rules of competition. *Advances in Strategic Management*, 15: 239–65.

Leadbeater, C. 1997. *The Rise of the Social Entrepreneur*. London: Demos.

Lee, T. W. 1998. *Using qualitative methods in organizational research*. Thousand Oaks, CA: Sage Publications.

Leonard-Barton, D. 1992. Core capabilities and core rigidities: A paradox in managing new product development. *Strategic Management Journal*, 13: 111–24.

Mair, J. and Martí, I. 2004. Social entrepreneurship: What are we talking about? A framework for future research. Working Paper 546. IESE Business School, University of Navarra, Barcelona.

Mair, J. and Noboa, E. 2003a. The emergence of social enterprises and their place in the new organizational landscape. Working Paper 523. IESE Business School, University of Navarra, Barcelona.

Mair, J. and Noboa, E. 2003b. Social entrepreneurship: How intentions to create a social enterprise get formed. Working Paper 521. IESE Business School, University of Navarra, Barcelona.

Miles, M. B. and Huberman, A. M. 1994. *Qualitative Data Analysis*. Beverly Hills, CA: Sage Publications.

Moore, G. 1991. *Crossing the chasm: Marketing and selling high-tech products to mainstream customers*. New York, NY: HarperBusiness.

NCCS. 2005. National Center for Charitable Statistics. Information available: http://nccsdataweb.urban.org/NCCS. Accessed 13 June 2005.

Nelson, R. R. and Winter, S. G. 1982. *An evolutionary theory of economic change*. Cambridge MA: Belknap Press of Harvard University Press.

O'Regan, K. and Oster, S. M. 2000. Nonprofit and for-profit partnerships: Rationale and challenges of cross-sector contracting. *Nonprofit and Voluntary Sector Quarterly*, 29(1): 120–40.

Pettigrew, A. M. 1990. Longitudinal field research on change: Theory and practice. *Organization Science*, 1(3): 267–92.

Prahalad, C. K. 2005. *The fortune at the bottom of the pyramid: Eradicating poverty through profits*. Upper Saddle River, NJ: Wharton School Publishing.

Rindova, V. and Kotha, S. 2001. Continuous morphing: Competing through dynamic capabilities, form and function. *Academy of Management Journal*, 44(6): 1263–80.

Schumpeter, J. A. 1934. *Theory of economic development: An inquiry into profits, capital, credit, interest, and the business cycle*. New York: Oxford University Press.

Shane, S. 2000. Prior knowledge and the discovery of entrepreneurial opportunities. *Organization Science*, 11(4): 448–69.

Shane, S. and Stuart, T. 2002. Organizational endowments and the performance of university start-ups. *Management Science*, 48: 154–70.

Shane, S. and Venkataraman, S. 2000. The promise of entrepreneurship as a field of research. *Academy of Management Review*, 25(1): 217–27.

Shaw, E. and Carter, S. 2004. Social entrepreneurship: Theoretical antecedents and empirical analysis of entrepreneurial processes and outcomes. Paper presented at 24th Babson-Kauffman Entrepreneurship Conference, Glasgow.

Skloot, E. 2002. Evolution or extinction? A strategy for nonprofits in the marketplace. *Nonprofit and Voluntary Sector Quarterly*, 29(2): 315–24.

Tsoukas, H. 1989. The epistemological status of idiographic research in the comparative study of organizations: A realist perspective. *Academy of Management Review*, 14(4): 551–61.

UNDP. 2001. *United Nations Development Report 2001*. Available: http://www.undp.org/hdr2001. Accessed 13 June 2005.

Utterback, J. M. 1994. Radical innovation and corporate regeneration. *Research Technology Management*, 37(4): 10.

Venkataraman, S. 1997. The distinctive domain of entrepreneurship research: An editor's perspective. In J. Katz and R. Brockhaus (eds), *Advances in entrepreneurship, firm emergence, and growth*. Greenwich: JAI Press.

WAC. 2004. Innovating information technologies to protect human rights. World Affairs Council of Northern California, February 2004, audio presentation. Available: http://wacsf.vportal.net/?fileid=3356.

Whetten, D. A. 1989. What constitutes a theoretical contribution? *Academy of Management Review*, 14(4): 490–5.

Yin, R. K. 1994. *Case Study Research: Design and Methods*. Newbury Park, CA: Sage Publications.

Zuckerman, E. 2004. Jim Fruchterman's talk at the Berkman Center, Harvard University. Blog. Available: http://blogs.law.harvard.edu/ethan/2004/09/03#a320.

12
Social Enterprise: Beyond Economic Outcomes and Individual Returns

Helen Haugh

Introduction

The study reported in this chapter examines the outcomes and impact of social entrepreneurship (SE). The extent of entrepreneurial activity in an economy can be measured in terms of antecedents (contextual factors associated with entrepreneurship), process (the extent of opportunity spotting and resource acquisition) and outcomes.

Traditionally, entrepreneurial outcomes have been studied from the perspective of financial performance and firm survival (Ucbasaran, Westhead and Wright, 2001). This emphasis – on objective financial and economic outcomes (Birley and Westhead, 1990; Chandler and Hanks, 1993) – fails to acknowledge the social and/or environmental gains that accrue from enterprising behavior. In addition, the impact of entrepreneurship is usually studied at individual, local, regional or macroeconomic level and few studies investigate multiple level impacts.

This chapter examines these issues by presenting the findings from a qualitative, longitudinal study of six social enterprises. First, the nature of entrepreneurial outcomes is considered. Next, the rural context of the study, the social enterprises, and their role in economic and social regeneration are presented. These are brought together in a theoretical classification of entrepreneurial outcomes, which is followed by an account of the methodology of the study and the presentation of results. The conclusion proposes the development of an outcomes indicator to record and monitor the multiple outcomes and impact of SE.

Outcomes of the entrepreneurial process

An entrepreneurial outcome is a desired level of activity (Todd and Ramanathan, 1993) or performance (Jenkins and Johnson, 1997), which specifies the intended effects (Buckmaster, 1999), achievements or consequences of supplying a service to targeted recipients (Wang, 2002). Outcomes therefore differ from output, which is the direct product made or service delivered. Outcome measures are useful internally (for monitoring and control purposes), and externally (for accountability, image management, developing trust and building and retaining confidence). Although different enterprises with different strategies require different information for assessing outcomes (Eccles, 1991), some common denominators are useful to benchmark performance among organizations.

When assessing firm performance, an emphasis on financial and economic outcomes (Birley and Westhead, 1990; Chandler and Hanks, 1993; Cooper, 1993) has the advantage of providing objective measures. These measures can be found in national entrepreneurship data (see for example http://www.gemconsortium.org), as well as surveys of social enterprise activity (Ecotec, 2002). Although perceived to be valid, reliable and comparable (Eccles, 1991), such measures tend to adopt a narrow view of outcomes. They often overlook indirect economic outcomes, such as improved employability; social outcomes, such as increases in perceived confidence, independence and empowerment; and environmental outcomes, such as improving the physical infrastructure. An individualistic, economic perspective tends to make collective entrepreneurship involving more than one person peripheral (Holmquist, 2003) and neglects the noneconomic outcomes that have the potential to transform society (Lindgren and Packendorff, 2003).

In addition, the impact of entrepreneurship tends to be studied narrowly, usually in relation to a single target group (the individual, local economy, regional or macroeconomic level) with few studies investigating multiple level impacts (Malecki, 1994). At the level of the individual, the outcomes of entrepreneurship have been categorized as extrinsic (wealth) or intrinsic (independence, autonomy, recognition, challenge, excitement and growth) (Bird, 1989; Kuratko, Hornsby and Naffziger, 1997).

While new enterprises have a direct economic impact on the individual (entrepreneur or employee/s) by providing income, they also have indirect economic effects, such as skills training to improve employability.

Furthermore, entrepreneurship generates individual noneconomic benefits such as fulfilling a need for achievement (McClelland, 1987), control (Busenitz and Lau, 1996), independence (Boyd and Gumpert, 1983; Birch, 1986; Bird, 1989) and the opportunity to participate in formal and informal social networks (Johannisson and Nilsson, 1989).

In this chapter, outcomes such as those above are labeled social outcomes. Although more difficult to quantify (Lyon et al., 2002), social outcomes are seen as an important by-product of entrepreneurship. Encouraging entrepreneurship has been found to help restore a philosophy of self-help (Johnson, 1998), generate social capital (Dhesi, 2000) and promote empowerment, independence and skills development (Dumas, 2001).

At the level of the organization, social outcomes arise from the establishment of the cultural identity of the firm, the opportunities for social interaction generated by the new venture, the creation of new organizational networks and the formation of interorganizational trust. In addition, the establishment of a physical base from which to run the enterprise has the potential to make a positive environmental contribution to the community and region in which it is based.

Another way in which entrepreneurship contributes to local economic development is through the addition of new enterprises to the economy, employment (Birch, 1979), incomes growth and increases in tax revenue. Indirect economic outcomes include raised skill levels of the local population and the increased circulation of money locally. Social benefits accrue in terms of improvement in the supply of, and hence access to, goods and services for local residents (OECD, 2003) and businesses (Lyon et al., 2002). The creation of new enterprises also plays a role in demonstrating motivation effects (OECD, 2003): exposing people to examples of enterprise, building trust-based networks within communities through collaboration, increasing the amount of interaction and transactions in a community (Flora, 1998) and empowering the community to exert greater levels of self-determination and control (Amin, Cameron and Hudson, 2002).

In a study of microenterprise in South Africa, Gibb and Adhikary (2000) found that the collective action associated with enterprise development added value to society through the strengthening of networks, which in turn generated benefits to individual network members. The positive relationship between local capitalism and beneficial local socioeconomic outcomes is supported by Tolbert, Lyson and Irwin (1998) and Human and Provan (1997).

At the regional level, impact studies to assess the outcomes of entre-preneurship have tended to use indicators such as jobs created and increases in business income and turnover. Wider impacts include the provision of goods and services, increases in regional money flows, savings in public expenditure, benefits to supply chains and building social capital.

The rural economy and social enterprise

The context of this study is the peripheral, rural region of north-east Scotland that covers an area of approximately 6313 sq km. It has 250 km of coastline and a population of 226,940.

Although the definition of 'rural' remains contested (Halfacree, 1993), common perceptions associate it with low population density and spatial isolation (Butler Flora and Flora, 1993). It also suggests a stable, natural environment with close community ties to a locality (McInerney, 1996). The rural economy is made up of interacting spheres of social, economic, cultural and political activity (Allanson et al., 1995). In a postproductivist countryside, the economic subsystem is characterized by high unemployment rates, falling farm populations and declining rural services (Keeble et al., 1992). The impact on the local economy of falling expenditure in rural businesses and popula-tion out-migration to urban areas (where employment opportunities are enhanced), has been a sustained decline in living standards for the rural poor.

Stimulating the creation of new enterprises can help tackle economic decline in rural areas (Lin, Buss and Popovich, 1990; D'Arcy and Guissani, 1996; Lyons, 2002) but is hampered by inaccessibility, poor communication, infrastructures and business services, and a shortage of human resources (OECD, 1998). These conditions combine to make the environmental context unattractive to entrepreneurs: it may simply be impossible for a for-profit business to be financially sustain-able. Nevertheless, those living in rural communities require goods and services and an alternative means of providing them needs to be found. In the UK, social, community and voluntary organizations have emerged to fill some of the market gaps.

Social enterprise is a collective term for a range of organizations that trade for a social purpose (DTI, 2002). They adopt one of a variety of different legal formats but have in common the principles of pursuing business-led solutions to achieve social aims, and the reinvestment of surplus for community benefit. Their objectives focus on socially desired, nonfinancial goals and their outcomes are the nonfinancial measures of the implied demand for and supply of services (Todd and Ramanathan, 1993). A decrease in rural transport, for instance, implies an increase in demand for community transport, and an increase in unemployment implies an increase in demand for intermediate labor market programs.

Community enterprises are a specific category of social enterprise that involve local people with local knowledge in the creation and management of sustainable, nonprofit enterprises that are accountable to their local community. In line with a community-based (Bowler and Lewis, 1991) or bottom-up (Scottish Office, 1995; Meyer-Stamer, 1997; Gibb and Adhikary, 2000) approach to development, community enterprises rely on the involvement of local people (as volunteers/ employees/trustees) for their creation, management and governance. They bring together deep local knowledge (which is used to identify product/service gaps in the community and acquire resources) with strong interpersonal ties (which help to create community-led solutions to local market failure).

The role of local people, however, extends beyond participation in the creation and management of the community enterprise to include identifying unmet needs, developing a means of satisfying those needs and maintaining accountability to multiple stakeholders. Many social enterprises rely on a combination of different sources of funds – such as grants, donations and earned revenue (Bank of England, 2003) – and each source requires an account of the effectiveness of its expenditure (Volkmann, 1999). In this way community enterprises are led by, accountable to and embedded in the values of the community they serve. They are underpinned by the belief that local community members are 'best placed to identify their own needs and solutions to them' (DoE/MAFF, 1995: 16), and that they should create their own strategies and action plans to deal with them (Bryden and Bollman, 2000). They embody the four values of community roots, community accountability, community benefit and community ownership of wealth and assets (Pearce, 1993).

While the encouragement of endogenous enterprise creation through community-based economic development is not new in rural communities (Lyons, 2002), in thin markets where economies of scale are hard to achieve, lack of resources, single industry dominance and a limited flow of entrepreneurial ideas create a sparse or difficult environment (Malecki, 1994). Although these factors have been found to limit the success of rural enterprise development programs (Lichtenstein and Lyons, 2001), the capacity of rural communities to respond to downward economic pressure by developing new sources of income and employment has been noted by Bryden and Bollman (2000). The contribution of this chapter is to examine the outcomes and impacts of rural community enterprises.

Classification of enterpreneurial outcomes

Few enterprises have escaped the need to establish outcome measures to communicate their effectiveness (Plantz, Greenway and Hendricks, 1997; Kendall and Knapp, 2000) and accountability to key stakeholder groups (Buckmaster, 1999). Interest is likely to increase as consumers and investors put pressure on for-profit organizations to consider the impact they have on the local communities where they operate and to ensure their impact is beneficial (Dennis, Neck and Goldsby, 1998; Reis and Clohesy, 2001).

Outcome measures are useful internally, to monitor and control business operations, and externally, to communicate and enhance the image of the organization in its community, to help identify partners for collaboration and to recruit talented staff and volunteers (Volkman, 1999). Typical measures of business outcomes include revenue, profitability, the introduction of new services and number of customers (Keldenberg and Gobeli, 1995); sales, profit and number of retail outlets (Jenkins and Johnson, 1997); and customer satisfaction, quality, market share, human resources and perceived value of goods (Eccles, 1991).

While financial and economic outcomes may have the appearance of validity, reliability and comparability, to ignore direct social and environmental, and indirect economic, social and environmental outcomes, is to underplay the wider contribution of entrepreneurship to society. Although the employment effect of social enterprises and community development initiatives remains small, their social impact – for example, assisting the excluded to become integrated into society and creating a nonmarket mechanism for meeting local needs – is of equal, if not greater, importance (Stohr, 1990).

Indigenous local development strategies may be better placed than top-down initiatives to capitalize on diverse local resources and commodify tangible and intangible local assets (Bryden and Munro, 2000). The community takes responsibility for its own economic and social regeneration (Herlau and Tetzschner, 1994) and important economic and noneconomic contributions to the community/locality (Flora

Table 12.1 Beyond direct economic outcomes

	Economic outcomes	Social outcomes	Environmental outcomes
Direct	• Number of new legal enterprises created • Number of jobs created • Number of socially-useful jobs created • Turnover from: trading service agreement contracts • Nontrading income: grants loans donations other • Tax revenue	• Supply of services to the community • Improved access to services • Improved quality of life • Contribution to social capital	• Improved appearance of physical environment • Reduction in unrecycled waste products • Contribution to local environmental capital
Indirect	• Raised skills of the local population to improve employment prospects • Increased innovation and creativity • Increased employment opportunities in other organizations (suppliers, catering and accommodation) • Increased money flows within community from: residents nonresidents	• Increases in level of: individual confidence independence satisfaction with life extent of personal networks productive use of free time personal development perceived self-esteem motivation enthusiasm teamworking skills	• Increased attractiveness of the region • Improved environmental context • Contribution to sustainability agenda • Contribution to regional environmental capital

Table 12.1 Beyond direct economic outcomes – *continued*

Economic outcomes	Social outcomes	Environmental outcomes
	• Increased perception of involvement in community activities • Increased awareness of community assets • Perception of increased community empowerment, control • Contribution to community vibrancy	

et al., 1992; Laukkenan and Niittykangas, 2003) can be generated. Outcomes such as increasing democracy, generating a sense of community and improving the business climate and community vitality are, however, notoriously difficult to measure. Although social accounting (Pearce, 2001; Dawson, 1998) would enumerate some of the more direct social impacts, less direct and longer term impacts may simply remain undocumented.

The tendency to date has been to prioritize economic outcomes ahead of noneconomic outcomes. This is illustrated by the ranking of outcomes of enterprise development programs as first order (employment), and second and third order (economic literacy, time management, budgeting and success in the mainstream labor market) (Servon and Doshna, 2000). It is increasingly important to capture data about the multiplicity of outcomes and impacts of entrepreneurship however, since 'what gets measured gets attention' (Eccles, 1991: 31). See Table 12.1.

Methodology

The aim of the research is to examine the origins, strategy and outcomes of social enterprise in the rural economy, drawing on data from case studies located in two administrative regions in north-east Scotland. Region A is 617 sq km, with 10 established villages/towns and many scattered farms and settlements and a population of 35,742. Since 1971, it has suffered a 27 per cent fall in provision of key facilities and is eligible for European Union (EU) structural funding (Objective 2) due to its high dependency on traditional economic sectors. Region B is 587 sq km with a population of 39,160, dispersed across 15 established villages/towns. It has suffered a 26 per cent decline in provision of key facilities since 1981 and part of Region B also benefits from EU Objective 2 funding, intended to facilitate the general development of rural areas and to reduce disparities between the region and the wider UK and European economies.

This area was chosen as a study site because of its history of successive blows to the rural economy (such as the decline in fishing and farming industries and the closure of major employers) and its low rate of business startup. Market failure could possibly be anticipated and alternative forms of economic activity might be present.

The current lack of academic research into social and community enterprises and the consequent dearth of theory about them led to the decision to adopt an exploratory, inductive, case study approach (Yin,

1994). Following Eisenhardt (1989), the aim was to build theory from a small number of case study organizations, using the interpretations, meanings and understandings gathered from individuals involved and associated with the case study organizations in their naturalistic setting.

In an extended attachment to the field, the author gathered data from multiple sources to create a holistic account of each community enterprise, the people it served and the region in which it was based. At the start of the study, the decision was made to collect longitudinal data – since each organization was small and still in the process of development, this would allow time for the outcomes and impacts to emerge.

Initially, through a local authority contact of the author, an economic development executive responsible for Regions A and B was approached for an interview. The aims of the research were explained and the interviewee was invited to identify organizations that could be considered good examples of social/community enterprise, and to seek an introduction to these organizations. This technique employs reputational sampling (Scott, 1991) in which case selection is based on reputation, allowing other aspects to emerge rather than be predefined. The initial interview identified two different organizations in two separate communities that might be suitable and the author was given contact details to pursue.

Entry to the field through an individual already connected to the fieldwork site was considered necessary since many small, relatively isolated and closed communities populate the region. Over a period of three months, frequent visits by the author to social, cultural and business events in the two communities helped to establish field relationships, gain trust and create direct, personal access to both communities. This led to the recruitment and commitment of six fledgling community enterprises to the study, code-named Transport, Web, Tourism, Care, Marina and Sport.

The study used in-depth interviewing with multiple informants from each enterprise as the principal research method. Interviews were conducted with the chief executive, volunteers, employees, trustees and community stakeholders from each community. The process of selecting informants followed the principles of theoretical sampling (Strauss and Corbin, 1998) such that each would contribute information to the developing theory. The in-depth interviews have been employed to elicit an authentic account of an individual's interpretation of events (Silverman, 2001). Informants were asked to relate, from their perspective, the origins and development of the enterprise they were involved with: to talk about its purpose, structure, funding, marketing, membership and extent of community participation. They were also asked to describe critical incidents, problems and difficulties that had been encountered in the life of the enterprise.

During the three-year study period, the author returned to the field to collect data from informants approximately every six months. After the first round of interviews, informants were asked to talk about the development of the enterprise since the previous interview, describing critical incidents and events at organizational, community and regional level. Throughout the study, in-depth interviews were also conducted with economic and community development coordinators responsible for the wider region, local authority employees responsible for regenerating fishing communities and elected councilors from each community.

A contact summary sheet was completed for every informant. Interviews that had been recorded were transcribed within 24 hours to reduce data loss. Where permission for recording was refused (due to sensitive content), or was impracticable (due to inappropriate venue or background noise) field notes were made as soon as possible after the interview.

The in-depth interviews were supplemented by participant observation by the author at site visits, community development meetings, community feedback events and social functions and festivals typical of the region. Participant observation enabled conversations as informal interviews and the frequent appearance of the author at community events led to the creation of a dense network of informants from each community and across the region. Detailed field notes were written after each period of observation.

Data was also collected from secondary sources, including census information, publications pertaining to the communities and regions, and descriptive material developed by each community enterprise. Both print and web-based information were accessed.

The textual data (interview transcriptions, handwritten field notes and printed media) were systematically analyzed for themes and references to outcomes and impacts. The analytical themes for each enterprise and community were noted and coded on a series of index cards, onto which additional details and cross-references, arising from within-case and cross-case analyses, were subsequently added. This led to the isolation of the data into distinct groups of outcomes and impacts. The process described is in line with qualitative data analysis proscribed by

Table 12.2 Summary of case study organizations

	CE1	CE2	CE 3	CE4	CE5	CE6
Description	Transport Enterprise	Web Enterprise	Tourism Enterprise	Care Enterprise	Marina Enterprise	Sport Enterprise
Location	Rural	Rural	Rural	Coastal	Coastal	Coastal
Aims	To provide door-to-door transport services for elderly and disabled people in local community	To provide an on-line community information service via website To provide IT training services for local people and businesses	To create a tourist attraction based on a local, historic artifact	To provide day care, education and training services for people with learning difficulties To create a tourist attraction based around local craft enterprises	To create a leisure marina and let berths at a commercial rate	To create a tourism and activity center based on local sports and crafts
Date started	1997	1998	1989	1998	1999	1998
Revenue potential	Low: nominal charge for users	Break even potential: nominal charge for local users; commercial rate for others	Short term – Low: charge made for publications Longer term – High: planned study and activity center	Break even potential: revenue from users of day care center facilities paid by local authority Rental income	Break even potential: from marina revenue	Low: project later abandoned due to lack of market potential
Economic outcomes	Job creation Expenditure in local facilities	Revenue generated from commercial work Revenue generated from tourists who have used the website	Revenue from tourists attracted to area	Fees for day care usage Revenue from visitors to craft center	Revenue from berth charges Revenue from tourists and visitors to Marina and local village	Projected accommodation and training charges for users Projected expenditure in local businesses

Table 12.2 Summary of case study organizations – *continued*

	CE1	CE2	CE 3	CE4	CE5	CE6
Noneconomic outcomes	Increased access to local facilities Increased independence for users	Circulation of information about local events and opportunities Increased competence in IT skills	Increased awareness of local cultural history Increased confidence from participation in project work	Modernization of old building Development of useful life skills for day care center users Increased confidence from enhanced employment prospects	Modernization of marina infrastructure Increased sense of prosperity due to number of visitors to Marina and village	Modernization of old building Anticipated utilization of a currently derelict building Community enthusiasm and confidence from project involvement

Glaser and Strauss (1967), Miles and Huberman (1994), Yin (1994), and Denzin and Lincoln (1998). The use of multiple sources allowed data triangulation (Denzin, 1978). The framework of outcomes and impacts began to take shape after the third round of interviews (approximately 18 months into the study). Subsequent data collection and analysis used an iterative process to strengthen the robustness of the categories.

In accordance with the nature of qualitative research and the small number of case studies, the findings create a rich description of the fieldwork without claiming to be representative of rural community enterprises more generally. The purpose of qualitative research is to develop a deep understanding of an issue from the informant's perspective ['verstehen'] from which theorizing can take place. A summary of each case study enterprise and its main outcomes is presented in Table 12.2.

Direct and indirect outcomes

The direct economic outcomes that arose from data analysis and categorization were: the establishment of an organization with a distinct legal identity; the income received; and the employment opportunities created. All six ventures adopted a recognized legal format: either a trust, or a company limited by guarantee/shares of £1. Thus, from six community enterprises examples of three legal entities were found. In all six case studies, income had been generated from external sources (grants, donations and revenue). At different times in the study, each enterprise had recruited at least one employee and by the end of the study, three had long term employment contracts with at least one employee. Thus, each venture had generated measurable, direct economic outcomes. Refer to Table 12.2.

In addition, each community enterprise had generated indirect economic outcomes. Income had been deployed to pay employees, purchase assets, attract business investment and host events that would bring visitors to the area. All employees were recruited locally, thereby increasing the likelihood that wages would be kept within the community and spent in local businesses. Whenever possible, assets were purchased locally – for Tourism, Care, Marina and Sport, this was integral to the process, since a proportion of funds had been raised specifically to purchase buildings/land for development in the community. Transport and Web had to obtain some assets (vehicles and information technology equipment) from organizations outside the community due to lack of availability, but purchased fuel, stationery and other requirements from local suppliers.

The Tourism Enterprise attracted national and international visitors, who contribute to local development by buying local goods and services, while Web and Care earned income from other businesses: Web marketed IT and web design services to other business clients; and Care earned rental income from its premises. These types of activities bring money into the community that is then circulated in the local economy through the payment of wages and other expenditure.

> But really, at the end of the day, we are all working to the same objective... which is to attract visitors, to try to create jobs and at the same time make people aware of the history within the area.
> I5, Tourism Enterprise.

> ... Apart from the training function, we are going to be creating jobs, with the craft workers, we are going to be able to let them earn money for themselves, start up their own small business... we are going to create an additional tourist attraction in the area which is needed.
> I1, Care Enterprise.

Although economic outcomes are the performance measure against which entrepreneurship is often assessed, they do not address the social and/or environmental purpose(s) which social enterprises are created to pursue. Informants referred to the following social outcomes: reducing social exclusion and enhancing integration through the delivery of transport services, IT training, education, leisure facilities, day care for disabled people and sport facilities for the community. The Transport Enterprise, for example, reduced social exclusion by providing access to healthcare services: patients were taken to medical centers in other villages, towns and cities, and elderly and disabled residents were taken on social outings. Web Enterprise enhanced integration by providing training to improve the education and life skills of local people, improving the employment prospects for the unemployed and helping people to lead independent lives.

> ...not everyone who comes here will have the ability to get a job, with [some of them]...they are here to develop their skills so that they can enjoy their life more. But I am particularly keen to encourage youngsters who, given enough training, and the right sort of training, can then become really integrated into society by getting a job.
> I8, Care Enterprise.

Environmental impacts referred to were: improving village streets, reno-
vating and reusing derelict buildings, and removing dangerous and dilapi-
dated structures. These measures improved the physical appearance of the
community, making it a more attractive place to live, work and visit.
The physical improvement of previously neglected buildings conveyed
symbolic messages that the community enterprise was instrumental in
creating beneficial impacts for the whole community and region.

Levels of impact

Moving on to the impact of the community enterprises, the outcomes
were coded and categorized in terms of where the impacts were made.
The outcomes were then categorized into individual, organizational,
local and regional levels. See Table 12.3.

For the individual, the direct economic impact was income from
employment. Indirect, longer term impacts were also identified – one
volunteer, for example, as a result of the knowledge and skills acquired
from involvement with the community enterprise, had subsequently
become self-employed. Her new business, selling locally grown produce,
in turn led to further economic gains for local producers.

Informants also referred to noneconomic, intangible benefits that
they had gained from their involvement in community enterprise.
These were articulated in references to feelings of increased independence, empowerment, motivation, enthusiasm and confidence in the
future; and included opportunities for personal development, increased
satisfaction, expanded personal networks and individual confidence
building for both employees and volunteers. Collectively, they were
coded as social outcomes.

> I think also though, part of the thing about volunteering is you look
> at the reason why people volunteer in the first place, and the benefits
> that come from volunteering for the volunteer. I mean just expanding
> the number of people that you know ... gaining confidence.
> I7, Web Enterprise.

> I suppose it's the satisfaction of putting something back from what
> you have out of it, kind of thing... I think most of the committee
> are looking for satisfaction of having done a job well.
> I3, Transport Enterprise.

Informants also reported that impacts extended beyond the individual, to
include the organization, the local community and the wider region.

Table 12.3 Outcomes indicator

Outcomes	Individual	Enterprise	Community	Region
Direct economic	Employment income	Number of employees Turnover Nontrading income Access to supply chains	Number of new legal enterprises in the community Number of jobs created in the community	Number of new community enterprises in the region Number of jobs created in community enterprises in the region
Indirect economic	Improved personal skills Improved employment prospects	Increased money flows Increased innovation and creativity	Additional jobs created (suppliers) Increased money flows Local taxation Increased prosperity of the community	Additional jobs created in the region Increased money flows Taxation Increased prosperity of the region Savings to public expenditure
Direct social	Increased access to services Improved quality of life	Creation of cultural identity of the enterprise	Provision of services Contribution to social capital	Provision of services Contribution to social capital
Indirect social	Increased: confidence, independenc satisfaction empowerment self-esteem networks	Opportunity for social interaction Organizational networks Interorganizational trust	Community vibrancy: independence empowerment self-determination cooperation social interaction involvement of community in activities	Regional vibrancy Increased attractiveness as a place to live, work and visit

Table 12.3 Outcomes indicator – *continued*

Outcomes	Individual	Enterprise	Community	Region
Direct environmental	More attractive place to work	Renovation of old buildings Redeployment of unused assets	Regeneration of physical infrastructure of community	Regeneration of physical infrastructure of the region
Indirect environmental	More attractive place to live and visit	More attractive place to live and visit	Increased attractiveness of the community as a place to live, work and visit Contribution to local environmental capital	Increased attractiveness of region as a place to live, work and visit Contribution to sustainability agenda Contribution to regional environmental capital

Apart from the income of the community enterprise, the impacts at organizational level were said by informants to be primarily social: improving group skills, increased opportunities for interpersonal communication and teamworking, as well as raising the skills base of the enterprise (such as IT skills at Web Enterprise) and the achievement of a national quality award for the organization (Investors in People) by Transport Enterprise.

At the level of the community, informants referred to improvements in the economic health and vibrancy of their village. Marina Enterprise, for example, was instrumental in regenerating the villages in which it is located by acting as a conduit for boat owners and visitors to facilities in the village. This was also reported by an employee to be one of the driving forces behind the Sport Enterprise.

> We thought, if the harbor dies, then the village will be the next thing.
> I1, Marina Enterprise.

> The purpose of the project is economic regeneration among other things, because the community is poor.
> I2, Sport Enterprise.

The social impacts referred to by informants included increased community empowerment, independence and control, as well as greater cooperation within the community as a result of more social interaction between local people.

> The community has benefited by people coming to the village ... it has brought visitors to the community and it is bringing in a lot of money into the community.
> I1, Marina Enterprise.

> The broad [benefit] is financial ... People who ...would like to start a business ... we can show them how to do it, and we can make it financially viable for them. ... We have got the general benefit of attracting tourists and the whole general economic thing....
> I8, Care Enterprise.

Finally, in the broadest conception of community, informants from Tourism, Care and Marina reported that their organization had the potential to contribute to the wealth and vitality of the wider region.

> For visiting yachts ... it is going to complement the whole area.
> I1, Marina Enterprise.

In the end it will change this area into something that's a real profitable tourism area.

I8, Care Enterprise.

Discussion

The data gathered in this study illustrate that community enterprises have the potential to make direct and indirect, economic, social and environmental contributions to the regeneration of a rural economy. The research process, however, makes clear just how difficult it is to find a method to assess those outcomes and impacts that do not lend themselves to objective, standardized enumeration measures. Despite this, the informants reported the outcomes and impacts to be real, existing in reasonably stable, regular sequences and verifiable relationships (Miles and Huberman, 1994).

One method of assessing the indirect outcomes and impacts of entrepreneurship is by social accounting. This measures attainment of wider organizational achievements specified at the start of the social accounting process. It will not measure unanticipated outcomes and impacts, however, and may overlook indirect economic, social and environmental outcomes, especially those generated at broader community and regional level. Furthermore, the costs of the social accounting process are borne by the individual organization: the high resource demands it places on organizations, particularly small ones, may limit its adoption to larger companies.

A second method involves conducting regular and wide-ranging community audits at village level to capture quality of life measures. These could then be monitored pre and post community enterprise creation. Amin, Cameron and Hudson (2002) provide an example of collecting data before and after the creation of a social enterprise is reported: participants in the social enterprise were videoed at the start of the enterprise (bitter and perceiving themselves as victims) and three years later (positive and forward looking). Ultimately, anecdotal evidence may be inevitable and – although collecting testimonials from people who have benefited from the social enterprise is one way of communicating its impact – some outcomes may simply be impossible to measure quantitatively (Amin, Cameron and Hudson, 2002).

The multiple outcomes and impacts of community entrepreneurship encourage us to think more broadly about how to capture performance data. For ease of use, it is proposed that an outcomes indicator, constructed from the categories identified in the study reported here, may offer a potentially useful instrument to gather such data. See Table 12.3.

The creation of a new measurement tool is not without contention since it will require resources that many smaller social enterprises either do not have (Hoefer, 2000) or which would be diverted away from social value-creating activities into an accountability process (Buckmaster, 1999). The longer term benefits of measuring and monitoring outcomes and impacts will, however, help social and community enterprises prove their effectiveness in achieving economic, social and environmental goals to stakeholders.

Conclusion

The community enterprises presented in this chapter have demonstrated their capacity to generate direct and indirect outcomes and impacts. The direct economic outcomes include the creation of new organizations, employment opportunities and income. The indirect economic outcomes relate to raising the skills levels of the local population, and to increases in the circulation and retention of money within the community and region. The creation of employment also generates savings in public expenditure (from reduced social security and benefit payments) and increased income from local and national taxation. The direct social outcomes are reduced social exclusion and enhanced integration, and indirect social outcomes are increased individual feelings of independence and empowerment and overall community vibrancy. The environmental outcomes are the improvement of the physical infrastructure of the community: the renovation and reuse of old buildings, the creation of sport and leisure facilities and the removal of dangerous structures. These outcomes improved the appearance of the community for local residents, employees and visitors, making it a better place to live, work and visit (spending money). Collectively, the community enterprises demonstrate that the concept of wealth creation can be broadened beyond economic wealth to include social and environmental dimensions.

The study examined six community enterprises in a peripheral region. The evidence of multiple outcomes and impacts endorses the fact that the performance evaluation of social and community enterprises should be multidimensional – and not reduced merely to economic outcomes. Although presented separately in this paper, in the field the outcomes and impacts were closely linked and overlapping.

The difficulty becomes one of creating a cost-effective method for collating outcomes and impacts. To this end, the outcomes indicator provides a potentially useful tool, which could be of use to other organizations and in other contexts.

The diversity of the ventures in these case studies shows that it is possible to regenerate a rural economy beyond frequently held assumptions that tourism exploitation is the sole means of regenerating fragile rural areas (Stobart and Ball, 1998). The social enterprise approach to exploiting market opportunities which bring much needed goods and services to rural communities creates a valuable policy tool for promoting economic and social regeneration.

As an exploratory study, this paper places social and community enterprise at the heart of community regeneration and future research might explore outcomes and impacts in other rural, and resource-poor urban, communities. This would help to establish whether or not the results of this study are unique to its organizations and research context. It would also allow the outcomes indicator to be tested and refined by further field work with a larger sample. If social enterprises are to continue to play an increasingly important role in the delivery of national regeneration policy, the need to provide evidence of their performance will become ever more pertinent. In addition, research that extends our understanding of the direct and indirect environmental outcomes and impacts of entrepreneurship will add greatly to our knowledge of entrepreneurial behavior and can also be useful to for-profit organizations.

From a more critical perspective, the outcomes and impacts presented in this chapter appear to be complementary and noncompetitive. This might be explained by the way in which each venture is embedded in a tight-knit community. It is feasible that in larger communities, competition between community enterprises for resources could create a situation in which the goals of different community enterprises are in conflict. The processes of negotiation and collaboration to resolve the conflict would be a very promising research topic with potentially valuable findings for many organizations, irrespective of their profit status and/or purpose.

Acknowledgment

The author would like to acknowledge the support of the Carnegie Trust for the Universities of Scotland for funding the fieldwork of this research.

References

Allanson, P., Murdoch, J., Garrod, G. and Lowe, P. 1995. Sustainability and the rural economy: An evolutionary perspective. *Environment and Planning A.* 27: 1797–814.

Amin, A., Cameron, A. and Hudson, R. 2002. *Placing the social economy.* London: Routledge.

Bank of England. 2003. *Review of finance for social enterprise.* London: Bank of England.

Birch, D. 1979. *The job generation process, final report to economic development administration.* MIT Project on Neighborhood and Regional Change. Cambridge, MA: MIT Press.

Birch, J. 1986. *Entrepreneurship.* New York: John Wiley.

Bird, B. 1989. *Entrepreneurial behavior.* Glenview, IL: Scott Foresman.

Birley, S. J. and Westhead, P. 1990. Growth and performance contrasts between types of small firms. *Strategic Management Journal,* 11(7): 535–57.

Bowler, I. and Lewis, G. 1991. Community involvement in rural development: The example of the Rural Development Commission. In T. Chapman and C. Watkins (eds), *People in the countryside, studies of social change in rural Britain*: 160–77. London: Paul Chapman.

Boyd, D. P. and Gumpert, D. E. 1983. Coping with entrepreneurial stress. *Harvard Business Review,* 61(5): 162–88.

Bryden, J. and Bollman, R. 2000. Rural employment in industrialized countries. *Agricultural Economics,* 22: 185–97.

Bryden, J. and Munro, G. 2000. New approaches to economic development in peripheral rural regions. *Scottish Geographical Journal,* 116(2): 111–24.

Buckmaster, N. 1999. Associations between outcome measurement, accountability and learning for nonprofit organizations. *International Journal of Public Sector Management,* 12(2): 186–97.

Busenitz, L. and Lau, C. 1996. A cross-cultural cognitive model of new venture creation. *Entrepreneurship Theory and Practice,* 20(4): 25–39.

Butler Flora, C. and Flora, J. L. 1993. Entrepreneurial social infrastructure: A necessary ingredient. *The Annals of the American Academy of Political and Social Science,* 529: 48–58.

Chandler, G. and Hanks, S. H. 1993. Measuring the performance of emerging businesses: A validation study. *Journal of Business Venturing,* 8(5): 391–408.

Cooper, A. C. 1993. Challenges in predicting new firm performance. *Journal of Business Venturing,* 8(3): 241–53.

D'Arcy, E. and Guissani, B. 1996. Local economic development: Changing the parameters? *Entrepreneurship and Regional Development,* 8: 159–78.

Dawson, E. 1998. The relevance of social audit for Oxfam GB. *Journal of Business Ethics,* 17(13): 1457–69.

Dennis, B., Neck, C. P. and Goldsby, M. 1998. Body Shop International: An exploration of corporate social responsibility. *Management Decision,* 36(10): 649–53.

Denzin, N. K. 1978. *The research act.* Englewood Cliffs, NJ: Prentice Hall.

Denzin, N. K. and Lincoln, Y. S. 1998. *Collecting and interpreting qualitative materials.* London: Sage.

DoE/MAFF. 1995. *Rural England: A nation committed to living in the countryside.* London: HMSO, Department of the Environment, Ministry of Agriculture, Fisheries and Food.

Dhesi, A. 2000. Social capital and community development. *Community Development Journal*, 35(3): 199–214.

DTI. 2002. *Social enterprise: A strategy for success.* London: Department of Trade and Industry. Available: http://www.sbs.gov.uk/default.php?page=/ socialenterprise/default.php.

Dumas, C. 2001. Evaluating the outcomes of micro-enterprise training for low income women: A case study. *Journal of Developmental Entrepreneurship*, 6(2): 97–129.

Eccles, R. G. 1991. The performance measurement manifesto. *Harvard Business Review*, 69(1): 131–7.

Ecotec. 2002. *Guidance on mapping social enterprise.* Final report to the Department of Trade and Industry Social Enterprise Unit. Available: http://www.sbs.gov.uk/content/socialenterprise/finalrep.pdf.

Eisenhardt, K. 1989. Building theory from case study research. *Academy of Management Review*, 14(4): 532–50.

Flora, J. L. 1998. Social capital and communities of place. *Rural Sociology*, 63: 481–506.

Flora, J. L., Green, G., Gale, E. A., Schmidt, F. E. and Butler Flora, C. 1992. Self-development: A viable rural development option? *Policy Studies Journal*, 20(2): 276–88.

Gibb, A. and Adhikary, D. 2000. Strategies for local and regional NGO development: Combining sustainable outcomes with sustainable organizations. *Entrepreneurship and Regional Development*, 12(2): 137–61.

Glaser, B. and Strauss, A. 1967. *The discovery of grounded theory: Strategies for qualitative research.* New York: Aldine.

Halfacree, K. 1993. Locality and social representation: Space, discourse and alternative definitions of rural. *Journal of Rural Studies*, 9: 23–37.

Herlau, H. and Tetzschner, H. 1994. Regional development: Who are the problem owners? *Entrepreneurship and Regional Development*, 6: 161–75.

Hoefer, R. 2000. Accountability in action? Program evaluation in nonprofit human service organizations. *Nonprofit Management and Leadership*, 11(2): 167–77.

Holmquist, C. 2003. Is the medium really the message? Moving perspective from the entrepreneurial actor to the entrepreneurial action. In C. Steyaert and D. Hjorth (eds), *New movements in entrepreneurship*: 73–85. Cheltenham: Edward Elgar.

Human, J. E. and Provan, K. G. 1997. An emergent theory of structure and outcomes in small firm strategic manufacturing networks. *Academy of Management Journal*, 49: 368–403.

Jenkins, M. and Johnson, G. 1997. Entrepreneurial intentions and outcomes: A comparative causal mapping study. *Journal of Management Studies*, 34(6): 895–920.

Johannisson, B. and Nilsson, A. 1989. Community entrepreneurship networking for local development. *Entrepreneurship and Regional Development*, 1: 1–19.

Johnson, M. A. 1998. Developing a typology of nonprofit micro enterprise programs in the United States. *Journal of Developmental Entrepreneurship*, 3(2): 165–84.

Keeble, D., Tyler, P., Broom, G. and Lewis, J. 1992. *Business success in the country-side: The performance of rural enterprise*. London: HMSO.

Keldenberg, D. O. and Gobeli, D. H. 1995. Total quality management practices and business outcomes: Evidence from dental practices. *Journal of Small Business Management*, 33(1): 21–33.

Kendall, J. and Knapp, M. 2000. Measuring performance of voluntary organizations. *Public Management*, 2(1): 105–32.

Kuratko, D., Hornsby, J. and Naffziger, D. 1997. An examination of owner's goals in sustaining entrepreneurship. *Journal of Small Business Management*, 35(1): 24–33.

Laukkenan, M. and Niittykangas, H. 2003. Local developers as virtual entrepreneurs – do difficult surroundings need initiating entrepreneurs? *Entrepreneurship and Regional Development*, 15: 309–31.

Lichtenstein, G. A. and Lyons, T. S. 2001. The entrepreneurial development system: Transforming business talent and community economies. *Economic Development Quarterly*, 15(1): 3–20.

Lin, N., Buss, T. F. and Popovich, M. 1990. Entrepreneurship is alive and well in rural America: A four state study. *Economic Development Quarterly*, 3: 254–9.

Lindgren, M. and Packendorff, J. 2003. A project-based view of entrepreneurship: Towards action-orientation, seriality and collectivity. In C. Steyaert and D. Hjorth (eds), *New movements in entrepreneurship*: 86–102. Cheltenham: Edward Elgar.

Lyon, F., Bertotti, M., Evans, M., Smallbone, D., Potts, G. and Ramsden, P. 2002. *Measuring enterprise impacts in deprived areas*. Report to the Small Business Service. Available: www.sbs.gov.uk/content/research/MeasuringEnt_Summary.pdf.

Lyons, T. S. 2002. Building social capital for rural enterprise development: Three case studies in the United States. *Journal of Developmental Entrepreneurship*, 7(2): 193–216.

Malecki, E. J. 1994. Entrepreneurship in regional and local development. *International Regional Science Review*, 16(1–2): 119–53.

McClelland, D. C. 1987. Characteristics of successful entrepreneurs. *Journal of Creative Behaviour*, 21: 219–33.

Meyer-Stamer, J. 1997. New patterns of governance for industrial change: Perspectives for Brazil. *The Journal of Developmental Studies*, 33: 364–91.

Miles, M. B. and Huberman, A. M. 1994. *Qualitative data analysis, an expanded sourcebook*. Thousand Oaks, CA: Sage.

OECD. 1998. New business in rural areas. *OECD Observer*. Feb–March, 210: 12–17.

OECD. 2003. *Entrepreneurship and local economic development*. Paris: OECD.

Pearce, J. 1993. *At the heart of the community*. London: Calouste Gulbenkien Foundation.

Pearce, J. 2001. *Social audit and social accounting*. Scotland: CBS Network.

Plantz, M. C., Greenway, M. T. and Hendricks, M. 1997. Outcome measurement: Showing results in the nonprofit sector. *New Directions for Evaluation*, 75, Fall: 15–30.

Reis, T. K. and Clohesy, S. J. 2001. Unleashing new resources and entrepreneurship for the common good: A philanthropic renaissance. *New Directions in Philanthropic Fundraising*, 32: 109–43.

Scottish Office. 1995. *People, prosperity and partnership*. Edinburgh: HMSO.

Scott, J. 1991. *Social network analysis*. London: Sage.

Servon, L. J. and Doshna, J. P. 2000. Microenterprise and economic development toolkit: A small part of the big picture. *Journal of Developmental Entrepreneurship*, 5(3): 1–20.

Silverman, D. 2001. *Interpreting qualitative data*. London: Sage.

Strauss, A. and Corbin, J. 1998. *Basics of qualitative research*. Thousand Oaks, CA: Sage.

Stobart, J. and Ball, R. 1998. Tourism and local economic development. *Local Economy*, 13(3): 228–38.

Stohr, W. B. 1990. On the theory and practice of local development in Europe. In W. B. Stohr (ed.), *Global challenge and local response*: 35–54. London: United Nations.

Todd, R. and Ramanathan, K. V. 1993. Perceived social needs, outcomes measurement and budgetary responsiveness in a not-for-profit setting: Some empirical evidence. *The Accounting Review*, 69(1): 122–37.

Tolbert, C. M., Lyson, T. A. and Irwin, M. D. 1998. Local capitalism, civic engagement and socio-economic well being. *Social Forces*, 77(2): 401–27.

Ucbasaran, D., Westhead, P. and Wright, M. 2001. The focus of entrepreneurial research: Contextual and process issues. *Entrepreneurship Theory and Practice*, 25(4): 57–80.

Volkman, R. 1999. Outcomes measurement: The new accounting standard for service organizations. *Fund Raising Management*, 30(9): 26–7.

Wang, X. 2002. Perception and reality in developing an outcome performance measurement system. *International Journal of Public Administration*, 25(6): 805–29.

Yin, R. K. 1994. *Case study research: Design and methods*. Applied Social Research Methods Series, 5. Thousand Oaks: Sage.

Part IV

Integrating Sustainability and the Environment

13
Introduction to Part IV – Ecopreneurship: Unique Research Field or Just 'More of the Same'?

Kai Hockerts

The two papers in Part IV of this volume approach the topic of social entrepreneurship (SE) from the angle of *environmental* or *sustainable* entrepreneurship. Does it make sense to have such a focus? At first sight ecological entrepreneurship, often also referred to as 'ecopreneurship' (Isaak, 1997: 80), seems to be a mere subset of SE. Accordingly one could argue that, where SE generally aims at the identification and exploitation of opportunities for the creation of public goods, ecopreneurship simply narrows the focus to one particular type of public good – namely the protection of the environment. If this warrants a unique research domain one could also argue for similar efforts to be undertaken in other domains of SE – such as poverty relief, health or education.

While such an argument is not baseless, I would nonetheless suggest that it is still worthwhile to consider the differences between what is referred to in the literature as 'social entrepreneurship' and 'ecopreneurship'. The motivation for this is not to erect a barrier between fields, but rather to help both domains learn from each other by pointing out the unique elements of each approach.

SE has been more often associated with nonprofit than with for-profit organizations, however, this is not true for what is studied under the label of ecological entrepreneurship. Isaak (1997: 80), for example, defines ecopreneurship as 'system-transforming, socially-committed environmental businesses characterized by breakthrough innovation'. The focus is thus strongly placed on ecological-purpose business ventures. Most authors studying ecopreneurship would probably agree with this definition (Hendrickson and Tuttle, 1997; Isaak, 1997; 1998;

Pastakia, 1998; Wüstenhagen, 1998a; Larson, 2000; Schaltegger and Petersen, 2001; Hockerts, 2003), although some scholars have also studied corporate ecopreneurship in large firms (Menon and Menon, 1997; Azzone and Noci, 1998; Keogh and Polonsky, 1998; Krueger, 1998; Lober, 1998; Schaltegger and Petersen, 2001), and in a public or nonprofit context (Bryant and Bryant, 1998; Lounsbury, 1998; Pastakia, 1998).

None of these authors refers to the efficient management of ecological NGOs or the greening of SMEs as ecopreneurship. Environmental management scholars have researched both areas, although not under the ecopreneurship label. Among the publications on ecopreneurship, several recurring topics can be identified that are also studied by scholars of SE. Authors have addressed the question of opportunity identification and exploitation, the motivation of ecopreneurs, and the role networks play in supporting ecopreneurship. Typologies of ecopreneurs have been proposed by Schaltegger and Petersen (2001) and Walley and Taylor (2002).

Comparing the social and ecological entrepreneurship literature, it becomes evident that more has been published on the first than on the second topic. However, it is interesting to note that nearly all of the latter are in scholarly journals applying rigorous academic research methods, whereas the majority of what has been published to date on SE was published in news magazines. In this context it is also interesting to note that there are a number of real world social entrepreneurs who identify themselves with that label while there are hardly any self-proclaimed ecopreneurs. The term seems to be used in academic circles only.

The phenomenon that ecopreneurs do not like to be singled out as such is also known to SE researchers. However, the reason for such reticence could not be more different. Social entrepreneurs rebelling against being labeled as such usually are concerned about the perceived proximity of the expression 'entrepreneur' to terms such as 'capitalist' or 'industrialist'. Such persons see their mission as furthering the public good through philanthropic means. Research on ecopreneurs on the other hand suggests that they often take offence at being identified as 'green' or 'ecological', a label they feel may turn out to be a burden when looking for investors and customers (Randelovic, O'Rourke and Orsato, 2002).

Here then lies also the main difference between social entrepreneur and ecopreneur. The second is strongly motivated by the ambition to be like any other (business) entrepreneur. More recently the label 'cleantech venturing' has emerged as a means to avoid the dreaded 'e-word'. In consequence cleantech venturing has become a considerable niche within the venture capital market: in 2005, the Cleantech Venture Network served over 900 affiliate investors. They report to have tracked more than US$4.5 billion invested in cleantech ventures since 2002 (Cleantech, 2005).

In this sizeable success lies one of the most interesting leads for SE research. What should social entrepreneurs make of the fact that some green ventures have succeeded in breaking through the glass ceiling of the venture capital world? Could there be models of social private equity that would be profitable both from an economic and a social point of view? An intertwining of researchers' agendas might deliver interesting results for the SE field.

A second lead that should interest SE scholars lies in what Wüstenhagen (1998b; 2003) describes as the tension between the 'multiplying Davids and greening Goliaths'. What role can social corporate intrapreneurship play and how does it relate to its entrepreneurial cousin? By focusing on social corporate intrapreneurship we approach the frontier to corporate social responsibility (CSR) research. However, while much has been written about CSR innovation there remains a considerable white space between these two research fields.

In the context of the first suggested research question the paper by Clifford and Dixon offers interesting insights. Although it is nonprofit, Green-Works, the company described, aims at becoming a profitable organization. The balancing act on the triple bottom line performed by Green-Works is instructive not just for other charities but could also prove valuable for many businesses in the waste management area. Clifford and Dixon have developed a case study based on rich descriptions from participant observation, interviews and document analysis. The founder and CEO of Green-Works, Colin Crooks, is described as a 'social ecopreneur' and the aim of the paper is to discover whether an organization with the mission of creating both social and environmental value can sustain an economically viable business while staying true to its core values. Their findings suggest that such an outcome is achieved by creating a network level strategy of mutual benefit to all stakeholders. The Green-Works business model provides large corporates with an opportunity to fulfill some of their own CSR goals and therefore is also an instructive model in the domain of corporate 'intrapreneurship'.

Seelos, Ganly, and Mair in their paper, on the other hand, consider how social entrepreneurs contribute to the UN-defined set of Millennium

Development Goals. This research angle opens interesting opportunities for studying the role 'Davids and Goliaths' can (and even must) play if the goals are to be achieved. The organizations examined here are found to contribute to a number of Millennium Goals including environmental sustainability, poverty elimination, education, reducing maternal and child mortality and combating disease. They represent a mix of both nonprofit and for-profit forms and operate in many of the world's least developed countries. While not all of these initiatives are 'ecopreneurial', the authors consider each of them to be providing alternative and unique business models for achieving global sustainable development. Importantly, Seelos, Ganly and Mair see these social entrepreneurial initiatives as potential partners not only for multilateral development organizations, but also for corporations entering developing markets.

Both papers show that sustainability and ecological entrepreneurship do not have to be topics apart from the SE domain. At the same time they are also testimony to the fact that there remain questions to be asked that the mainstream SE literature may find useful to consider. Both areas can only benefit from closer integration.

References

Azzone, A. R. and Noci, G. 1998. Seeing ecology and 'green' innovations as a source of change. *Journal of Organizational Change Management*, 11(2): 94–111.

Bryant, T. A. and Bryant, J. E. 1998. Wetlands and entrepreneurs: Mapping the fuzzy zone between ecosystem preservation and entrepreneurial opportunity. *Journal of Organizational Change Management*, 11(2): 112–34.

Cleantech. 2005. Cleantech Venture Network. http://cleantech.com. Accessed 30 September 2005.

Hendrickson, L. U. and Tuttle, D. B. 1997. Dynamic management of the environmental enterprise: A qualitative analysis. *Journal of Organizational Change Management*, 10(4): 363–82.

Hockerts, K. N. 2003. Sustainability innovations, ecological and social entrepreneurship and the management of antagonistic assets. PhD Thesis, University St. Gallen.

Isaak, R. 1997. Globalization and green entrepreneurship. *Greener Management International*, 18: 80–90.

Isaak, R. 1998. *Green logic, ecopreneurship, theory and ethics*. Sheffield: Greenleaf.

Keogh, P. D. and Polonsky, M. J. 1998. Environmental commitment: A basis for environmental entrepreneurship? *Journal of Organizational Change Management*, 11(1): 38–49.

Krueger, N. 1998. Encouraging the identification of environmental opportunities. *Journal of Organizational Change Management*, 11(2): 174–83.

Larson, A. L. 2000. Sustainable innovation through an entrepreneurship lens. *Business Strategy and the Environment*, 9: 304–17.

Lober, D. J. 1998. Pollution prevention as corporate entrepreneurship. *Journal of Organizational Change Management*, 11(1): 26–37.

Lounsbury, M. 1998. Collective entrepreneurship: The mobilization of college and university recycling coordinators. *Journal of Organizational Change Management*, 11(1): 50–69.

Menon, A. and Menon, A. 1997. Enviropreneurial marketing strategy: The emergence of corporate environmentalism as market strategy. *Journal of Marketing*, 61(1): 51–67.

Pastakia, A. 1998. Grassroots ecopreneurs: Change agents for a sustainable society. *Journal of Organizational Change Management*, 11(2): 157–73.

Randelovic, J., O'Rourke, A. and Orsato, R. 2002. The emergence of green venture capital. Working Paper 2002/51/CMER. INSEAD, Fontainebleau.

Schaltegger, S. and Petersen, H. 2001. *Ecopreneurship – Konzept und Typologie*. Lüneburg: Center for Sustainability Management.

Walley, E. E. and Taylor, D. 2002. Typologies of green entrepreneurs. Proceedings of the Business Strategy and the Environment Conference. September 2002, Leeds.

Wüstenhagen, R. 1998a. Technologische und soziale innovationen als gleichgewichtige säulen von ecopreneurship im energiebereich. Thesenpapier zur 11. Oikos-Konferenz – Innovationen für eine nachhaltige entwicklung: Akteure – Plattformen – Zeitpläne, 1–3 July 1998, St. Gallen.

Wüstenhagen, R. 1998b. *Greening Goliaths vs. Multiplying Davids. Pfade einer coevolution ökologischer massenmärkte und nachhaltiger nischen*. St Gallen: Institut für Wirtschaft und Ökologie IWÖ-HSG.

Wüstenhagen, R. 2003. Greening Goliaths vs. Multiplying Davids: Entrepreneurship as the missing piece in the corporate sustainability debate. Greening of Industry Network Conference. October 12–15, 2003, San Francisco.

14

Green-Works: A Model for Combining Social and Ecological Entrepreneurship

Anne Clifford and Sarah E. A. Dixon

Introduction

How can social and ecological entrepreneurs create and develop an economically viable business whilst retaining the core environmental and social values that motivated them in the first place? Can sound business practice be genuinely consistent with idealism and environmental best practice? This research into the strategies adopted and the challenges faced by Green-Works, a UK nonprofit company, makes three contributions to the research in social and ecological entrepreneurship. Firstly it demonstrates a strong link between entrepreneurialism and environmentalism. The entrepreneurial flair of the CEO, who sees waste as an opportunity rather than a problem, enables his successful pursuit of a triptych of environmental, social and economic goals. Secondly, Green-Works' business model demonstrates that economic sustainability is possible for social and ecological enterprises. Thirdly, the research reveals the value of network level strategy for enabling a variety of organizations to achieve their objectives in terms of the triple bottom line.

The research is presented as follows. First, the theoretical grounding for social and ecological entrepreneurship is provided. Then the research setting at Green-Works is described, followed by details of the methodology, which comprised a single qualitative case study. The findings are broadly categorized under the headings: an entrepreneurial organization; balancing the triple bottom line; and creating networks. The findings are discussed and the business model of Green-Works is elucidated. The final section describes the implications of this research for practicing managers and for theory development.

Social and ecological entrepreneurship

What motivates companies to embrace sustainability? Moreover, why should they, given that such measures are usually seen to lead to escalating costs? (Lanoie and Tanguay, 2000). Global sustainability requires innovative newcomers to unseat incumbent firms in the Schumpeterian process of creative destruction (Hart and Milstein, 1999). There is no common terminology for these newcomers, who are becoming less obsessed with single issues and more likely to embrace a trinity of social, environmental and economic values (Menon and Menon, 1997). Isaak (1997: 85) uses the term *'ecopreneur'*, defining an ecopreneurial organization as one that is a *'system-transforming, socially committed...breakthrough venture'*, a definition that seems to encompass both ecological and social enterprise. However, the term ecopreneur draws the focus too narrowly upon the environmental aspects, and we therefore apply the term 'social ecopreneur', in a slightly different sense to Pastakia (1998), in order to encompass the triple drivers of these organizations: environmental, social and economic, the latter being inherent in the concept of entrepreneurship.

What kind of an organization does the social ecopreneur create? Does it differ from other small entrepreneurial firms? Venkataraman (1997) considers that traditional entrepreneurs generate social value as a by-product of economic value, whereas for social entrepreneurs (and therefore other mission-driven individuals such as ecopreneurs) the reverse is true. Balancing the often competing demands of the wide variety of stakeholders (Hall and Vredenburg, 2003) representing the triptych of economic, social and environmental concerns is a key skill for the social ecopreneur. Securing funding can be particularly onerous since the ecopreneurial business concept is novel and therefore without precedent (Linnanen, 2002). Another challenge faced by social ecopreneurs is managing their reputation – trading on a reputation for sustainability can be difficult, partly because of the shifting sands of what is considered 'green' (Azzone and Nucci, 1998). Anita Roddick complained that, as the face of The Body Shop (one of environmentalism's few business exemplars), she was expected to meet standards worthy of Mother Teresa (Financial Times, 1994).

This research seeks to examine how a balance is attained in one small social and ecological firm. The insights suggest that, rather than hindering entrepreneurialism, idealistic values can be translated into valuable economic assets (largely by providing corporations with the opportunity to adopt a means of ethical purchasing), which, in its

offering of social and environmental benefits, goes well beyond traditional green procurement. Crucially, these benefits reflect market conditions in that they are both quantifiable, reflecting the UK Chancellor
Gordon Brown's call for measurable corporate social responsibility
(CSR) outcomes (DTI, 2004), and delivered through a service that is
differentiated further by its high level of professionalism.

Research setting

Set up by its CEO Colin Crooks in 2000, Green-Works is a nonprofit
organization, which is now a registered charity (although at the time of
the research Green-Works was a social enterprise). It operates a business model that is unique in the UK: companies with office furniture
that is surplus to demand because of relocation or refurbishment sign
up to Green-Works' membership scheme. Green-Works then collects
the furniture and the items are refurbished by a team of people drawn
from disadvantaged sectors of the community. Landfill dumping and
the use of virgin materials in creating new furniture is avoided and
community benefits are secured both via the employment and training
of disadvantaged people and through the provision of cheap but high
quality furniture, largely to nonprofit organizations. The corporates
benefit from a one-stop furniture disposal service that also helps them
fulfil their CSR mandates. Green-Works runs one outlet itself and franchises its operation across the country with a variety of partners, all of
which are nonprofit and have expertise in the employment and training of disadvantaged people. Amies (2000) describes this model as
social franchising.

Methodology

This research adopted an exploratory approach within a phenomeno-
logical research paradigm, emphasizing sense-making and deriving
understanding. This has been the predominant approach for research
into the strategy of sustainable organizations. The field researcher vol-
unteered for the organization over a period of two months in 2004,
this high degree of access benefiting the single case study approach
with its emphasis on understanding particular settings (Dyer and
Wilkins, 1991).

Multiple means of data collection – semi-structured interviews,
microethnography and document analysis – increased the robustness
of the research via triangulation (Eisenhardt, 1989). With the excep-

tion of the CEO, the interviewees were all reported anonymously. Their views are rather similar, but often diametrically opposed to those of the CEO, hence the need to separate the two. The interview questions, together with their links to the basic research questions, are given in Appendix 14A. Microethnography, as a scaled-down version of ethnography, was undertaken during the time available, the objective being to understand the culture of the organization through participant observation. Field notes, including both observation and reflection, were taken over the course of 17 days' site visits, in various degrees of covertness in order to try to avoid stimulating unnatural behavior. The document analysis was relatively restricted since few documents were available due to Green-Works informal modus operandi.

Data collection and analysis were overlapped (Eisenhardt, 1989), providing flexibility in data collection and allowing a more thorough investigation of emerging themes, for example the discovery of the importance of networks to Green-Works. Throughout the process memos were written, coded and placed in a data display database (Miles and Huberman, 1994). See example in Table 14.1.

Table 14.1 Typical entries in data display

Data source	Research question	Subtheme	Issue	Representative quotation/episode
Interviewees				
Resp 3	ECN	Funding	Danger of grants	In our business I think it would be uncomfortable to have funding above 10%
Resp 5	STRGY	Long term focus	Lack of planning	...but if you're going to be thinking 'established company' then you have to at least have a very vague idea as to which spot on the horizon you're aiming for
Resp 1	STRGY	Outsourcing CSR	Finding new markets	This [partnership] could've been make or break for them (Harrow Green)
Resp 4	STRGY	Social franchising	Skills from partners	Green-Works tries to stop office furniture going to landfill. It's no use trying to save very unemployable people if you're no good at it

Table 14.1   Typical entries in data display – *continued*

Data source	Research question	Subtheme	Issue	Representative quotation/ episode
Interviewees				
Resp 4	CHL	Balance	Green goals are primary	Green-Works tries to stop office furniture going to landfill. It's no use trying to save very unemploy-able people if you're no good at it
Documents				
Doc 6	ECN	Funding	Self-funded	Our daily operations are now entirely funded by commercial activity
Doc 11	ETHC	Quality	Comment from member	'They are savvy and street-smart and seem very well organized and pleasant to deal with'
Micro-ethnography				
Day 5	ETHC	Consistency	Minor quibble	No organic milk in the kitchen though fair trade coffee is there
Day 3	STRGY	Culture	Opportunism is all	'Very bureaucratic' is a term that's been bandied about today as a criticism

Notes: As shown for respondent 4 some comments were given more than one coding ca. 1,000 individual coded entries in total

Key to research questions:
STRGY   What are the strategies of this organization and how are they created?
ETHC   How does the organization fulfil its ethical mandate?
ECN   How does it keep itself economically viable?
CHL   What are the other key challenges it faces?

The coding system was designed to link the data from all sources into the original research questions. After coding, the data were sorted and clustered into matrices by different criteria, for instance by respondent or by data source (Miles and Huberman, 1994). A conceptually ordered display was devised. Immediately after this process the field researcher produced a 'stream of consciousness'. A series of if-then tactics was developed using enumerative and eliminative induction (Miles and Huberman, 1994). From this, a preliminary logic model (Yin, 2003) was created with a view to establishing a tentative conceptual framework. The final conclusions were cross-checked with the original 'stream of consciousness' and with Green-Works staff.

Three methods were used to increase the robustness of the research in terms of construct validity and reliability: triangulation of data sources as described above, the use of thick description (Geertz, 1973) using primarily the microethnography; and maintaining a chain of evidence (Yin, 2003).

Findings

An entrepreneurial organization

We are a young organization driven by commitment and enthusiasm to prove that waste is an opportunity rather than a problem: an opportunity to save valuable resources and an opportunity to create jobs.
Colin Crooks, CEO

This statement shows Green-Works' CEO to be a classic entrepreneur, an individual who sees opportunities where others do not. He is also a visionary, who hates waste, but he has the brain of a pragmatist. Driven by an intuitive sense that a latent market for reusing and recycling office furniture existed, he disregarded both competitor activities (Table 14.2: 1) and unfavourable market research data (Table 14.2: 2). In a process of *'probe and learn'* (Lynn, Morone and Paulson, 1996), Green-Works incorporated learning from preliminary versions of the end product into each subsequent version, thus achieving continual modest improvements designed to meet customers' needs.

Table 14.2   An entrepreneurial organization

Theme	Ref	Comment
Creating a novel business concept	1	I didn't actually want to be influenced by the current market because I disagree with the way it's currently done. *(CEO)*
	2	I don't see how you could frame a question to give you a sensible answer. But actually, when you go to them and say, this is real, the truck is actually outside and we can do this – and this is the direct benefit you can get from this: then I think that the answer is a different one. But you have to make that commitment, you have to say, it is real, it's not a theoretical proposition, it's a real proposition. *(CEO)*
Continuous growth	3	It seems to me that I have a duty to continue, I can't just say I should stop 'cause this is a nice comfortable level of business [*note of evangelism in CEO's eyes and voice here*]...it's almost pointless. I've just begun to address the issue. So I've got to keep on going. *(CEO)*

Table 14.2   **An entrepreneurial organization** – *continued*

Theme	Ref	Comment
Structure vs opportunism	4	I do find the whole thing about devising structures and systems a bit tedious. But I love the result. I tend to recruit around me, people that are better tuned to doing those sorts of things. And who are hopefully enthused by the energy I bring to it,... and hopefully I don't frighten them too much, hopefully they don't slow me down too much and we get a nice happy medium. *(CEO)*
	5	The beauty of Green-Works is... entrepreneurial flair is encouraged. *(Manager)*
Short time horizons	6	...in the last few years it's been a bit tighter, so these projects that are happening now are the product of mid to late 90s economic growth, and where that growth has stagnated around the millennium, perhaps in 6, 7, 8 years' time these projects simply won't exist...if we drop 10% of that corporate income then the bottom falls out of the profit and loss account. *(Manager)*
	7	What will you do if the money runs outs? *(Researcher)* Dunno! Get the metal detector out. *(CEO)*
Adapting to a larger company	8	..I'm slower than I was and less opportunistic, and I have to consider that an opportunity that backfires now could take 40 jobs with it. *(CEO)*
	9	...we are so different from any other social enterprise which marks us out... we've put the sector into mainstream business. *(Manager)*

By 2004 Green-Works had begun to make a modest profit. The notion of simply maintaining the same level of activity did not merit consideration, primarily because the ultimate reason for growth is the CEO's need to further his mission (Table 14.2: 3). However, the CEO's seemingly insatiable appetite for growth has been tempered by the need for a structure to support and foster that growth. He has in part overcome this challenge through recruitment (Table 14.2: 4); in particular, by the selection of a management team with a strong planning orientation. At the same time he continues to promote an entrepreneurial culture (Table 14.2: 5). Despite company growth, planning horizons remain short and the approach opportunistic (Table 14.2: 6, 7). The growth of the company on the one hand represents greater responsibilities, but on the other hand its success puts the company into the mainstream, creating credibility (Table 14.2: 8, 9).

Balancing the triple bottom line

The CEO is driven by his ideals:

> 'I absolutely hate waste... the whole point about hating waste is because it could do something else.'

His idealism is palpable:

> 'I would be in many ways thrilled if one of two things happened. One, that the corporate sector suddenly became less wasteful.... if we had a small part in that, by highlighting the waste, they suddenly decided, this is crazy – if Green-Works could do it we could do it internally... Or, if the rest of the waste management industry could catch up and say, we can out-Green-Works Green-Works, we'll do it commercially, then I would really have achieved sustainability. And we would be out of business.'

These values are shared by his managers (Table 14.3: 1, 2): environmentalism is part of the bedrock of the company's culture (Table 14.3: 3, 4).

Table 14.3   Balancing the triple bottom line

Theme	Ref	Comment
Staff share ideals	1	[Reducing waste] is, you know, an important message, this is our future, for the next generations. *(Manager)*
	2	I can either set myself the target of GBP40,000 of income every month for the company, or I can set myself a target of 500 tonnes of furniture to come through us. If I set myself a financial target, I just start thinking of myself as a bit of a slippery salesman, which I'm not at all, whereas if I set myself a target of 500 tonnes ... I can kind of think of myself as someone who is saving this whole chunk of furniture from going to a landfill site and then all of that is being redistributed...*(Manager)*
Walking the walk	3	Are you going [to Woolwich] by car? *(Member of staff)* No such luck! We're environmentalists, we go by train. *(CEO)*
	4	On finding out that a truck had attracted a fine for an unspecified traffic offence, the CEO said that he would pay for parking tickets, but absolutely not for penalties relating to travelling in bus-lanes, a distinction typical of an environmentalist.

Table 14.3 **Balancing the triple bottom line** – *continued*

Theme	Ref	Comment
Benefiting from partners' expertise	5	It's no use trying to save very unemployable people if you are no good at it. So we're trying to learn, we're trying to get in organizations who deal in providing jobs and training, things like that. *(Manager)*
Clear goals	6	The major goals that have been set for us by the board are 10 thousand tonnes of furniture being sent through us in the next three years and get it up to a rate of about 70/80% reuse in some way, shape or form. *(Manager)*
Matching CSR needs	7	The corporate citizenship, or otherwise, of someone like [a named blue-chip company] is absolutely fundamental, it's something that [its chairman] thinks that he needs to be spending 3 hours a week thinking about, and that's the same, probably, for every...FTSE 100 company. *(Manager)*
	8	I have been impressed by the level of information that we receive from Green-Works. *(Donor)*
	9	[It] ticks all boxes. *(Donor referring to Green-Works' employment policy and provision of cheap furniture to nonprofits as well as the avoidance of landfill)*
Start-up capital and funding	10	We had real trouble, despite the fact that I had an exceptionally long track record with the bank – 25 years of banking with them. Couldn't even get a GBP500 overdraft. Quite ludicrous. *(CEO)*
	11	You find that... [a grant] has got a curved end on it which says, we need these outputs, and you start to achieve a completely different set of outputs to the ones that you originally set out on. *(CEO)*
Delivering a high quality service	12	They are savvy and street-smart and seem very well organized and pleasant to deal with. *(Donor)*
	13	We, bar none, have said we'll do something and we've done it. The internal mechanics of doing it have sometimes been painful, but...on time, on budget, that's why we're very commercially orientated because we work to things like on time and on budget. A community organization doesn't talk like that, doesn't think like that. *(Manager)*
Self-funding	14	Our daily operations are now entirely funded by commercial activity ... [since] Green-Works is unashamedly trying to make a buck. [The reason?] We've got to grow and try and make some money to grow some more...there's more [furniture] out there, we want to divert more...from landfill. *(CEO)*

Table 14.3   **Balancing the triple bottom line** – *continued*

Theme	Ref	Comment
Revenue streams	15	[Income is] loaded to the corporate side, which is an ethical decision. *(Manager)*
Outsourcing the social element	16	Green-Works has a few jobs at the warehouse but there's not much training in place, there's no procedure for: right, we're going to go and get some people who are desperately unemployable, we have people who could probably be employed somewhere else...Now we've got a warehouse...and it's operational and running smoothly, we can start looking at that. *(Manager)*
Tensions about commerciality	17	As a business, I think we've already crossed the bridge in the sense that people view us – other social enterprises, other charities – are very wary of the big commercial beast that we are. *(Manager)*
	18	[Green-Works is] a pretty commercially-minded but not financially-motivated organization ...we're not after a great return on capital or anything like that. *(Manager)*

Crooks' hatred of waste extends to people – the notion of disadvantaged individuals unable to secure employment is an anathema to him. Providing such individuals with employment and training, which was originally contracted out to community partners and franchisees because of a lack of expertise in the area, (Table 14.3: 5) is a key part of the business model.

Whilst the literature highlights problems in establishing what being 'green' means and in deriving useful measurements, it is, for Green-Works, an unequivocal concept: namely, reducing the UK's landfill burden by a quantifiable amount whilst aiming (and nowadays succeeding) to recycle 100 per cent of its donations. Measuring 'greenness' and linking this to clear strategic goals is easy in this context (Table 14.3: 6). Every piece of furniture it receives is tracked individually, from initial donor to end consumer. Its team have calculated that at July 2004 their customers – largely nonprofits – saved around GBP half a million by buying such cheap (but good quality) office furniture. Triple bottom line reporting is used, along with the Global Reporting Initiative's environmental measurement system, to assess the impact of its actions. This assiduousness in tracking and measurement is considered by Green-Works to be pivotal in its ability to attract donors for whom the CSR agenda is becoming increasingly important (Table 14.3: 7) as is the quantification of CSR benefits. An anonymous qualitative survey demonstrated the value of this tactic: Green-Works was valued for its provision of information (Table 14.3: 8), as well as for the duality of environmental and social benefits (Table 14.3: 9), all of which gives the donors specific data to put in their annual reports as opposed to a donation to charity, whose benefits are usually less tangible.

Green-Works' idealism runs in tandem with an awareness of the importance of economic sustainability – particularly important given the perceived ineptness of ecopreneurs in managing their finances (Linnanen, 2002). The economic viability of the business is illustrated by the operating surplus made (See Table 14.4) which is reinvested in the business.

Table 14.4   Economic viability: Green-Works' Financial Report 03/04

	Income (£)		Expenditure (£)
Internal			
Membership and renewals	80,585	Warehouse fees	296,073
Donations, grants and sponsorships	115,158	Wages incl. consultancy	357,958
Reception and collection fees	424,065	Marketing/other office expenses	56,782
Furniture sales	105,001	General operational costs	65,543
Third party carriers	139,020	Third party carriers	123,365
Misc incl. interest	26,639		
Franchises			
Franchise fees	6,850	Furniture and other purchases	10,704
Furniture sales	23,207	Third party carriers	550
Total	**920,525**		**910,975**
Net pretax profit	**9,550**		

The problems in finding startup capital highlighted by Linnanen (2002) were experienced by Green-Works (Table 14.3: 10) and aggravated by the CEO's rejection of grant funding (Table 14.3: 11). However, initial cash-flow problems were rapidly overcome, primarily by charging the donor organizations a modest premium over the cost of landfill. This premium reflects the value added by the quantifiable CSR benefits to what is already a well-received service (Table 14.3: 12, 13). In doing this Green-Works has subverted the traditional social enterprise model, whereby customers are charged below cost price (Renewal.net, 2003), thus allowing the organization to become self-funded (Table 14.3: 14) as well as facilitating low prices to its nonprofit customers (Table 14.3: 15). Another innovation is a system whereby Green-Works' tariffs are split between two of the donor's departments (Table 14.5). The membership fee is often paid in advance, thus further alleviating any potential cashflow problems.

Table 14.5   Green-Works' pricing scheme

	Facilities management department	CSR department
Benefits sought	Logistical solution: one-stop furniture removal	PR; association with Green-Works brand; HR relations
Fees paid to Green-Works	Reception/collection fees	Membership fees
Payment timing	On delivery	(Often) in advance
Nature of benefits	Tangible	Intangible/tangible (reporting)
Premium paid	Moderate	High
Price sensitivity	Moderate	Low

The literature review in this chapter has highlighted the problems inherent in balancing classic triple bottom line values. However, there is agreement amongst the management team that Green-Works' principal goal is environmental sustainability. The focus on green matters is reflected in staff motivations: two out of the four managers interviewed stated that they were motivated primarily by environmentalism, with the other two focused respectively on helping the community and working for (and learning from) an entrepreneur.

There is some tension about Green-Works' commerciality within the business (Table 14.3: 17) with even the least idealistic manager feeling that the balance has tipped too far towards making money. However, the comments from another (Table 14.3: 18) emphasize that profitability is not the end-game – it is helping to reduce waste which, in its turn, requires a commercial approach to be sustainable. This marriage between idealistic values and commercial acumen is perhaps best epitomised by one ethnographic observation noting the CEO's daily metamorphoses from ecowarrior in full cycling kit to a city-slicker in a well-cut suit and back again. It is hard not to form the impression that this willingness to embrace the symbols of a classical perception of business efficiency is a metaphor for the essence of Green-Works' success.

Creating networks

Pivotal to Green-Works' success is its embeddedness within a series of networks created by the CEO and the management. An early example of the development of such networks took place when the CEO, in typically entrepreneurial style, seized the opportunity proffered by a bank planning what was then the biggest corporate move in UK history. This allowed Crooks to secure two out of three of the benefits described by Gnyawali and Madhavan (2001) through networks: assets (the furniture) and status in the form of credibility, deemed so important for ecopreneurs with their unknown, untested businesses (Linnanen, 2002; 14.3: 7, 8, 9 and Table 14.6: 1). As an example of the third benefit cited by Gnyawali and Madhavan (2001), information (in this case about local markets), together with a further injection of assets (expertise in employing and training people from disadvantaged backgrounds and warehousing facilities) were secured again through Crooks' inveterate networking (Table 14.6: 2, 3). He already knew of an East End charity that was looking for opportunities to invest in the creation of jobs with a low skills base and joined forces with them. Green-Works supplied the furniture; they provided the human resources (including training) and the warehousing. Thus was born a viable business model based on a pattern of partnerships.

This second series of networks, which evolved into the social franchising model, is in the words of one manager, *'really a key part of our capacity'*. It and other partnerships – with community groups and commercial operators – foster the unusual combination of high growth with low risk (Table 14.6: 4). A high proportion of the costs borne by Green-Works comes from charges relating to its own warehouse, and therefore contracting out this activity to partners and franchisees elsewhere, reduces the need for hefty investment in further outlets thereby facilitating rapid expansion.

Another key partner is a commercial office relocation firm. It offers what it terms the *'green package'*, but contracts out the environmentalist element of the offering to Green-Works, giving itself significant competitive advantage: *'They were aware that if they didn't get onto the environmental bandwagon one of their competitors would'* (Green-Works Manager). Other charities and social enterprises may feel that entering

Table 14.6   Creating networks

Theme	Ref	Comment
Building credibility	1	[It is] important to have prior success. (*Corporate donor commenting on Green-Works' track record*)
Entrepreneurial networking	2	We've got opportunistic antennae that are out there looking and I have about 20 opportunities in my line at any one time that I am looking for partners to share with. So it's not exactly extraordinary that people pop up one day, so long as I've got the idea of what I'm looking for ....it isn't luck. *(CEO)*
	3	He [Crooks] wants to be out there networking, talking to people, coming up with ideas and seeing them through. *(Manager)*
Reducing risk	4	If business dries up... with us, OK, we're in breach of contract but we can wind things down without a financial knock-on effect. *(Manager)*
The advantages of partnerships	5	I think a lot of these wishy-washy, airy-fairy, very cuddly charitable organizations, they think that they have to take the world on themselves, whereas you can take the world on yourself, but if you happen to have an underbelly of partners and sub-contractors and such like to allow you to do that... *(Manager)*
Governmental contacts	6	...we're getting into a whole series of government-based documents. I don't know how many times we've featured in the DEFRA* stuff... *(Manager)*

*DEFRA – Department for Environment, Food and Rural Affairs

into such agreements is tantamount to a Faustian pact, an attitude dismissed by Green-Works (Table 14.6: 5).

A further web of partnerships encompasses the well-chosen board. With a raft of highly relevant skills, it is comprised of journalists, fellow social entrepreneurs, local government contacts and volunteers all enjoying synergistic relationships with Green-Works. Governmental support is also important in validating the Green-Works operation (Table 14.6: 6), which has benefited from the publicity surrounding ministerial visits and the Mayor of London, Ken Livingstone, naming Crooks as London's 'Green Ambassador'. In return, Green-Works in general (and Crooks in particular), acts as a torch-bearer for governmental moves towards delivering sustainable social solutions.

These networks facilitate the balancing act between social, environmental and economic goals described in the section above not just within the social enterprise itself, but also in terms of the division of roles between the different organizations in the network.

Discussion

We have examined Green-Works as an example of social ecopreneurship under three broad headings: an entrepreneurial organization; balancing the triple bottom line; and creating networks. Taking firstly *an entrepreneurial organization* we have demonstrated that the CEO exhibits the classic characteristics of an entrepreneur, such as vision and risk-taking. The potent mix of this flair with ideals, vision, ingenuity, networking and knowledge of the market, means that Green-Works can leverage CSR, environmental and social issues (for instance waste of both resources and people) and secure governmental involvement (regulation and the desire to propagate certain goals through social enterprise) to create an economically, environmentally and socially sustainable business. Idealistic values, which in other circumstances may have been a hindrance, have been transformed by entrepreneurial flair into valuable assets contributing to Green-Works' economic success.

Crooks' commercial approach should, according to Walley and Taylor (2002), be at odds with his mission. They suggest that for social and ecological entrepreneurs economic and sustainability orientation, are, literally, poles apart. However, if Leibenstein (1968) is right, entrepreneurs have a nose for slack in the system and a desire to do something about it: that is their basic function. This is reflected in Crooks' near-obsession with waste reduction and his ability to see value where others do not – in redundant office furniture. Social and ecological entrepreneurship might be an even more natural offshoot of entrepreneurship than has previously been thought.

Anderson (1998: 138) described entrepreneurship as a *'splendid vehicle'* for social change. This research builds upon his and other work and suggests that *social ecopreneurship* using a franchising model is a very effective way of large-scale dissemination of an individual's environmental vision. Crooks thinks that the microindustry Green-Works represents is close to becoming a norm; this, in tandem with his missionary motivation, resonates with speculation from Carroll (1997) that industries are often founded by evangelical individuals dedicated to a vision of a better world. If Green-Works really is able to keep delivering its lofty triptych of environmental, social and economic goals it could become an avatar for the waste industry, for social franchising in the nonprofit world, for the provision of CSR solutions and, indeed, for any commercially-minded social enterprise with an appetite for growth.

Under *balancing the triple bottom line* we saw that economic viability was achieved whilst meeting environmental and social goals (Menon and Menon, 1997). This is best illustrated by Figure 14.1 – the business model.

Reuse of furniture provides both a benefit to the environment and an engine for jobs, thus meeting social and environmental goals. Economic viability is achieved largely through Green-Works' status as a social enterprise (securing it a range of free goods) and its lack of investment in assets (facilitated by social franchising), which, together with an ingenious and novel pricing model, allow it to overcome the social and ecological entrepreneur's usual cash-flow problems. This is somewhat akin to the suggestion of Seelos and Mair (2004) that social enterprises may flourish in partnership with corporations since the advance payment of membership fees functions rather like an interest-free loan. The model ensures that economic goals are met.

However whilst financial success is considered necessary for sustainability, it is only a means to an end. Green-Works' primary goal

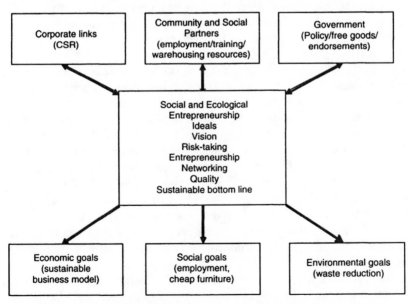

Figure 14.1 A model for combining social and ecological entrepreneurship

of reducing the country's landfill burden is an unequivocal and measurable environmental mission. This acts as a lodestar for determining the company's overall direction and, indeed, its culture, thus negating any suspicion of the tension between ethics and entrepreneurialism highlighted by Morris, Schindehutte, Walton and Allen (2002).

The achievement of a triple bottom line needs to be considered in the context of network level strategy (De Wit and Meyer, 2004). In *creating networks* we saw the importance of Green-Works' embeddedness in a web of complex and symbiotic relationships with a whole network of organizations involved in social enterprise, CSR and ecological activities. Among the most important are those it has forged with its corporate donors – for whom it has addressed the market for CSR benefits by offering a duality of measurable environmental and social outcomes. By incorporating these outcomes into the notion of quality, the firms are charged a premium, thus changing the rules of the game (Hamel, 2000) in the field of social enterprise. This innovative pricing scheme (Table 14.5) ultimately benefits the customers, to whom Green-Works can afford to offer extremely low prices. That the donor-oriented element of the operation – from which Green-Works derives the vast majority of its income – is a service, renders the exercise even less price-sensitive especially since the donors report such ease of use. Free goods, received as expertise and networking opportunities from the corporate community through its well-chosen board, serve to further bolster the model.

Also of vital importance are Green-Works' relationships with its community partners and franchisees. Through the latter it has established a business model that is new to the UK, namely a franchised social enterprise. This model facilitates rapid dissemination of the environmental and social vision via relatively risk-free growth, whilst minimizing acquisition of expensive assets and leaving, at least in its early stages, the employment and training of disadvantaged people to these experts.

The governmental relationships built up by Crooks, and also by his managers, have gained Green-Works both media coverage and endorsement through ministerial visits and the winning of awards. Probably the key benefit from this source that Green-Works enjoys is the government's zeal in promoting CSR as part of its environmental and social policy.

Green-Works, large corporates and social franchises are thus 'embedded' within a mutually advantageous network (Gnyawali and Madhavan, 2001; Granovetter, 1985). Firms have a limited set of core competencies and core business processes but, at the same time, they are beset by an increasing number of requirements to meet social, environmental and economic objectives. As Crooks himself has said: 'My philosophy is much more holistic than just a straightforward debate about, let's protect the environment... it's key that these things are linked together. I don't see them as 1, 2 and 3, I seem them as embedded'. The requirements of corporates to meet triple bottom line objectives, the policies of governments to promote sustainability and social enterprise, and the endeavors of community and social partners to provide training and employment are tightly interlinked in a network created by Green-Works.

We maintain that this research has thus provided empirical evidence of Granovetter's theory (1985) that economic action is embedded in structures of social relations in modern industrial society. Green-Works is an example of the way that small firms in a market setting persist 'because a dense network of social relations is overlaid on the business relations connecting such firms and reduces pressures for integration'. (Granovetter, 1985: 504). Thus, Crooks' idealistic wish that corporates might take on the activity of ecological waste management themselves seems unlikely to be fulfilled and the position of such social and ecological enterprises is secure.

Implications

The aim of this study was to discover whether social ecopreneurs can operate an economically viable business whilst still retaining the core values that motivated its creation in the first place. Green-Works is an example of such a business. At the heart of its success is an essential entrepreneurialism and its embeddedness within a network of organizations working together to achieve mutually beneficial aims.

Although this research was restricted to one UK case study – a model that has evolved in part through policies and business trends specific to the UK – we believe that implications may be derived for other organizations. The achievement of a triple bottom line needs to be considered in the context of network level strategy (De Wit and Meyer, 2004). We have described how Green-Works, large corporates and social franchises are 'embedded' within a mutually advantageous network (Gnyawali and Madhavan, 2001; Granovetter, 1985). The Green-Works business model presents large corporates with a possibility to meet their social and environmental targets in a way that is *quantifiable*. The environmental benefit can be counted in the number of desks saved from landfill and the social benefit can be calculated as the number of extra jobs created and the savings achieved by nonprofits buying the furniture.

Hart and Milstein (1999) maintain that visionary companies in incumbent positions have an opportunity to drive the redefinition and redesign of their industries towards global sustainability. A development route for these companies (described as 'corporates' in this chapter) can be to work within a network by supporting social ecopreneurs.

The Green-Works network is complex. It includes large corporates, as well as social franchisees, board members, and links to government and local authorities. The key message for any social and ecological enterprise is therefore to develop a network, to embed the organization within a symbiotic business model. In this way, what may be a fundamentally unprofitable business dealing with waste management for example, can be transformed by free or low cost goods provided symbiotically by other members of the network.

This research has demonstrated: firstly, a natural fit between social and ecological enterprise and entrepreneurialism; secondly, a business model offering economic sustainability for social and environmental enterprises; and thirdly, the value of network level strategy for enabling a variety of organizations to achieve their objectives in terms of the triple bottom line. We therefore suggest three avenues for future research. What further evidence is there of the natural fit between idealism and entrepreneurialism as established in this organization, or is a tension between the two more prevalent? Do other viable business models for social and ecological enterprise exist in the UK and elsewhere? How can network and organizational embeddedness theory be further advanced in relation to the CSR and the global sustainability debate?

Appendix 14A   Interview guide and links to original research questions

---

Q1   What are the organization's major goals?
 Research questions: STRGY
 Prompts: evolution of model, decision making processes, time horizons, opportunism vs planning
Q2   What do you think gives you competitive advantage?
 Research questions: STRGY, CHL
 Prompts: governmental relations, skills, unpredictable market processes
Q3   How do you measure performance?
 Research questions: STRGY, ETHC, ECN
 Prompts: environmental management system, waste management, stakeholders, profit orientation

Appendix 14A   Interview guide and links to original research questions – *continued*

Q4   How important is growth to Green-Works?
Research questions: STRGY, ECN
Prompts: funding/startup capital, importance of regulations/
instruments/CSR, social franchising

Q5   How do you manage supply and demand?
Research questions: ECN
Prompts: fluctuations, effects of publicity

Q6   Apart from the things we've already mentioned what are the key
challenges you face?
Research questions: CHL
Prompts: small team, risk of green-washing, leadership styles, balancing
wide range of demands

Q7   Do you think that Green-Works operates in a way that is different to its
nonsustainable counterparts?
Research questions: STRGY, CHL
Prompts: culture, integration of management and staff, having to be
greener than green

Q8   Describe your marketing policy
Research questions: STRGY, CHL
Prompts: tight budgets, word of mouth, awards, education, commercialism
vs ethics

Key to original research questions:
STRGY: What are the strategies of this organization and how are they created?
ETHC: How does the organization fulfill its ethical mandate?
ECN: How does it maintain economic viability?
CHL: What other key challenges does it face?

References

Amies, M. 2000. Not for profit franchising. *Franchising World*, 32(6): 38–9.
Anderson, A. R. 1998. Cultivating the Garden of Eden: Environmental entrepreneuring. *Journal of Organizational Change Management*, 11(2): 135–44.
Azzone, A. R. and Noci, G. 1998. Seeing ecology and 'green' innovations as a source of change. *Journal of Organizational Change Management*, 11(2): 94–111.
Carroll, G. R. 1997. Long-term evolutionary change in organizational populations: Theory, models and empirical findings from industrial demography. *Industrial and Corporate Change*, 6: 119–45.
De Wit, B. and Meyer, R. 2004. *Strategy: Process, content, context* (3rd edn). London: Thomson.
DTI (Department of Trade and Industry). 2004. *Corporate social responsibility: A government update*. Available: http://www.societyandbusiness.gov.uk/pdf/dti_csr_final.pdf. Accessed 11 Aug 2004.
Dyer, W. G. J. and Wilkins, A. L. 1991. Better stories, not better constructs, to generate better theory: A rejoinder to Eisenhardt. *Academy of Management Review*, 16: 613–19.

Eisenhardt, K. M. 1989. Building theories from case study research, *Academy of Management Review*, 14: 532–50.

Financial Times. 1994. Halo slips on the raspberry bubbles. 8–27/28 August.

Geertz, C. 1973. *The interpretation of cultures: Selected essays*. New York: Basic Books.

Gnyawali, D. R. and Madhavan, R. 2001. Cooperative networks and competitive dynamics: A structural embeddedness perspective. *Academy of Management Review*, 26(3): 431–45.

Granovetter. 1985. Economic action and social structure: The problem of embeddedness. *American Journal of Sociology*, 91: 481–501.

Hall, J. and Vredenburg, H. 2003. The challenges of innovating for sustainable development. *MIT Sloan Management Review*, 45(1): 61–8.

Hamel, G. 2000. The end of progress. *Business Strategy Review*, 11(3): 69–78.

Hart, S. L. and Milstein, M. B. 1999. Global sustainability and the creative destruction of industries. *MIT Sloan Management Review*, 41(1): 23–33.

Isaak, R. 1997. Globalisation and green entrepreneurship, *Greener Management International*, 18: 80–90.

Lanoie, P. and Tanguay, G. A. 2000. Factors leading to green profitability. *Greener Management International*, 31: 39–50.

Leibenstein, H. 1968. Entrepreneurship and development. *American Economic Review*, 58: 72–8.

Linnanen, L. 2002. An insider's experiences with environmental entrepreneurship. *Greener Management International*, Summer (38): 71–80.

Lynn, G. S., Morone, J. G. and Paulson, A. S. 1996. Marketing and discontinuous innovation: The probe and learn process. *California Management Review*, 38(3): 8–37.

Menon, A. and Menon, A. 1997. Enviropreneurial marketing strategy: The emergence of corporate environmentalism as market strategy. *Journal of Marketing*, 61(1): 51–66.

Miles, M. B. and Huberman, A. M. 1994. *Qualitative data analysis: An expanded sourcebook*. Thousand Oaks, London and New Delhi: Sage Publications.

Morris, M. H., Schindehutte, M., Walton, J. and Allen, J. 2002. The ethical context of entrepreneurship: Proposing and testing a developmental framework. *Journal of Business Ethics*, 40(4): 331–61.

Pastakia, A. (1998). Grassroots ecopreneurs: Change agents for a sustainable society. *Journal of Organizational Change Management*, 11: 157–73.

Renewal.net. 2003. *Social Enterprise*. Available: http://www.renewal.net/Documents/RNET/Overview/Local%20Economies/SocialEnterprise.DOC. Accessed 11 August 2004.

Seelos, C. and Mair, J. 2004. Entrepreneurs in service of the poor – models for business contributions to sustainable development. Working Paper, IESE Business School, University of Navarra, Barcelona.

Venkataraman, S. 1997. The distinctive domain of entrepreneurship research. In J. Katz (ed.), *Advances in entrepreneurship, firm emergence and growth*. Vol. III: 119–38. Greenwich, Conn: JAI Press.

Walley, E. E. and Taylor, D. W. 2002. Opportunists, champions, mavericks...? A typology of green entrepreneurs. *Greener Management International*, Summer: 31–43.

Yin, R. K. 2003. *Case study research. Design and methods* (3rd edn). Thousand Oaks, London and New Delhi: Sage Publications.

15
Social Entrepreneurs Directly Contribute to Global Development Goals

Christian Seelos, Kate Ganly and Johanna Mair

Introduction

In 1987, Gro Harlem Brundtland put forward the global objective of achieving sustainable development (UN General Assembly, 1987). She had been tasked by the United Nations General Assembly in 1983 to 'make available a report on environment and the global *problématique* to the year 2000 and beyond, including proposed strategies for sustainable development' (UN General Assembly, 1983). In her report, she explicitly assigned priority to satisfying the essential needs of the poor, such as those for 'food, clothing, shelter, jobs', and also to provide them with the 'opportunity to satisfy their aspirations for a better life'. This should be achieved, however, without 'compromising the ability of future generations to meet their own needs' (Brundtland, 1987). Brundtland thus identified the main goal for global efforts to trace a path of balanced social and economic development which was also compatible with a notion of social equity across the dimensions of space and time. Her report left open the question of how such balanced development could be achieved:

> No single blueprint of sustainability will be found, as economic and social systems and ecological conditions differ widely among countries. Each nation will have to work out its own concrete policy implications. Yet irrespective of these differences, sustainable development should be seen as a global objective. (Brundtland, 1987: 50)

To instill new momentum in the efforts to achieve sustainable development (SD), the UN Millennium Declaration was adopted in September 2000 at the largest-ever gathering of heads of state. It committed countries – rich and poor – to doing all they could to eradicate poverty, promote human dignity and equality and achieve peace, democracy and environmental sustainability (UN General Assembly, 2000). In order to operationalize the notion of SD, the United Nations (UN) defined a set of Millennium Development Goals (MDGs). These MDGs comprise eight quantifiable and monitorable goals (with 18 targets and 48 specific indicators) for global development and poverty eradication by 2015. Goals include health, education, gender equality and environmental issues. While a multitude of projects was immediately launched among aid agencies, governments and multilateral institutions to address these pressing problems, the UNDP Human Development Report 2003 (UNDP, 2003: v) stated that:

> ... despite these welcome commitments in principle to reducing poverty and advancing other areas of human development, in practice – as this Report makes very clear – the world is already falling short.... More than 50 nations grew poorer over the past decade. Many are seeing life expectancy plummet due to HIV/AIDS. Some of the worst performers – often torn by conflict – are seeing school enrolments shrink and access to basic health care fall. And nearly everywhere the environment is deteriorating.

The World Development Report 2004 released by the World Bank, clearly states that economic growth is essential to reaching the MDGs and that 'the projected growth in per capita GDP will by itself enable five of the world's six developing regions to reach the goal for reducing income poverty' (World Bank, 2004: 2). However, the report also maintains that many services contributing to health and education are failing poor people. The reason for this failure appears to be the fact that public spending effectively does not reach the poor, or if it does manage to reach them, service provision is inefficient and of inadequate quality.

We have recently argued that neither development organizations nor multinational companies may be in the best position to discover the innovative solutions necessary to achieve sustainable development on a global scale (Seelos and Mair, 2005a; 2005b). One of the main reasons is that development problems generally consist of large sets of interconnected problems that are context specific: usually they cannot be solved through direct intervention because the chain of causality is unclear (Easterly, 2001). Furthermore, helping poor people directly through donations of food, medicine or through services such as education and medical care does not change the system that produced poverty in the first place. The least accessible group in societies, the so-called 'ultra poor', have extremely high reproduction rates and therefore create new poverty faster than direct development efforts can help them to escape the poverty trap in which many of them are caught. Indeed, population growth projections until 2045 indicate that of the 2.2 billion additional people, 1.5 billion will come from the lowest income group and only 0.026 billion from the highest income group (World Bank, 2005).

Context dependency often prevents a 'best practice' approach to these problems and thus the replication of 'solutions' will be limited. We argue that social entrepreneurs are able to discover unique solutions within a local context and thereby contribute more effectively to social, human and economic development. Social entrepreneurs invent service provision models that cater to the very basic needs of individuals and they also change and institutionalize behavior, norms and rules that enable communities and societies to allocate resources more fairly and formalize individual rights. While their 'solutions' and models may not lend themselves to replication because they are context dependent, the process of finding solutions, that is, the entrepreneurial process of discovery, might be replicable in diverse settings and on a global scale. To better understand the extent to which social entrepreneurs contribute to sustainable development, we have addressed the following questions:

1. Do social entrepreneurs directly contribute to recognized sustainable development goals?
2. Are social entrepreneurs able to act on a global scale and, most importantly, in the poorest countries?

Methodology

Study population

As much literature in this field has highlighted, the term 'social entrepreneurship' (SE) still lacks a clear definition (Dees, 1998; Johnson, 2000; Mair and Martí, 2005) and seems to consist of a diverse range of initiatives in both developing and developed countries (Bornstein, 1998; Fowler, 2000; Seelos and Mair, 2005a; 2005b). A wide set of financial models of income generation exist, both internal and external to operations, as well as a number of different structural features ranging from nonprofit, nongovernmental organizations to commercial structures and even a mix of both within a single brand umbrella (Alvord, Brown and Letts, 2004; Austin, Stevenson and Wei-Skillern, 2003; Thompson, Alvy and Lees, 2000): all seem consistent with the term SE. We chose the Schwab Foundation list of *Outstanding Social Entrepreneurs* as the study population for its clarity and consistency of definition and for its global reach (Schwab Foundation, 2005). We introduce the criteria of the Schwab Foundation for recognizing 'outstanding social entrepreneurs' later in this chapter. In our analysis we have drawn on various sources of data on these initiatives: interviews with founders, existing teaching case studies (case studies on several initiatives were prepared by the authors), case studies prepared by the Schwab Foundation and other public resources such as websites, newspaper articles, features, and so on.

Measures for impacting sustainable development

The method of assessing contributions to global, sustainable economic development was to ask how the many organizations within the sample of social enterprises directly impact the eight MDGs set by the UN as a standard for achieving a more equitable level of global development (United Nations, 2005a). This was achieved by comparing the independent assessments of two researchers who examined each initiative in order to: a) understand its mission; b) understand its product/service provision model and; c) evaluate the outcome or level of product/service provision. To make a qualitative judgement, the models of the Schwab Foundation social entrepreneurs were mapped to the 18 individual targets specified by the MDGs. Discrepancies between the two independent assessments were resolved by reaching consensus through debate among the three authors.

Defining the 'poorest countries'

In particular, the population of social entrepreneurs was examined to determine if any are impacting the MDGs in the Least Developed Countries (LDCs) as defined by the UN. This study will also consider social entrepreneurs who are impacting these goals in countries with a very low Human Development Index (HDI) ranking as defined by the United Nations Development Program (UNDP).

The Millenium Development Goals

In September 2000, 192 member states of the UN made a commitment to achieving a number of specific goals aimed at stimulating economic and human development in countries with very low incomes and extremely basic living standards. High on the agenda were the eradication of poverty and hunger, education for all, gender equality and health. The goals were derived from the UN Millennium Declaration which addressed the burning issues of inequality among nations in an increasingly interconnected and interdependent world. The resolution of the UN General Assembly stated that 'we have a collective responsibility to uphold the principles of human dignity, equality and equity at the global level' (UN General Assembly, 2000: 1). Furthermore, it continued:

We believe that the central challenge we face today is to ensure that globalization becomes a positive force for all the world's people. For while globalization offers great opportunities, at present its benefits are unevenly shared, while its costs are unevenly distributed. We recognize that developing countries and countries with economies in transition face special difficulties in responding to this central challenge. Thus, only through broad and sustained efforts to create a shared future, based on our common humanity in all its diversity, can globalization be made fully inclusive and equitable.

To this end, a set of eight MDGs were created and 18 specific targets set. Each goal also has a set of indicators to be employed in the measurement of the world's progress towards achieving the goals by 2015. These goals and targets are now incorporated into all of the UNDP and the World Bank's benchmarking on development issues. Table 15.1 lists the MDGs and their associated targets.

Table 15.1 The Millennium Development Goals and targets

Goals	Targets
1. Eradicate extreme poverty and hunger	1. Halve between 1990 and 2015, the proportion of people whose income is less than one dollar per day 2. Halve between 1991 and 2015, the proportion of people who suffer from hunger
2. Achieve universal primary education	3. Ensure that by 2015, children everywhere, boys and girls alike, will be able to complete a course of primary schooling
3. Promote gender equality and empower women	4. Eliminate gender disparity in primary and secondary education, preferably by 2005, and in all levels of education no later than 2015

Table 15.1   The Millennium Development Goals and targets – *continued*

Goals	Targets
4. Reduce child mortality	5. Reduce by two-thirds, between 1990 and 2015, the under-five mortality rate
5. Improve maternal health	6. Reduce by three-quarters between 1990 and 2015, the maternal mortality ratio
6. Combat HIV/AIDS, malaria and other diseases	7. Have halted by 2015 and begun to reverse the spread of HIV/AIDS 8. Have halted by 2015 and begun to reverse the incidence of malaria and other diseases
7. Ensure environmental sustainability	9. Integrate the principles of sustainable development into country policies and programs and reverse the loss of environmental resources 10. Halve by 2015, the proportion of people without sustainable access to safe drinking water and basic sanitation 11. By 2020, to have achieved a significant improvement in the lives of at least 100 million slum dwellers
8. Develop a global partnership for development	12. Develop further an open, rule-based, predictable, nondiscriminatory trading and financial system 13. Address the special needs of the least developed countries 14. Address the special needs of landlocked developing countries and small island developing states 15. Deal comprehensively with the debt problems of developing countries through national and international measures in order to make debt sustainable in the long term 16. In cooperation with developing countries, develop and implement strategies for decent and productive work for youth 17. In cooperation with pharmaceutical companies, provide access to affordable essential drugs in developing countries 18. In cooperation with the private sector, make available the benefits of new technologies, especially information and communications

The Schwab Foundation social entrepreneurs

The Schwab Foundation defines a social entrepreneur as someone who:

- Identifies and applies *practical* solutions to social problems by combining innovation, resourcefulness and opportunity
- *Innovates* by finding a new product, a new service, or a new approach to a social problem
- Focuses first and foremost on *social value creation* and in that spirit, is willing to *share openly* the innovations and insights of the initiative with a view to its wider replication
- *Doesn't wait to secure the resources* before undertaking the catalytic innovation
- Is *fully accountable* to the constituencies she/he serves
- Resists being trapped by the *constraints of ideology or discipline*
- Continuously *refines and adapts* the approach in response to feedback
- Has a vision, but also a *well-thought out roadmap* as to how to attain the goal
  (Schwab Foundation, 2005)

Typically the Schwab Foundation elects members to its network of 'Outstanding Social Entrepreneurs' when their enterprise is in its growth and expansion phase. Rather than offering cash grants, the Schwab Foundation gives social entrepreneurs the opportunity to network with members of the World Economic Forum and among each other thus providing access to valuable networks, knowledge and experience on a global scale. The selection process is lengthy and thorough, and the Foundation has a number of criteria for awarding membership to the network. According to the Schwab Foundation (2005), the successful social enterprise must demonstrate: innovation, reach and scope, replicability, sustainability, direct positive social impact, mutual value added for both the Schwab network and the social entrepreneur; and it must have the ability to be a role model. Using these criteria, since its inception in 1998, the Schwab Foundation has selected an average of ten 'Outstanding Social Entrepreneurs' each year. In 2004, 15 were added to the network.

In 2005, the Schwab network consisted of a total of 84 social entrepreneurs who managed 74 social enterprises. For the purposes of this study the total population of 74 enterprises was considered. Appendix 15A contains a list of the Schwab selected social enterprises considered in this study.

How are social entrepreneurs helping achieve millennium development goals?

Having analyzed the models, products and services of the total population of 74 social enterprises of the Schwab network, we consider 50 to directly contribute to targets defined by the MDGs and a further 6 to indirectly contribute or to have an impact over time (See Appendix 15A). From the information available, the remaining 18 do not seem to clearly affect the specific MDGs although many of them fulfill other UN goals which were, in fact, also outlined in the Millennium Declaration of 2000, such as human rights issues, landmine clearance and so on. Thus it can be said that, of our sample, 68 per cent of initiatives have a *direct impact* on MDGs, eight per cent *indirectly impact* MDGs and 24 per cent *might not have a distinct impact*.

Of the group of initiatives which did not seem to have an impact on specific MDGs, most were ruled out because they operate in relatively developed countries and, although targeting the socially disadvantaged, on a global scale they are not eradicating extreme poverty, hunger or gender inequality, nor preventing needless death and disease. For example, Barka addresses the needs of homeless people with psychological problems in Poland by creating communities in once abandoned rural houses. It also offers socioeducational programs and provides employment through its local cottage industries. Whilst Barka's aim to improve the quality of life for a minority of the population is admirable, the context of a country with at least a basic social safety net precludes consideration of the MDGs. Other well-conceived social enterprises such as Habitat for Humanity and Endeavor Global, are aimed at a higher socioeconomic stratum, helping to stimulate a fledgling middle class by facilitating home ownership and entrepreneurship in developing countries. Innovative and commendable initiatives, such as Witness, which combats human rights abuses using video technology or Benetech which puts technology at the service of the visually impaired, develops human rights monitoring tools and now aims to produce humanitarian landmine detectors, address issues that are not covered by MDGs.

Among the social enterprises directly impacting MDGs, the majority are working to reduce poverty, empower women and conserve natural resources. The microfinance initiatives in this study offer a range of service models tailored to their specific communities, each targeting a sector of the population with extremely low income levels and little or no collateral thus enabling them to provide food, shelter and medicines for their families. In particular, Kashf Foundation and BRAC target their services towards women and provide additional educational and support programs to help them make the most effective use of their resources. Other social enterprises aimed at women are more specific. For example Phulki, in Bangladesh, operates 55 work-based daycare facilities for women employed in factories, government offices and businesses; it aims to show factory owners that, by investing in childcare they will benefit from a happier, more productive workforce.

The social enterprises having an impact on environmental concerns addressed by the MDGs are often solving several problems at once. IDEAAS for instance, provides low cost electricity to impoverished rural families in Brazil attacking both poverty and environmental degradation through the use of solar electricity and training in environmentally sustainable farming methods. Agriculture and technology-based initiatives such as ANEC, APABEB, ApproTEC and Honey Care help farmers to climb out of poverty by maintaining a sustainable income in a volatile and increasingly competitive market. Other social entrepreneurs make the organic and ecofriendly nature of their products the unique selling point: Duck Revolution, Transfair USA, Irupana and Sekem are good examples.

Other targets which social entrepreneurs are also impacting to some degree are the provision of primary education, reducing child and maternal mortality and combating the spread of HIV/AIDS and other diseases. One social enterprise which is helping to achieve education goals is Escuela Nueva. Originating in Columbia but now inspiring educational reform in 35 Latin American and Caribbean countries, it provides an alternative approach to primary education, especially in neglected rural areas, which has dramatically improved mathematical and language skills among populations where grade repetition, student dropout and low teacher morale were once the norm. Education and health are traditionally seen as the responsibility of the government, yet many of the social enterprises in this study have managed to make an impact in these areas when other approaches have failed. In India, for example, the *Comprehensive Rural Health Project* targets two specific MDGs, maternal health and child mortality, by training local village health workers and facilitating community participation. Market-based approaches to the problems of healthcare delivery such as *Project Impact* and the *Aravind Eye Hospital* are also enjoying success.

The six social enterprises which we have deemed as having an indirect impact on the MGDs or which may have an impact over time highlight some interesting cases (see Appendix 15A). The Institute for OneWorld

Health (IOWH) refers to itself as the world's first nonprofit pharmaceutical company (IOWH, 2005). Its goal is to target neglected diseases by developing donated compounds through the clinical trial phases into marketable, low-cost drugs for sufferers in developing countries. IOWH has drugs in its pipeline which may help combat malaria and other deadly diseases (MDG six, target eight); however, as of August 2005, IOWH had not yet launched a drug. The potential for IOWH to impact health goals in the future could be enormous but we cannot include this social enterprise in our list of active contributors. In a similar vein, CAMBIA is a biotechnology organization which aims to democratize the biotech innovation process and to disseminate knowledge about advanced agricultural technologies throughout the developing world. This could have great repercussions for farmers in these countries and possibly also for the environment yet we cannot point to a specific achievement which has directly impacted any of the MDGs.

The targets associated with goals one to seven have been set by the UN to be achieved mainly by developing countries themselves, often with the help of aid supplied by OECD nations. The eighth MDG, on the other hand, outlines targets for the creation of a global partnership for development which is to be achieved by the OECD countries working with various multilateral agencies, NGOs and private companies. It is interesting to note that social entrepreneurs are also impacting four out of these seven targets: helping to promote open trade, reducing youth unemployment and providing access to drugs and technology. The only targets upon which social entrepreneurs are not having a direct impact are those operating at a macro level where results can only really be achieved by governments making unilateral agreements and contributing aid. More specifically, these targets are: assisting the LDCs to achieve economic growth; assisting the Land-Locked and Small Island Developing Countries (LLDCs and SIDCs) to achieve economic growth; and reducing the debt burden of developing countries overall. As we will discuss in the next section however, many of the social enterprises in this study are indeed having an impact in the world's LDCs and are, therefore, indirectly helping to reduce debt and stimulate economic growth from the ground up.

Where are social entrepreneurs having an impact?

Social entrepreneurs have a global reach

One of the research questions addressed in this study is whether social entrepreneurs are able to operate globally, including in the poorest countries. As shown in Figure 15.1, at the time of this study, of the 74 initiatives, 15 were operating in North America, 19 in Latin America, eight in Europe, seven in Africa, 23 in Asia and two in Australia. However, it should be noted that many initiatives are operating in several countries. Figure 15.1 only shows the headquarter locations and thus underrepresents the collective global scope of the initiatives.

Since the Schwab entrepreneurs have a success-bias in the sense that the initiatives have survived the initial startup phase and have proven impact and scale; their ability to create social value on a global scale, the wide variety of their structural organization and the value creation models they have discovered, all support the proposition that they emphasize local discovery rather than replication of best practices. Attempts to 'clone' the Grameen Bank model in India, Nepal, and Vietnam in the 1990s have proven much more difficult than anticipated (Todd, 1996). There is, however, indication that some basic principles of successful models can be employed in different contexts. For example the Kashf Foundation, an initiative in Pakistan, was designed and built from the model of the Grameen Bank in Bangladesh. However, local insights and experimentation by the founder Roshaneh Zafar were necessary to 'customize' the model to the particular culture, problem sets and resources of Pakistan (Zafar, 2005).

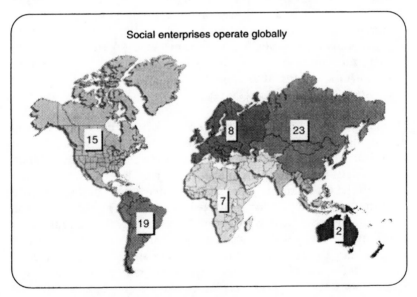

Figure 15.1 Distribution of Schwab Foundation social entrepreneurs

The world's LDCs and the Human Development Index

Another aim of this study is to assess whether social entrepreneurial initiatives can demonstrate that they are achieving their aims in the world's LCDs, where the biggest inequalities and large-scale poverty occur, and where the issue of meeting the MDGs is most urgent. The UN Office of the High Representative for the Least Developed Countries, Land-Locked Developing Countries and Small Island Developing States (OHRLLS) was established by the UN General Assembly (2001) to have special focus on these nations and their progress towards the MDGs. The criteria for identifying the LDCs, as defined by OHRLLS, are as follows:

- a low-income criterion, based on a three-year average estimate of the gross domestic product per capita (under US$750 for inclusion, above US$900 for graduation);
- a human resource weakness criterion, involving a composite Augmented Physical Quality of Life Index (APQLI) based on indicators of: (a) nutrition; (b) health; (c) education; and (d) adult literacy; and
- an economic vulnerability criterion, involving a composite Economic Vulnerability Index (EVI) based on indicators of: (a) the instability of agricultural production; (b) the instability of exports of goods and services; (c) the economic importance of non-traditional activities (share of manufacturing and modern services in GDP); (d) merchandise export concentration; and (e) the handicap of economic smallness (as measured through the population in logarithm); and the percentage of population displaced by natural disasters (United Nations, 2005b).

The many other multilateral institutions focused on economic and human development, such as the World Bank, the World Health Organization (WHO) and the United Nations Development Program (UNDP), defer to these criteria and use them in their own analyses. To be added to the list a country must meet all three criteria and to graduate from the list a country must meet the thresholds for at least two of the three criteria in two consecutive triennial reviews by the Committee for Development Policy (CDP). The first review in 2003 added Timor Leste to the group and suggested that Cape Verde and Maldives be recommended for graduation. The next review will take place in 2006 and Samoa has since also been recommended for graduation. After the review a recommendation will be made to the General Assembly, which

Table 15.2   Least Developed Countries
2004 Gross National Income (GNI) in USD per capita in parenthesis (Atlas methodology, World Bank 2005). For comparison: the US GNI per capita in 2004 was 41,400. Countries where social enterprises operate are shown in bold.

Afghanistan (n.a.)	**Madagascar (300)**
Angola (1030)	**Malawi (170)**
Bangladesh (440)	Maldives (2510)
Benin (530)	**Mali (360)**
Bhutan (760)	Mauritania (420)
Burkina Faso (360)	**Mozambique (250)**
Burundi (90)	Myanmar (n.a.)
Cambodia (320)	**Nepal (260)**
Cape Verde (1770)	**Níger (230)**
Central African Republic (310)	**Rwanda (220)**
Chad (260)	Samoa (1860)
Comoros (530)	Sao Tome and Principe (320)
Democratic Republic of Congo (120)	Senegal (670)
Djibouti (1030)	Sierra Leone (200)
Equatorial Guinea (n.a.)	Solomon Islands (550)
Eritrea (180)	Somalia (n.a.)
Ethiopia (110)	Sudan (530)
Gambia (290)	Timor-Leste (550)
Guinea (460)	Togo (380)
Guinea Bissau (160)	Tuvalu (n.a.)
Haiti (390)	**Uganda (270)**
Kiribati (970)	**Tanzania (United Republic of)**
Lao (People's Democratic Republic)	**(330)**
(390)	Vanuatu (1,340)
Lesotho (740)	Yemen (570)
Liberia (110)	**Zambia (450)**

is responsible for the final decision on the list of LDCs. Table 15.2 lists the 50 countries classed as 'least developed' by the UN in 2005.

Since headquarter locations for many initiatives as depicted in Figure 15.1 are not necessarily the locations where Schwab social entrepreneurs are actually operating, we have analyzed the countries in which they are active in more detail. These include the following LDCs: Afghanistan, Angola, Benin, Chad, Congo, Ethiopia, Gambia, Lesotho, Malawi, Mozambique, Niger, Tanzania, Uganda, Haiti, Timor-Leste, Bangladesh, Cambodia, Laos and Nepal. Thus, 19 or 38 per cent of the LDCs are being serviced by Schwab Foundation social entrepreneurs. Of the 50 social enterprises from the sample population which are directly contributing to MDGs, 32 per cent are operating in the LDCs of the world.

The vulnerability criterion for being declared an LDC ensures that countries in special need are included in the list. In addition, the fundamental recognition of structural handicaps excludes large economies; therefore the population must not exceed 75 million (United Nations, 2005b). For this reason not all of the LDCs appear neatly clustered at the bottom of development rankings such as the HDI, or the World Bank's compilation of World Development Indicators. Indeed, it is often the case that key indicators used to compile these rankings are not monitored in the world's LDCs and some, Afghanistan for example, do not have an HDI ranking.

Each year both the World Bank and the UNDP publish statistics, which rank countries based on their level of development. Since 2000, these and other multilateral organizations now incorporate the specific indicators used to measure progress towards the MDGs along with other key indicators for economic development. The major difference between these two reports is that the World Bank's World Development Indicators, provides lists, tables and rankings according to data for each of the separate indicators, while the UNDP's HDI attempts to combine a large array of different indicators into one ultimate ranking for human development which also takes into account less easily measurable factors relating to quality of life. The Human Development Report 2004 takes the approach that the basis of development is to enlarge human freedoms and to expand human capabilities by expanding the choices that people have to live full and creative lives (UNDP, 2004). It further states that these capabilities must be universally valued and that they must be basic to life in the sense that their absence would obviate many other choices:

It is easier to measure national incomes than human development. And many economists would argue that national income is a good indicator of human well-being. While there is evidently a strong relationship, since economic growth is an important means to human development, human outcomes do not depend on economic growth and levels of national income alone. They also depend on how these resources are used – whether for developing weapons or producing food, building palaces or providing clean water. And human outcomes such as democratic participation in decision-making or equal rights for men and women do not depend on incomes. For these reasons the Report presents an extensive set of indicators (33 tables and almost 200 indicators) on important human outcomes achieved in countries around the world, such as life expectancy at birth or under-five mortality rates, which reflect the capability to survive, or literacy rates which reflect the capability to learn. They also include indicators on important means for achieving these capabilities, such as the gaps between men and women in schooling or political participation. (UNDP, 2004: 127)

The Human Development Report focuses on four important capabilities: to lead a long and healthy life; to be knowledgeable; to have access to the resources needed for a decent standard of living; and to participate in the life of the community (UNDP, 2004). All of these capabilities are covered by the MDGs although the targets set for them are extremely basic such as halving the proportion of people living on less than USD1 a day. For this reason it is important to focus development efforts where they can do the most good. It is the aim of this paper to demonstrate that a good percentage of social entrepreneurs are doing just that.

Given the importance of taking into account all of the factors contributing to human well-being and development, the holistic HDI ranking is used here to assess the contributions of our population of social entrepreneurs rather than a single indicator such as Gross National Income (GNI) per capita such as is available in the World Bank's World Development Indicators.

By breaking down the population of 50 social enterprises which are directly contributing to MDGs according to the HDI rank of the LDCs these social entrepreneurs are operating in, we established that 60 per cent of these initiatives are servicing the bottom 30 per cent of countries in the HDI (Figure 15.2).

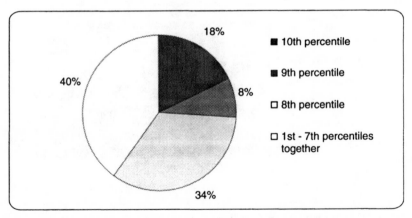

Figure 15.2 Social enterprises impacting MDGs in the bottom 30 per cent of the HDI

While the majority of the UN designated LDCs occur in the bottom 20 per cent of the HDI (the exceptions are Bangladesh, Cambodia, Laos and Nepal), Schwab social entrepreneurs who are impacting MDGs also work with a large percentage of those ranking in the bottom 30 per cent. These countries include India and Pakistan, which are precluded from the LDC list by their size and yet, according to the HDI, have a similar or lower level of development to Bangladesh.

Having established that at least 68 per cent of the total population of Schwab Foundation social entrepreneurial initiatives are directly impacting MDGs and that 60 per cent of those impacting MDGs are operating in countries ranked in the bottom 30 per cent of the HDI, this study will now consider which MDGs are being most affected by their work and which initiatives are the best examples of this practice.

A detailed analysis of social entrepreneurs impacting global development goals

Figure 15.3 displays the number of social enterprises from our total population making an impact on each individual MDG along with the number doing this work within countries in the bottom 30 per cent of the HDI. Analysis of the data shows that the social enterprises in our sample are having the most impact on goals for eradicating poverty, achieving gender equality, environmental sustainability and helping to

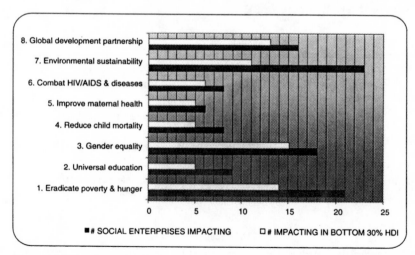

Figure 15.3 Number of social enterprises impacting Millennium Development Goals

Table 15.3 Mapping of Schwab Foundation Social Entrepreneurs to MDGs

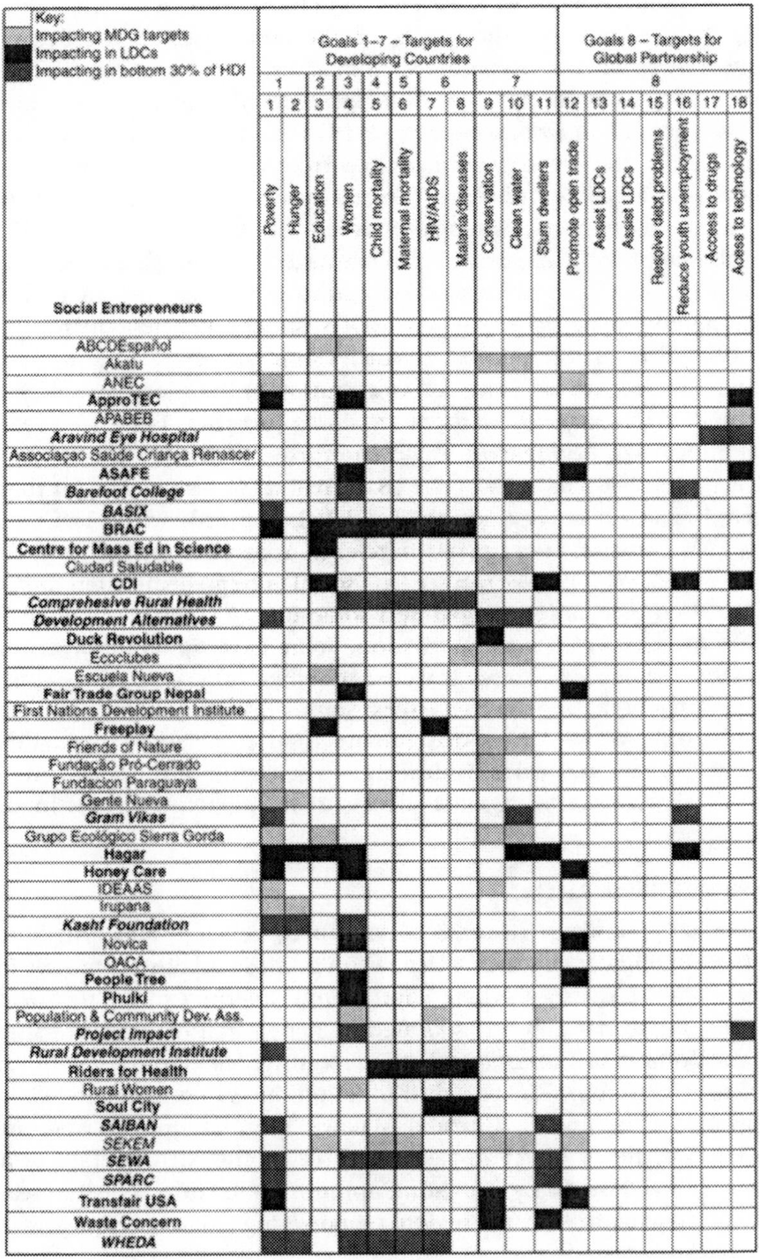

Key:
- Impacting MDG targets
- Impacting in LDCs
- Impacting in bottom 30% of HDI

Goals 1–7 – Targets for Developing Countries

Goals 8 – Targets for Global Partnership

Column headers:
1. Poverty
2. Hunger
3. Education
4. Women
5. Child mortality
6. Maternal mortality
7. HIV/AIDS
8. Malaria/diseases
9. Conservation
10. Clean water
11. Slum dwellers
12. Promote open trade
13. Assist LDCs
14. Assist LDCs
15. Resolve debt problems
16. Reduce youth unemployment
17. Access to drugs
18. Access to technology

Social Entrepreneurs

- ABCDEspañol
- Akatu
- ANEC
- ApproTEC
- APABEB
- *Aravind Eye Hospital*
- Associação Saude Criança Renascer
- ASAFE
- *Barefoot College*
- *BASIX*
- BRAC
- Centre for Mass Ed in Science
- Ciudad Saludable
- CDI
- *Comprehesive Rural Health*
- *Development Alternatives*
- Duck Revolution
- Ecoclubes
- Escuela Nueva
- *Fair Trade Group Nepal*
- First Nations Development Institute
- Freeplay
- Friends of Nature
- Fundação Pró-Cerrado
- Fundacion Paraguaya
- Gente Nueva
- *Gram Vikas*
- Grupo Ecológico Sierra Gorda
- Hagar
- Honey Care
- IDEAAS
- Irupana
- *Kashf Foundation*
- Novica
- OACA
- People Tree
- Phulki
- Population & Community Dev. Ass.
- *Project Impact*
- *Rural Development Institute*
- Riders for Health
- Rural Women
- Soul City
- *SAIBAN*
- *SEKEM*
- *SEWA*
- *SPARC*
- Transfair USA
- Waste Concern
- *WHEDA*

create a global partnership for development and that, with the possible exception of environmental sustainability, a large majority is doing this in countries with the lowest levels of human development.

It should be noted that most of the enterprises in the Schwab network will have at least some kind of an impact on poverty, however many operate in countries with a high level of human development and do not fall anywhere near the MDG threshold of USD1 a day. For this reason they have been excluded from our count of enterprises making an impact on poverty. When it comes to attacking poverty on a global scale, the difference between an organization providing employment and support for disadvantaged individuals in the LDCs compared to the most developed countries, is vast. In order to be making an impact on any of the MDGs, social entrepreneurs need to be operating in the poorest countries and the worst conditions of human development. From the distribution of their locations we can show that the majority of them are doing just that. Table 15.3 maps the 50 Schwab Foundation social enterprises which are contributing directly to MDGs to each of the 18 individual targets and codes them according to where they operate. For details of exactly which LDCs and low HDI countries they operate in refer to Appendix 15A.

From this mapping we can see that social entrepreneurs often impact more than one target or goal and sometimes a great many goals in their quest to fulfill a social mission. Some have opted to target one specific goal and go deeper into the problem; others are addressing a wide range of interconnected issues. Some organizations focus on one region only while others disseminate their innovation throughout many different countries. Following is a selection of the social enterprises which have been most successful in impacting MDGs in the LDCs.

ApproTEC (KickStart)

ApproTEC (KickStart since 2005) identifies, develops and distributes low-cost technologies such as irrigation pumps and oilseed presses for small scale industries where capital investments can be recovered within six months. It was founded in Kenya in 1991 and has since opened offices in Tanzania and, more recently, Mali (both listed by the UN as LDCs). ApproTEC also distributes products in surrounding countries including Sudan, Uganda, Malawi, Mozambique, Zambia and Senegal. It has a direct impact on three of the MDGs: eradicating poverty and hunger by providing appropriate technologies to create sustainable incomes in the region; empowering women who represent a majority of recipients; and disseminating technology to developing countries. ApproTEC focuses on agricultural technologies to fight poverty. It began by penetrating deeply in one area (Kenya, Tanzania) and is now expanding into targeted areas where it can have a high impact as it gains capacity.

BRAC

Since it was founded in 1972, BRAC's mission has been to empower and uplift the poor through a combination of microfinance with health, education, social development and environmental programs. Its holistic approach enables it to impact six of the MDGs which it perceives as interconnected. BRAC tackles: poverty and hunger with microfinance using an innovative village organization model; lack of education by providing nonformal schooling programs; health problems (including child and maternal mortality, HIV/AIDS and malaria) through facility-based services, community volunteers and partnerships; and environmental issues through its social development programs. It has achieved deep penetration in one LDC, Bangladesh, and is one of the largest self-sustaining NGOs in the world. In 2002 BRAC entered Afghanistan, an LDC designated as 'in special need' by the UN, and in 2004, following the devastating December Tsunami, began operations in Sri Lanka.

Riders for Health

Riders for Health overcomes the problems of delivery and distribution for health services in developing countries by operating and maintaining a fleet of motorcycles and other vehicles, and by offering training in maintenance and driving skills, in regions where vehicles are normally used until they break down and left to decay by the roadside. This enables health workers in rural Africa to visit large numbers of people spread over huge territories more often and to deliver services more efficiently. Founded in 1998 in the UK, it operates in Gambia, Nigeria and Zimbabwe with a pilot program underway for Uganda. Riders for Health impacts three of the MDGs associated with health: reducing child mortality, reducing maternal mortality and combating HIV/AIDS, malaria and other deadly diseases.

Transfair USA

Founded in 1998, Transfair USA works to establish 'fair trade' practices for agricultural products from developing countries. It develops close relationships with growers, manufacturers and retailers to certify products with the fair trade label. It is one of 19 members of Fair Trade Organizations International and the only third party certifier of fair trade products in the US. While based in the US, Transfair USA provides certification services to producers in over 32 countries including the LDCs: Congo, Ethiopia, Gambia, Haiti, Nepal, Tanzania and Timor-Leste; and many low HDI countries such as Cameroon, Kenya, Zimbabwe, India and Papua New Guinea. This enables it to have an impact on three MDGs: eradicating poverty and hunger by helping to provide growers with a decent living; achieving environmental sustainability through encouraging organic farming practices; and promoting global fair trade.

The social enterprises in this study represent many different organizational forms and reflect a broad array of social goals. Some are for-profit entities while others are purely nonprofit and some take on hybrid forms (Mair and Noboa, 2003). All have managed to achieve scale through various methods: branching, affiliates, social franchising or plural forms (Wei-Skillern, Battle Anderson and Dees, 2002). Most have a social mission which aims to affect societal transformation (Alvord, Brown and Letts, 2004) and the majority of them are focused on the issues tackled by the MDGs. Among those that are directly impacting MDGs we have identified various forms. Some initiatives, such as Riders for Health and ApproTEC focus on one issue or a small number of related issues in a particular area and expand to other countries as they gain capacity. Others, such as BRAC aim to tackle poverty and all its related problems covering the full spectrum of the MDGs but concentrated on creating a large scale and successful enterprise. BRAC is now testing its model in other regions; however its holistic approach grew out of a focus on the specific problems of Bangladesh. On the other hand, Transfair USA is a good example of an initiative that has taken a specific approach global. Within the sample population there are a multitude of social enterprises impacting MDGs with innovative and unique context-based approaches to solving global development problems.

Conclusion

Of the 50 social enterprises contributing to the achievement of the MDGs, 16 or 32 per cent are operating in the LDCs and a further 14 are operating in countries ranked in the bottom 30 per cent of the HDI. This means that 60 per cent of these initiatives are working to alleviate poverty, disease and death, and to increase the overall quality of life by expanding human capabilities and choices in the poorest of countries. Among them are certain social enterprises which could well be making a significant impact, either by attacking a broad range of the worst problems in the least developed places, or by concentrating in a particular area and going deeper into the problem. For example, many of the social enterprises on the Indian subcontinent take a much more holistic approach to tackling poverty by attacking a range of the problems that contribute to it. BRAC in Bangladesh is probably one of the best examples of this broad approach; it aims to mobilize the latent capacity of the poor to uplift themselves through self-organization with projects in microfinance, health, education and environment (Seelos and Mair, 2005c). In contrast, many African-based initiatives, such as ApproTEC and Riders for Health, tend to focus on particular problems and very specific methods of dealing with them. These regional differences and context-based approaches could provide rich ground for further research.

Most importantly, this study demonstrates that, of the social enterprises that are impacting MDGs directly, the majority are doing this in the countries where the most benefit would be gained. Sixty per cent of these initiatives are operating in countries in the lowest 30 per cent of the HDI and 32 per cent are directly targeting MDGs in the LDCs as determined by the UN. These social enterprises usually work from the ground up, fighting poverty directly by breaking the cycle and offering a proactive way out; whether by buying a low-cost water pump from ApproTEC to irrigate and sustain a small plot of land, or by training as a village health worker to give something back to the local community with the help of BRAC and many other organizations. Social entrepreneurs help to reinvigorate local economies and maintain healthy productive labor forces in ways which stimulate self-sustainability rather than create aid dependency. The UNDP's Millennium Project report of 2005 states that achieving the MDGs by 2015 is an ambitious task but can be done if there are intensive efforts to actively engage and empower civil society, promote entrepreneurship and the private sector and mobilize domestic resources in low-income countries (UN Millennium Project, 2005). This study shows that social enterprises are doing exactly that.

Our data indicate that social entrepreneurs constitute a novel set of partners for multilateral development organizations who are struggling to achieve the MDGs by the set date of 2015. Furthermore, social entrepreneurs are building resources in the form of human and social capital and intangible assets such as trust and credibility that may put them in a prime position to become the partners of corporations to develop new markets and new types of service offerings (Seelos and Mair, 2005b), and to contribute directly to large-scale economic development as well.

Appendix 15A   List of Schwab Foundation social entrepreneurs

Social enterprise	Description and focus	Impact: If yes how? – If not why not?	Where?
ABCDEspañol	Simple and effective system that teaches reading, writing and mathematics skills to children and adults	**Direct impact on MDGs:** 2. Universal education; 3. Gender equality	**Based in:** Colombia; **Other:** Guatemala, Honduras, Nicaragua, El Salvador, Costa Rica, Panama, Dominican Republic
Akatu Institute for Conscious Consumption	Brings together business and civil society to foster and promote conscientious consumption	**Direct impact on MDG:** 7. Environmental sustainability	Brazil
ANEC	Empowers small scale commercial grain farmers to compete in the mass market global economy	**Direct impact on MDGs:** 1. Eradicate poverty and hunger; 8. Global development partnership (technology)	Mexico
ApproTEC (now KickStart)	Identifies, develops and distributes technologies for small scale industries where capital investments can be recovered in 3–6 months	**Direct impact on MDGs:** 1. Eradicate poverty and hunger; 3. Gender equality; 8. Global development partnership (technology)	LDCs: Tanzania, Mali; **Lowest 30% HDI:** Kenya (based in Kenya)
Aravind Eye Hospitals	Supplies affordable eye care to patients who can't usually pay and performs over 200,000 sight restoring operations per year	**Direct impact on MDG:** 8. Global development partnership (drugs and technology)	Lowest 30% HDI: India
Arcandina	Produces entertaining, educational TV programs and movies for children promoting environmental and citizenship values	**Indirect impact on MDG:** 7. Environmental sustainability	Ecuador

Appendix 15A   List of Schwab Foundation social entrepreneurs – *continued*

Social enterprise	Description and focus	Impact: If yes how? – If not why not?	Where?
APAEB – Associação dos Pequenos Agricultores do Muncípio de Valente	Cooperative of sisal farmers which has built a bridge to international markets, organizing and training small agriculturalists to market their products	**Direct impact on MDGs:** 1. Eradicate poverty and hunger; 8. Global development partnership (technology)	Brazil
Associação Saúde Criança Renascer	Supplements hospital care for children from low-income communities and enables poverty-stricken mothers and families to prevent recurring illness	**Direct impact on MDG:** 4. Reduce child mortality	Brazil
ASAFE – Association pour le Soutien et L'Appui a la Femme Entrpreneur	Provides business training and development services, alternative financing and access to e-commerce to support women entrepreneurs	**Direct impact on MDGs:** 3. Gender equality; 8. Global development partnership (technology)	LDCs: Benin, Chad, Congo, Guinea; **Lowest 30% HDI:** Cameroon (based in Cameroon)
Barka	Provides basic needs of food and shelter for homeless individuals and offers training and employment through small business workplaces	**No impact on MDGs** as it operates in a country with a social safety net and a high level of human development	Poland
Barefoot College	Operates a network of community colleges which train poor rural jobless youths to become 'barefoot' doctors, teachers, engineers and designers	**Direct impact on MDGs:** 3. Gender equality; 7. Environmental sustainability; 8. Global development partnership (youth employment)	**Lowest 30% HDI:** India

Appendix 15A   List of Schwab Foundation social entrepreneurs – *continued*

Social enterprise	Description and focus	Impact: If yes how? – If not why not?	Where?
BASIX	Provides microcredit to the landless poor and self-employed and also to the small businesses that employ them	**Direct impact on MDG:** 1. Eradicate poverty and hunger	Lowest 30% HDI: India
Benetech	Aims to put high technology at the service of the socially disadvantaged from those with physical disabilities to human rights abuses	No impact on MDGs as it operates mainly in a country with a social safety net and a high level of human development; no human rights goals	USA
Bily kruh bezpeci	Volunteer-based support network for victims of violent crime, providing counseling, legal aid and assistance in dealing with institutions	No impact on MDGs as it operates in a country with a social safety net and a high level of human development	Czech Republic
Bosnian Handicrafts	Production and retail business that trains and employs women refugees displaced by the Bosnian war	No impact on MDGs as it operates in a country with a social safety net and a high level of human development	Bosnia
BRAC	Mobilizes the latent capacity of the poor to uplift themselves through self-organization with projects in microfinance, health, education and environment	**Direct impact on MDGs:** 1. Eradicate poverty and hunger; 2. Universal education; 3. Gender equality; 4. Reduce child mortality; 5. Improve maternal health; 6. Combat HIV/AIDS and diseases	LDCs: Afghanistan, Bangladesh (based in Bangladesh); **Other:** Sri Lanka

Appendix 15A   List of Schwab Foundation social entrepreneurs – *continued*

Social enterprise	Description and focus	Impact: If yes how? – If not why not?	Where?
CAMBIA – Centre for the Application of Molecular Biology to International Agriculture	Aims to democratize the biotech innovation process and to disseminate knowledge about advanced agricultural technologies in the developing world	**Indirect or future impact** on MDGs: 7. Environmental sustainability; 8. Global development partnership	**Lowest 30% HDI:** India, Pakistan, Nigeria, Kenya, Zimbabwe; **Other projects include:** Vietnam, Indonesia, Mexico, Brazil, Egypt; **Based in:** Australia
Centre for Citizenship Education	Promotes civic participation by facilitating multistakeholder educational policies and programming to improve schooling	No impact on MDGs as it operates in a country with a social safety net, primary education for both girls and boys and has a high level of human development	Poland
Centre for Mass Education in Science	Offers an alternative curriculum to traditional rote learning with emphasis on economically relevant life skills and educating girls	**Direct impact on MDG:** 2. Universal education	**LDC:** Bangladesh
City Year	Voluntary national service program aiming to bring together young people from different ethnic backgrounds and teach them civic engagement	No impact on MDGs as it operates in countries with a social safety net and a high level of human development	USA, South Africa
Child Helpline International	Provides a 24-hour helpline for vulnerable children in need of education, shelter, protection from abuse, counseling and other emergency services	**Indirect or future impact** on MDGs: 1. Eradicate poverty and hunger; 4. Reduce child mortality	**Lowest 30% HDI:** India

Appendix 15A   List of Schwab Foundation social entrepreneurs – *continued*

Social enterprise	Description and focus	Impact: If yes how? – If not why not?	Where?
Ciudad Saludable	Provides waste management services at lower cost than local government, recycles waste and promotes health messages	Direct impact on MDG: 7. Environmental sustainability	Peru
CDI – Committee for the Democratization of Information Technology	Promotes social inclusion of low income communities by providing information technologies as tools for building and exercising citizens' rights	Direct impact on MDGs: 2. Universal education; 8. Global development partnership (technology and youth employment)	LDC: Angola; Based in: Brazil; Other: Guatemala, Honduras, Argentina, Chile, Columbia, Mexico, Uruguay, South Africa, Japan
Comprehensive Rural Health Project	Community-based health care program for the rural poor which trains local women to become rural health workers; targets child and maternal mortality	Direct impact on MDGs: 3. Gender equality; 4. Reduce child mortality; 5. Improve maternal health; 6. Combat HIV/AIDS and diseases	Lowest 30% HDI: India
Development Alternatives	Develops technologies and products for the poor with the dual aims of helping create income and regenerating the environment. These products must also be commercially viable	Direct impact on MDGs: 1. Eradicate poverty and hunger; 7. Environmental sustainability; 8. Global development partnership (technology)	Lowest 30% HDI: India
Duck Revolution	Sustainable organic farming method which integrates organic rice and duck production significantly increasing yields while reducing environmental damage and farmers' workloads	Direct impact on MDG: 7. Environmental sustainability	Lowest 30% HDI: Cambodia, Laos; Based in: Japan; Other: Vietnam, Philippines, Korea, Malaysia

Appendix 15A   List of Schwab Foundation social entrepreneurs – *continued*

Social enterprise	Description and focus	Impact: If yes how? – If not why not?	Where?
Easy Being Green P/L	Furniture resource center which aims to provide public housing tenants with quality furniture thus changing their approach to their surroundings and raising their self-image resulting in less desertion and lower security costs	No impact on MDGs as it operates in countries with a social safety net and a high level of human development	UK, Australia, New Zealand
Ecoclubes	Network run by youth volunteers in 12 Latin American countries which promotes environmental action in the areas of: waste management, water quality, dengue control and protection of wildlife	Direct impact on MDGs: 6. Combat HIV/AIDS and diseases (malaria); 7. Environmental sustainability	**Based in:** Argentina; **Other:** Paraguay, Brazil, Uruguay, Chile, Bolivia, Panama, Costa Rica, Honduras, Guatemala, Spain
Endeavor Global	Fosters economic growth in developing countries by stimulating and supporting entrepreneurs servicing the emerging business and middle classes	No impact on MDGs as it targets those well above the poverty line of USD1 a day and aims to support an emerging middle class	**Based in:** USA; **Affiliates world-wide:** Latin America, Africa, Asia, Middle East, Europe, North America, Australia and the Pacific
Escuela Nueva	Provides an alternative approach to primary education, especially in neglected rural areas, by reshaping the roles of teachers, administrators, students and the community	Direct impact on MDG: 2. Universal education	**Based in:** Colombia; **Other:** Guatemala, Honduras, Guyana, Brazil, Ecuador, Dominican Republic, Chile

Appendix 15A List of Schwab Foundation social entrepreneurs – *continued*

Social enterprise	Description and focus	Impact: If yes how? – If not why not?	Where?
Fair Trade Group Nepal	Cooperative that engages with local producers of handicrafts and provides training, administration, marketing, distribution, decent salaries and social benefit programs focused on women	**Direct impact on MDGs:** 3. Gender equality; 8. Global development partnership (trade)	LDC: Nepal
First Nations Development Institute	Aims to assist indigenous North American and other peoples to control and develop their assets through grants and microfinance; has also developed literacy, health and other programs.	**Direct impact** on MDG: 7. Environmental sustainability	USA
Freeplay Energy Group and Foundation	Combats both widespread illiteracy and poor access to electricity in subSaharan Africa by developing and distributing radios and other products based on an ingenious wind up technology	**Direct impact on MDGs:** 2. Universal education; 6. Combat HIV/AIDS and diseases; 8. Global development partnership (technology)	LDCs: Afghanistan, Angola, Ethiopia, Ghana, Mozambique, Niger, Rwanda, Tanzania, Zambia; **Lowest 30 % HDI:** Cote d'Ivoire, Kenya; **Other:** South Africa
Friends of Nature	Works to raise environmental awareness in China; trains volunteers to teach children, usually in remote rural areas about environmental stewardship	**Direct impact on MDG:** 7. Environmental sustainability	China

Appendix 15A List of Schwab Foundation social entrepreneurs – *continued*

Social enterprise	Description and focus	Impact: If yes how? – If not why not?	Where?
Fundação Pró-Cerrado	Works to preserve the 'Cerrado' (savannah) biome in Brazil; teaches disadvantaged youth about the environment and places them in industry jobs	**Direct impact on MDG:** 7. Environmental sustainability	Brazil
Fundacion Paraguaya de Cooperacion y Desarollo	Self-sustaining microcredit program which actively promotes both sustainable development and entrepreneurship to youth using business mentors	**Direct impact on MDGs:** 1. Eradicate poverty and hunger; 7. Environmental sustainability	Paraguay
Gente Nueva	Youth organization; international education and volunteer programs; acts as umbrella for several programs: Un Kilo de Ayuda (fights malnutrition in children), Compartamos (microcredit), Mi Tienda (supplies small rural retailers at low wholesale prices)	**Direct impact on MDGs:** 1. Eradicate poverty and hunger; 4. Reduce child mortality	**Based in:** Mexico; Other: Brazil, Argentina, Chile, Spain, Belgium, France
Gram Vikas	Works with villages in the impoverished rural area of Orissa to build community collectives which then create a 'village corpus' fund; the fund is then used to finance health, water, education and energy projects	**Direct impact on MDGs:** 1. Eradicate poverty and hunger; 7. Environmental sustainability; 8. Global development partnership (youth employment)	**Lowest 30% HDI:** India

Appendix 15A   List of Schwab Foundation social entrepreneurs – *continued*

Social enterprise	Description and focus	Impact: If yes how? – If not why not?	Where?
Grupo Ecológico Sierra Gorda	Works to protect a unique biosphere – the 'Sierra Gorda' in Mexico and to address the survival needs of the local indigenous population by sustainable resource use and efficient natural resource management	**Direct impact on MDGs:** 1. Eradicate poverty and hunger; 2. Universal education; 7. Environmental sustainability	Mexico
Habitat for Humanity	Unique solution to low-income housing; affiliates in 83 countries sell housing and offer construction and mortgage services at very low rates enabling families to gain the stability of homeownership at less than the cost of renting	**No impact on MDGs** as it targets those well above the poverty line of USD1 a day and aims to support an emerging middle class	**Based in:** USA; **Affiliates world-wide:** Latin America, Africa, Asia, Middle East, Europe, North America, Australia and the Pacific
Hagar	Targets very poor women and children in rural areas who often drift to the cities becoming beggars and prostitutes; offers vocational training and follows up with employment opportunities in its commercial enterprises	**Direct impact on MDGs:** 1. Eradicate poverty and hunger; 2. Universal education; 3. Gender equality; 7. Environmental sustainability	LDC: Cambodia
Honey Care	Manufactures and sells innovative honey production technology to very poor farmers (often women); offers microfinance, marketing and training; acts as both purchaser and distributor within the value chain	**Direct impact on MDGs:** 1. Eradicate poverty and hunger; 3. Gender equality; 8. Global development partnership (trade)	LDC: Tanzania; **Based in:** Kenya

Appendix 15A   List of Schwab Foundation social entrepreneurs – *continued*

Social enterprise	Description and focus	Impact: If yes how? – If not why not?	Where?
IDEAAS	Provides low cost electricity to impoverished rural families; attacks both poverty and environmental degradation through solar electricity and training in environmentally sustainable farming methods	**Direct impact on MDGs:** 1. Eradicate poverty and hunger; 7. Environmental sustainability	Brazil
Independence Care System (ICS)	First worker-owned healthcare agency in the US; employees mostly Latin American and African American; specifically directed at improving quality of care for people with physical disabilities and/or low incomes	**No impact on MDGs** as it operates in countries with a social safety net and a high level of human development	USA
International Network of Street Papers (INSP)	Network of 50 street papers in 26 countries providing employment for homeless people; promoting media independence, knowledge sharing and self-help; and providing a voice for those who live on the street	**No impact on MDGs** as it operates in a country with a social safety net and a high level of human development	**Based in:** UK; **Other:** Australia, Brazil, Canada, Gambia, Namibia, South Africa, Uruguay, USA and many European countries
Irupana	Buys the organically grown products of indigenous farmers and sells direct from Irupana stores which actively	**Direct impact on MDG:** 1. Eradicate poverty and hunger	Bolivia

Appendix 15A   List of Schwab Foundation social entrepreneurs – *continued*

Social enterprise	Description and focus	Impact: If yes how? – If not why not?	Where?
	incorporates farmers into the value chain as owners offering market access, technical assistance and credit facilities		
Ithuteng Trust	Rounds up delinquent adolescents on the path to becoming career criminals and puts them through a 'shock treatment' program which involves spending a weekend in prison with criminals and terminal AIDS patients	**Indirect impact** on MDG: 6. Combat HIV/AIDS and diseases	South Africa
Kashf Foundation	Microcredit institution which has adapted the Grameen model; it specifically focuses on the economic transformation of women by offering loan and insurance products	**Direct impact** on MDGs: 1. Eradicate poverty and hunger; 3. Gender equality	**Lowest 30% HDI:** Pakistan
IOWH – Institute for OneWorld Health	The first nonprofit pharmaceutical company, IOWH aims to target neglected diseases by developing donated compounds through the clinical trial phases into marketable low-cost drugs for the Third World where these diseases are rampant	**Indirect or future impact** on MDG: 6. Combat HIV/AIDS and diseases	**Based in:** USA; Other: potential impact in many developing countries

Appendix 15A   List of Schwab Foundation social entrepreneurs – *continued*

Social enterprise	Description and focus	Impact: If yes how? – If not why not?	Where?
Nepal Press Institute	Trains journalists and promotes freedom of the press; helps deliver information on nutrition, health, minority rights and environmental issues in simple village languages; encourages small towns to create their own press	No impact as there are no MDGs covering freedom of the press	LDC: Nepal
Novica	Handicrafts reseller which buys direct from local artisans who set their own prices, and sells their products online all over the world	Direct impact on MDGs: 3. Gender equality; 8. Global development partnership (trade)	Lowest 30% HDI: Zimbabwe, Ghana, India; Based in: USA; Other: Peru, Brazil, Indonesia, Mexico, Thailand
OACA – Oficina de Asesoría y Consultoría Ambiental	Initiative to sustainably manage social, environmental and economic needs of urban environments; has spun off a for-profit consultancy – Ecolab which advises companies on how to comply with new environmental regulations	Direct impact on MDG: 7. Environmental sustainability	Peru
Parceiros Voluntarios	Prepares people, corporations, schools and universities for volunteer work. Also prepares nonprofit organizations to receive these volunteers and deploy their skills	Indirect impact on MDGs: potentially all of them	Brazil

Appendix 15A List of Schwab Foundation social entrepreneurs – *continued*

Social enterprise	Description and focus	Impact: If yes how? – If not why not?	Where?
People Tree Limited	The FairTrade Company in Japan and its UK branch – People Tree – create fashion garments from fair trade fabrics in places such as Bangladesh, India and Nepal, and Latin America and market them in the UK	**Direct impact on MDGs:** 3. Gender equality; 8. Global development partnership (trade)	**Based in:** UK, Japan; **LDC:** Bangladesh; **Lowest 30% HDI:** India
Phulki	Pioneering work and community-based daycare for women working in factories, government offices and businesses; aims to show factory owners that investing in childcare returns a happier, more productive workforce	**Direct impact on MDG:** 3. Gender equality	**LDC:** Bangladesh
Population and Community Development Association	Established in 1984; began providing family planning information and distributing contraception; now focuses on combating HIV/AIDS using similar methods; also operates 14 for-profit businesses which help sustain it	**Direct impact on MDGs:** 3. Gender equality; 6. Combat HIV/AIDS and diseases; 7. Environmental sustainability	Thailand
Project Impact	Manufactures and distributes quality and cost effective hearing aids to underserved markets in India and other developing countries; uses a	**Direct impact on MDGs:** 3. Gender equality; 8. Global development partnership (technology)	**Lowest 30% HDI:** India

Appendix 15A   List of Schwab Foundation social entrepreneurs – *continued*

Social enterprise	Description and focus	Impact: If yes how? – If not why not?	Where?
	cross subsidization model to provide free products to those who can't afford them		
RDI – Rural Development Institute	Organization of land and policy experts that helps poor farmers in developing countries gain ownership of land and helping to alleviate poverty on a grand scale	**Direct impact on MDG:** 1. Eradicate poverty and hunger	**Lowest 30% HDI:** India
RENCTAS	Works to dramatically decrease and lower tolerance for animal trafficking by forming partnerships and strategic alliances with government and business entities	No impact as there are no MDGs covering animal trafficking	Brazil
Riders for Health	Supports health workers in rural Africa by operating a fleet of motorcycles and other vehicles and running training on maintenance and driving skills so that the vehicles survive the harsh conditions and so do the patients	**Direct impact on MDGs:** 4. Reduce child mortality; 5. Improve maternal health; 6. Combat HIV/AIDS and diseases	**LDC: Gambia; Lowest 30% HDI:** Nigeria; Zimbabwe
Rubicon Programs Incorporated	Addresses the problems of poverty among African Americans, recent immigrants, the homeless and the severely mentally disabled by providing employment and targeted services through several businesses	No impact on MDGs as it operates in a country with a social safety net and a high level of human development	USA

Appendix 15A   List of Schwab Foundation social entrepreneurs – *continued*

Social enterprise	Description and focus	Impact: If yes how? – If not why not?	Where?
Rural Women	Promotes the education and support of rural women living with very traditional values about their roles in society and performs a supervisory role to the government	**Direct impact** on MDG: 3. Gender equality	China
Soul City	Multimedia initiative that seeks to integrate health and development issues into serialized prime time TV shows which challenge attitudes about HIV/AIDS, youth sexuality, violence against women and other issues	**Direct impact** on MDG: 6. Combat HIV/AIDS and diseases	**LDCs:** Lesotho, Malawi, Mozambique, Zambia; **Lowest 30% HDI:** Botswana, Namibia, Swaziland, Zimbabwe; **Based in:** South Africa
SAIBAN	Intervenes in the inefficient cycle of land development and sale by making small plots available to very poor families with credit thus discouraging participation in the informal and often corrupt housing market	**Direct impact** on MDGs: 1. Eradicate poverty and hunger; 7. Environmental sustainability	**Lowest 30% HDI:** Pakistan
Sekem	Holistic social enterprise combining organic farming with the production and marketing of phytopharmaceuticals, health products, textiles and organic food products; provides education, training and health services for workers	**Direct impact** on MDGs: 2. Universal education; 4. Reduce child mortality; 5. Improve maternal health; 7. Environmental sustainability; 8. Global development partnership (*...*)	Egypt

Appendix 15A   List of Schwab Foundation social entrepreneurs – *continued*

Social enterprise	Description and focus	Impact: If yes how? – If not why not?	Where?
SEWA – Self Employed Women's Association	Provides support for poor self-employed women in places with large informal economies by creating cooperatives and producer groups; offers health care, insurance, legal advice and IT facilities to its members	Direct impact on MDGs: 1. Eradicate poverty and hunger; 3. Gender equality; 4. Reduce child mortality; 5. Improve maternal health; 7. Environmental sustainability	Lowest 30% HDI: India
SPARC – Society for the Promotion of Area Resource Centres	Formed a three-way alliance with the National Slum Dwellers Federation of India and Mahila Milan (a federation of women's collectives) in order to improve the lives of slum dwellers and lift them out of extreme poverty	Direct impact on MDGs: 1. Eradicate poverty and hunger; 7. Environmental sustainability	Lowest 30% HDI: India
Teach for America	Recruits and trains recent college graduates and places them as full-time paid teachers in urban and rural public schools; addresses the education needs of children from low income areas who have fewer opportunities	No impact on MDGs as it operates in a country with a social safety net and a high level of human development	USA
The Way Home	Supports the homeless, unemployed and other socially vulnerable groups; promotes resocialization and offers housing, training, clothing, workshop employment and HIV/AIDS prevention programs	No impact on MDGs as it operates in a country with a social safety net and a high level of human development	Ukraine

Appendix 15A List of Schwab Foundation social entrepreneurs – *continued*

Social enterprise	Description and focus	Impact: If yes how? – If not why not?	Where?
Transfair USA	Works to establish Fair Trade practices for agricultural products; develops close partnerships with both growers in developing countries and manufacturers and retailers to certify products with the Fair Trade label	**Direct impact on MDGs:** 1. Eradicate poverty and hunger; 7. Environmental sustainability; 8. Global development partnership (trade)	**Based in:** USA; **LDCs:** Congo, Ethiopia, Gambia, Haiti, Nepal; Tanzania, Timor-Leste, Uganda; **Lowest 30% HDI:** Zimbabwe, Kenya, India, Cameroon, Papua New Guinea
Waste Concern	Waste disposal company which processes organic waste and produces organic fertilizers; provides jobs for the urban poor, stimulates behavioral change and addresses environmental problems	**Direct impact on MDG:** 7. Environmental sustainability	**LDC:** Bangladesh
Witness	Combats human rights abuses with the use of visual communications technology which encourages people to record such abuses; supplies the technology to partners and trains them in its use	**No impact** as there are no MDGs covering human rights abuses	**Based in:** USA
WHEDA – Women's Health and Economic Development Association	Umbrella organization for 121 women's groups; provides microfinance, training and advice on issues ranging from healthcare and nutrition to economic empowerment and helps women to form cooperatives	**Direct impact on MDGs:** 1. Eradicate poverty and hunger; 3. Gender equality; 4. Reduce child mortality; 5. Improve maternal health; 6. Combat HIV/AIDS and diseases	**Lowest 30% HDI:** Nigeria

Appendix 15A   List of Schwab Foundation social entrepreneurs – *continued*

Social enterprise	Description and focus	Impact: If yes how? – If not why not?	Where?
Working Today	Membership organization introducing a flexible form of trade unionism for independent and freelance workers linking them to legal, insurance, tax and retirement planning services	No impact on MDGs as it operates in a country with a social safety net and a high level of human development	USA

Acknowledgment

This paper has been prepared with the support of the European Academy of Business in Society (EABIS), as part of its Research, Education and Training Partnership Program on Corporate Responsibility. This program has been made possible due to the financial support of EABIS' founding corporate partners, IBM, Johnson & Johnson, Microsoft, Shell and Unilever.

References

Alvord, S. H., Brown, L. D. and Letts, C. W. 2004. Social entrepreneurship and societal transformation: An exploratory study. *The Journal of Applied Behavioral Science*, **40**(3): 260–82.

Austin, J., Stevenson, H. and Wei-Skillern, J. 2003. Social entrepreneurship and commercial entrepreneurship: Same, different or both? Working Paper 04-029, Harvard Business School.

Brundtland, G. H. 1987. *Our common future: The World Commission on Environment and Development.* Oxford: Oxford University Press.

Bornstein, D. 1998. Changing the world on a shoestring. *Atlantic Monthly*, **281**(1): 34–9.

Dees, J. G. 1998. The meaning of social entrepreneurship. Paper, Center for the Advancement of Social Entrepreneurship, Fuqua School of Business, Duke University, Durham. Available: http://www.fuqua.duke.edu/centers/case/documents/dees_SE.pdf

Easterly, W. R. 2001. *The elusive quest for growth: Economists' adventures and misadventures in the Tropics.* Cambridge MA: MIT Press.

Fowler, A. 2000. NGDOs as a moment in history: Beyond aid to social entrepreneurship or civic innovation? *Third World Quarterly*, **21**(4): 637–54.

IOWH. 2005. http://www.oneworldhealth.org. Accessed 5 May 2005.

Johnson, S. 2000. Literature review on social entrepreneurship. Canadian Centre for Social Entrepreneurship, University of Alberta School of Business, Canada. Available: http://www.bus.ualberta.ca/ccse/Publications.

Mair, J. and Martí, I. 2005. Social entrepreneurship research: A source of explanation, prediction and delight. *Journal of World Business*, forthcoming.

Mair, J. and Noboa, E. 2003. *The emergence of social enterprises and their place in the new organizational landscape.* Working Paper 523, IESE Business School, University of Navarra.

Schwab Foundation. 2005. www.schwabfoundation.org.

Seelos, C. and Mair, J. 2005a. Social Entrepreneurship: Creating new business models to serve the poor. *Business Horizons*, **48**(3): 247–52.

Seelos, C. and Mair, J. 2005b. Sustainable development, sustainable profit. *European Business Forum*, (20): 49–53.

Seelos, C. and Mair, J. 2005c. *BRAC – Enabling social capability and economic development.* Working Paper. IESE Business School, University of Navarra.

Thompson, J., Alvy, G. and Lees, A. 2000. Social entrepreneurship: A new look at the people and the potential. *Management Decision*, **35**(5): 328–38.

Todd, H. 1996. *Cloning Grameen Bank*. London: Intermediate Technologies Publications, Ltd.

UNDP. 2003. *Human Development Report 2003. Millennium development goals: A compact among nations to end human poverty*. New York, Oxford: Oxford University Press.

UNDP. 2004. *Human Development Report 2004. Cultural liberty in today's diverse world*. Washington: UNDP.

UN General Assembly. 1983. Process of preparation of the environmental perspective to the year 2000 and beyond. Resolution 38/161, 19 December 1983.

UN General Assembly. 1987. Report of the World Commission on Environment and Development. Resolution 42/187, 11 December 1987.

UN General Assembly. 2000. United Nations Millennium Declaration. Resolution 55/2, 18 September 2000.

UN General Assembly. 2001. Third United Nations Conference on Least Developed Countries. Resolution 56/227, 24 December 2001.

UN Millennium Project, 2005. *Investing in development: A practical plan to achieve the Millennium Development Goals overview*. Washington: UNDP.

United Nations. 2005a. www.un.org/millenniumgoals.

United Nations. 2005b. www.un.org/ohrlls.

Wei-Skillern, J., Battle Anderson, B. and Dees, J. G. 2002. Scaling social innovations: A report from the front lines. CASE Working Paper series 4, Fuqua School of Business, Duke University.

World Bank. 2004. *World Development Report 2004. Making services work for poor people*. Washington: Oxford University Press.

World Bank. 2005. www.worldbank.org.

Zafar, R. 2005. Interview with authors, March 2005: Barcelona, Spain.

Index

N.B. (references to tables, figures and appendices appear in bold-italic)

Printed in the United States
116909LV00001BC/4/A